NDS

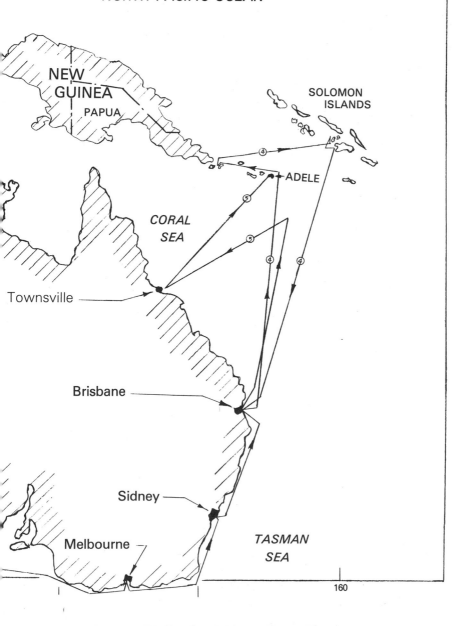

NORTH PACIFIC OCEAN

NEW
GUINEA
PAPUA

SOLOMON
ISLANDS

ADELE

CORAL
SEA

Townsville

Brisbane

Sidney

Melbourne

TASMAN
SEA

160

Pigboat 39

Pigboat 39

An American Sub Goes to War

Bobette Gugliotta

THE UNIVERSITY PRESS OF KENTUCKY

Technical consultation and drawings by Guy F. Gugliotta
(Captain, United States Navy, retired)

Copyright © 1984 by The University Press of Kentucky

Scholarly publisher for the Commonwealth,
serving Bellarmine College, Berea College, Centre
College of Kentucky, Eastern Kentucky University,
The Filson Club, Georgetown College, Kentucky
Historical Society, Kentucky State University,
Morehead State University, Murray State University,
Northern Kentucky University, Transylvania University,
University of Kentucky, University of Louisville,
and Western Kentucky University.

Editorial and Sales Offices: Lexington, Kentucky 40506-0024

Library of Congress Cataloging in Publication Data

Gugliotta, Bobette,
  Pigboat 39.

  Bibliography: p.
  Includes index.
    1. World War, 1939-1945—Naval operations—Submarine.
  2. S-39 (Submarine)   3. World War, 1939-1945—Naval
  operations, American.   I. Gugliotta, Guy F.   II. Title.
  III. Title: Pigboat thirty-nine.
  D783.5.S2G84   1984   940.54'51   84-15295
  ISBN 0-8131-1524-8

To the men and women who people these pages,
and all others like them

Contents

Illustrations

I am for having history rise up off her knees
and take a natural posture. . . . I would have
history familiar rather than heroic.
　　　　　　　—WILLIAM MAKEPEACE THACKERAY

The United States Asiatic Fleet seldom tasted
victory. It drank the cup of defeat to the bitter
dregs. Nevertheless, the fortitude of that Fleet
in the face of almost certain disaster inspired
the rest of the Navy in the forty months of war
that followed, and its exploits will always be
held in proud and affectionate remembrance.
　　　　　　　　—SAMUEL ELIOT MORISON

Preface

There are many admirable books, both fiction and nonfiction, about submarines. Jules Verne started it, and the end is not yet in sight. But until now, a rounded picture of what submarine life was like on board an obsolete, cantankerous S-boat early in World War II, when the U.S. Asiatic Fleet met one defeat after another, has not to my knowledge been put in print.

I suffered through those years as a bride, too close to it all then to realize the complexities, to understand not only the dangers but the humor, stress, discomfort, endurance, foibles, and courage of the men and women involved. Several years ago I began to think about getting all that down on paper. It also seemed to me that real women had been shortchanged in nonfiction and stereotyped in fiction. I wanted to do something about that, too.

For starters, I had the perfect technical consultant. My husband, Guy F. Gugliotta—who spent ten years of his naval career in submarines, serving on board three S-boats during World War II and as a skipper of one of them—was also interested in the project. Then I remembered that years ago I had crossed out the personal parts from all the letters he had sent me during the year 1940 when the *S-39* operated out of Manila, and still had the typed manuscript full of original material tucked away.

But the credibility of a nonfiction work of this kind would lie in how many original narratives we could garner from other people connected with *S-39* from approximately 1939 to 1942, when she went aground, the period I had decided to write about. We put notices in a multitude of service magazines, sent out an SOS to many organizations, and planned a trip to Washington in pursuit of logbooks, patrol reports, and original blueprints of the boat.

In 1981, the Submarine Veterans of World War II (SubVets) held their annual convention in Sacramento, California—practically in our back yard—

and we hightailed it up there. In 24 hours we came away with two valuable tape recordings from men who had been sailors on the *S-39* at the right time. They gave us leads to other sources, and thereafter people kept surfacing. Each time I thought a section of the book was complete, somebody else would get the word and telephone or write: "I want to be in it, too."

There are no heroes in *Pigboat 39* unless everyone is. Little people add up to big events and face them like heroes. All our thanks go to those (listed in the bibliography) who shared their memories with us; their continuing enthusiasm sustained a long and demanding job during the three years we worked to create another page of World War II history. Sometimes I cried, sometimes I laughed aloud, at some of the stories that comprise the fabric of the book. I hope the reader will react that way, too. The dialogue is reconstructed from incidents told in tape recordings, letters, and telephone conversations, as well as official source materials (such as patrol reports).

Special thanks for reading and criticism of the manuscript go to Rear Admiral Eugene B. Fluckey, USN (ret.); Captain Wilfred E. Holmes, USN (ret.); Captain Paul B. Ryan, USN (ret.); Captain Frank K.B. Wheeler, USN (ret.); Lieutenant Commander Paul F. Sayles, USN (ret.); and Mrs. May Sayles.

We are also grateful to the following Australian friends for their rapid response to various questions that arose: Bruce D. Hoy, curator, Aviation, Maritime and War Branch, National Museum and Art Gallery, Papua, New Guinea; Robert K. Piper, RAAF Historical Officer; and J.M. MacKenzie, Naval Historical Officer, Department of Defence. And more thanks to John B. Gibbons and George McKnight for generously adding to our supply of photos of the *S-39* and crew.

Pigboat 39

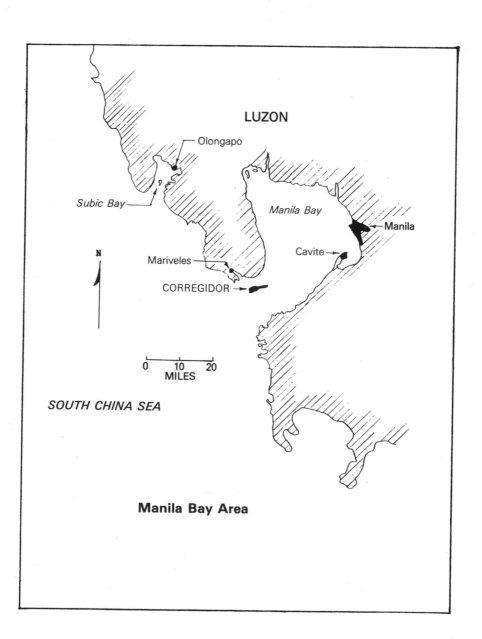

LUZON

Olongapo

Subic Bay

Manila Bay

Manila

Mariveles

Cavite

CORREGIDOR

N

0   10   20
     MILES

SOUTH CHINA SEA

Manila Bay Area

1. Mabuhay!

The Model A taxi chugged to a halt, and the tall, slender young man who erupted from it hesitated for a second on the runningboard, then leaped across the pondlike puddle of water that confronted him. He was Ensign Lawrence G. Bernard, unaware as yet that pockmarked country roads were standard for the Philippines in 1940. Larry was as green as the forests of Baguio about his new assignment, and his eagerness to start his first submarine duty was matched only by his fear that all the spit and polish he'd put into appearing in proper uniform, complete with coat and tie as instructed, was about to collapse in one of the tropical deluges that came without warning at Olongapo.

He had never seen anything like it in Deadwood, South Dakota, where he grew up; or in Long Beach, California, where he'd seen duty aboard the flagship *California* or in New London, Connecticut, where he'd just graduated from submarine school. The "China Station" had appealed to him and his wife Caroline as an adventure, not an endurance test. And it was only February. The real rainy season hadn't started yet.

The little brown taxi driver flashed a toothy smile and drove off, shouting back, "Mabuhay" (the Philippine equivalent of Hawaii's "aloha"), but Larry was too preoccupied with straightening out his wrinkled jacket to respond. Where his khakis weren't streaked with rain, they were streaked with sweat, because the spasmodic sheets of water that made the Olongapo dock a wavering mystery had done nothing to cool the air. Walking with as much dignity as he could muster while dodging potholes, he made his way to the lone sailor, swathed in yellow slicker and hat, who paced the dock.

"Can you tell me where to find the *S-39?*" Larry called.

The sailor thumbed to his left, but volunteered, "No officers aboard her, sir. They're all up to the house where they stay when we're in overhaul."

"Where's that?"

The thumb changed directions. "Thataway, sir, you can't miss it. It's a big white house with a long white porch."

A worrier by nature, Larry hoped he'd make it to the big white house with the long white porch before the sky launched another onslaught and the whole world looked wrapped in cellophane again. He slipped a bit, taking the steps two at a time in his eagerness. Calm down, he told himself; dignity is the order of the day. After all, you're not only an officer and a gentleman, you'll be a father in seven months. But the last thought was so unnerving that he quickly walked across the porch and peered through the window at the scene inside. An old player piano pushed against one wall was bracketed by a pair of wicker rocking chairs. The rest of the large room seemed to be taken up by men sitting at tables with stacks of chips in front of them. Stepping through the doorway, Larry said to the nearest man, who had just slapped down his cards. "Are there any officers from the S-39 here?"

The man yelled, "Hey Red, here's some fresh meat for you," and motioned to the far end of the room.

As Larry approached, all too conscious of his wilted collar and the damp tie riding his adam's apple, a bare-chested redhead, dressed—like the others—only in shorts and sandals, glanced at him and said, "Pull up a chair." Uncapping a bottle of beer, which he plucked from an ice-filled bucket on the floor, he passed it to Larry and pushed a couple of blue chips out in the center of the table. "Bet fifty," he said, and the lean-faced man next to him responded, "I fold." The poker game went on.

As he gratefully tugged at the cold beer and studied the calendar on the wall, showing for February a doll-like Malay girl draped in a scanty valentine heart, Larry began to get the word. He was never going to report in formally, and the redhead who didn't stand on ceremony had to be his new skipper, James "Red" Coe.

That night Larry tried sleeping below deck, but after a pair of stifling nightmare hours in the heat, he followed the crowd topside, where George Lautrup, executive officer, showed him how to rig up a cot where officers and men slept side by side. Larry had heard that, depending upon the skipper, submarine life could be very informal. It was proving true; he had also heard that S-boats weren't exactly queens of the sea, possessing none of the amenities of the larger, newer, faster fleet submarines. He believed that, too. In a few hours Larry had already experienced the 39's lack of air conditioning, the Rube Goldberg complexities of her head, and the primitive shower facilities.

Thoroughly awake now, his mind ran through the facts he'd acquired about his new assignment. With the exception of the few months immediately following her commissioning in 1923, the S-39's 16 years of service had been on the China station. She weighed in at about 800 tons with a submerged speed of nine knots (sustainable for only limited periods) and a surface speed of twelve knots; her hull was designed to stand depths of no more than 200 feet. Larry had read that her Mark 10 torpedoes were very little different from those used on U.S. submarines in World War I and that the air injection diesel engines, though not beyond the possibility of repair by the crew, were crotchety and ponderous. Last but not least, it had been officially reported in 1925 that "experience in maneuvers indicates that these vessels [S-boats] cannot be considered as a satisfactory type of fleet submarine." Having run through all the negatives, he knew that he was still damned glad to be aboard. Then he fell asleep.

During the night a battalion of Olongapo mosquitoes, coming upon a new body that hadn't built up resistance yet, zeroed in and gorged on Larry's exhausted hide from stem to stern. When he awoke, he found his vision somewhat hampered by the fact that one eye was swollen tightly shut. Not a vain man, he was still glad that his bride Caroline was in Manila where she couldn't see him.

The ship came out of dry-dock in late afternoon, and once everything was squared away, George Lautrup turned to him and asked, "Larry, do you think you can take the duty tonight? We have to have a battery charge. Do you know anything about batteries?"

With more confidence than he felt, Larry promptly replied, "Yes, they told us all about that at sub school."

Lautrup nodded. "It's our last night here in Olongapo, and we're going ashore—probably be back by about midnight. If you have any trouble, ask Chief Bridges—he's an old hand."

The battery charge was finished by 2330, and Larry, dead on his feet, pillowed his head on his arms and fell fast asleep at the table in the stifling six-by-ten wardroom. In the midst of a confusing dream where someone had just handed him a brand new baby and asked him if he wanted to name it Larry or Caroline, he heard an insistent voice repeating, "Mr. Bernard, Mr. Bernard, Mr. Bernard . . . " and awoke with a start.

"Rollins here, sir," the quartermaster said, kindly supplying his name to the dazed new officer. "We just got a message by blinker to bring the boat alongside the pier and pick them all up."

Larry thought he was still dreaming. The *39* was anchored out; it was midnight. "Does he mean get a boat somewhere and send it in?"

Keeping a straight face, Quartermaster Rollins said, "No sir, the captain said to bring the submarine alongside. I've started preparations."

Up on the bridge, with the tactful Rollins behind him, Larry stood for a moment in the quiet night, seeing a row of distant lights that he didn't know marked the location of the popular Tia Juana bar just outside the base. Then he gave his first order as a submariner: "Make all preparations to get underway."

He started out cautiously, making half a knot at most. He'd kick it ahead one

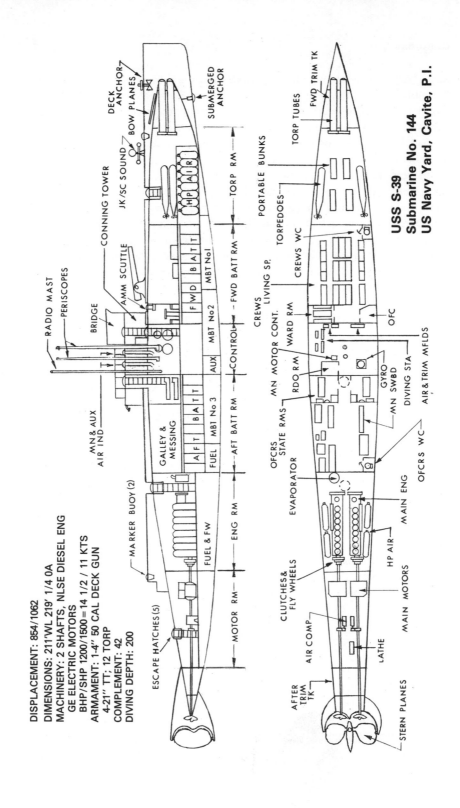

DISPLACEMENT: 854/1062
DIMENSIONS: 211'WL 219' 1/4 0A
MACHINERY: 2 SHAFTS, NLSE DIESEL ENG
GE ELECTRIC MOTORS
BHP/SHP 1200/1500 = 14 1/2 / 11 KTS
ARMAMENT: 1-4" 50 CAL DECK GUN
4-21" TT; 12 TORP
COMPLEMENT: 42
DIVING DEPTH: 200

USS S-39
Submarine No. 144
US Navy Yard, Cavite, P.I.

third speed then after thirty seconds had elapsed he'd stop. They approached the pier by inches. Although Larry was directing, "Right this, left that," it became more obvious by the minute that the quartermaster was steering the way he wanted to. When Larry glanced at him questioningly, Rollins said soothingly, "Everything's going fine, sir," and Larry thought, "Rollins has been bringing submarines alongside for ten years; he's just pretending I'm doing it. I'd better shut up and enjoy the experience."

The submarine crept in slowly, putting her bow neatly alongside the pier. One by one the officers jumped on board. Larry didn't even have to tie up.

"Good job," George Lautrup said. "I'll take it now."

As Larry gratefully turned over the responsibility, he noticed Pop Bridges, chief of the boat, hovering in the background, his lined, nutcracker face briefly illuminated as he held a match to his cigarette. Pop and Quartermaster Rollins exchanged nods. That was the end of Mr. Bernard's first full day aboard the *S-39*. Later on, he realized that the whole incident was typical of serving with Red Coe. Different skippers have different styles, and Coe's was relaxed responsibility. Coe had probably weighed the factors; a clear night with a calm and glassy sea, a quartermaster on board with years of experience, a chief of the boat second to none, and an eager new ensign whose worries would begin to dissolve with action. Besides, Coe wouldn't have had the patience to sit there on the dock indefinitely. He wasn't the type. Mosquitoes or not, Larry slept that night. In a few days he'd see Caroline and be able to share the whole experience with her.

Gunner's Mate Joseph S. Browning watched Larry Bernard's first days with interest; they brought back memories of his own beginnings in submarine service. When Browning first glimpsed *S-39*, she was sitting on keel blocks in dry-dock at Cavite. The rusty holes in the ancient outer hull looked cavernous, and the play of light and shadow in the setting sun made her resemble a wrinkled crone who ought to be arrested for indecent exposure. What a comedown for a guy who put the USS *Enterprise* into commission in 1938, Browning thought. What a change after serving on a brand-new aircraft carrier.

The feeling of having been shanghaied grew as he made his way to the deck of the submarine. He saluted the man on watch and asked where he should go to report in. The man gave him directions to the ship's office and a long, slow look. Browning couldn't tell if the look implied commiseration, derision, or just plain astonishment that another fool was about to become an S-boat sailor. Whatever it was, Browning began wishing he'd never had the urge to see the Far East.

As he slugged his way across the yard, he thought of home for the first time in a long time. Joseph Browning had been born and raised on a small farm near Greenville, Kentucky—tobacco and coal country. As the Depression had worsened, Browning had quit school after the eighth grade. He had to get out and support himself because there were other kids in the family, other mouths to feed.

He worked wherever he could find a job—a few days here, a week there. There were the rich brown tobacco fields of Muhlenberg County. There were mineral springs and resort hotels at Dawson Springs that hired extra help in the summer. The competition was ferocious; all Kentucky was on the prowl for work. But when you were down to your last penny and had no prospects at all, muskellunge could be caught in the Green River and cooked over a campfire.

Joseph Browning finally made his way to Louisville, where he considered himself lucky to find a job at a White Tower hamburger stand. At least he was close to bread, meat, and fried onions. But then he found out that there was food, drink, and shelter to be had for free if Uncle Sam would accept you, plus a chance to make a few bucks and learn a trade. He joined the Navy. For three years he minded his own business, had some good duty. Then he went on board the USS *Chaumont*, thirsty for big adventure in the mysterious Orient. En route he was assigned to USS *S-39*.

Just as Browning had suspected, from machinery to furniture, the old boat was as beat-up as the leftovers at a church rummage sale. But in spite of it all, Browning discovered within a couple of weeks that he liked submarines. Pop Bridges, chief of the boat, was an old souse but a great sailor. The skipper had a sense of humor and let it show. And Browning met an attractive Spanish girl who had attended college in the States. When she invited him to a party at Malacañan Palace, the White House of the Philippines, he was flying much higher than he ever had off the decks of the *Enterprise*. He was hooked and happy.

Tall, seventeen-year-old Allyn Christopher was struggling, as usual, with a loaded tray of dirty dishes. He knew he was beginning to look more emaciated than just skinny, and he now understood the meaning of the title "messcook" that went with his job: it was all mess and no cook. Only the guy who was called just "cook" dreamed up menus and created goodies. After three months serving the engineer's mess in the sweltering temperature of the crew's galley on the submarine tender *Canopus*, Christopher's big-boned frame had only 120 pounds of meat on it, a far cry from what he'd weighed back on the farm in Grand Forks, North Dakota. Now when he went ashore, his white liberty uniform hung on him. It was part of a fellow's pride that his bell-bottoms fit slick, but as Christopher watched the hot dishwater add more steam to the already steamy air, he allowed that his pride had been taking a beating one way or another ever since he'd been railroaded off the destroyer *Dewey* in Pearl Harbor and shanghaied out to the Asiatic Fleet.

As he carefully lowered the stack of dishes onto the sink, Christopher flinched at his recollections of his first assignment. Not a humble type by nature, he realized that starting at the bottom was inevitable. His first job on the destroyer had been cleaning the firesides, a part of the boiler that held the burning fuel and hot gases of combustion. It was the dirtiest, sootiest work of all for a lowly fireman apprentice. Following that, he became a messcook in the chief's quarters, and then captain of the cleanest head in the Navy. Finally, the powers-that-be decided he was smart enough to stand watch on the bridge, and Christopher felt that he had begun to climb the ladder of success at last.

When it came time to go out for gun practice, they put him on the speed cones, devices used to tell what speed the ship was doing. He was glad that the captain was present along with the engineer and the officer of the deck so they could see how efficiently he performed his tasks.

"Do you know the difference between one-third and two-thirds?" the officer of the deck asked solemnly.

Christopher replied, "Of course, sir," but they should have asked much more.

At that moment the *Dewey* was just passing the flagship *Pennsylvania*. With great aplomb young Allyn rigged the speed cones upside down one-third—which meant backing down. This order, if executed, could have terminated in a collision and court martial. The officers immediately began discussing Christopher's ability in terms that could not be mistaken for praise. That was Wednesday. On Thursday Allyn Christopher's transfer papers were ready. On Friday he was standing on the dock in downtown Honolulu, ready to board the transport *Chaumont*. Without a single aloha or pikake lei he'd been banished to the Asiatic Fleet.

The *Chaumont* had no extra hammocks or bunks for an unexpected guest so Christopher bedded down on the movie deck every night after the show was over. When he got to the Philippines, he was sent to the *Canopus,* where he was assigned once more to the messcook duty he hated. The Philippines were so much hotter than Hawaii that if it wasn't hell, it was damned close to it.

As he scratched the prickly heat that splotched his body at random, rapidly becoming raw skin on bones, he heard the messroom yeoman say, "Hey Christopher, you're going to have to do another turn." Then, reading Christopher's face, he added, "The only way you can get out of it is to go aboard submarines."

It only took a little while for Christopher to glance over the side of the tall tender, muse for a minute on how small those little black things looked, and decide he had nothing to lose. He volunteered for submarines and was assigned to the *S-39.*

With a clean jumper slung over his shoulder and a safety pin holding up his pants around his shrunken waist, he whipped lightheartedly down the gangway and made his way across the six S-boats tied up alongside the *Canopus*. He'd just placed a foot on the deck of *S-39* when he noticed a weatherbeaten chief sitting like a movie director in a special chair with white, fringed canvas awning over his head. Pop Bridges looked up, the brilliance of the tropical sun highlighting the deep grooves around his mouth as well as the more delicate crosshatch wrinkles on his jowls. "You coming aboard here, son?" he asked softly.

Christopher sucked in his guts to make a good impression. "Yes, sir."

"Don't call me sir," the chief said. "I'm glad you're coming aboard."

"Me too," Christopher agreed, happy that somebody was beginning to appreciate him at last.

"They're waiting for you in the galley." Chief Bridges paused. "We need another messcook."

It was a low blow. Allyn Christopher looked up at the tender he'd just left and thought, it can't be any hotter down here than it was up there.

The submarine tender *Canopus* serviced a squadron of (two divisions) 12 submarines. Acquired by the U.S. Navy in 1921, *Canopus* had originally been a merchant ship of the Grace line named the *Santa Leonora*. She had machine shops and forges, carried enlisted men's uniforms and small stores of all kinds, and boasted messes for officers and men, movie facilities, barbers, medical treatment, and postal services. *Canopus* had real showers, unlimited ice cream, and cold drinking water. She was a floating town. After a long stretch on an old S-boat (pigboat to submariners because of foul living conditions) to go aboard *Canopus* could be heaven. To serve aboard her, whatever work you did, had its compensations, since she hardly ever got underway—everybody joked about having to dredge out the coffee grounds under her keel in order to move her. What's more, it was possible to get liberty almost every night, which insured longevity with a Manila girlfriend if you had energy and money enough to afford one.

Still, the *Canopus* had spawned many a submariner; a number of the men who served aboard her decided, sooner or later, to leave the mother ship (they often called her Mama San, meaning honorable mother) and try the offspring down below. Some did it out of curiosity, some because they wanted the extra pay, a smaller organization, or more action.

One of the rare times when the *Canopus* became a seagoing vessel was reluctantly experienced by Thomas Parks. He had wanted nothing so much as to be assigned to the old carrier *Langley,* first of her breed to land planes and now relegated to the role of aircraft tender in the Philippines. Tom's older brother Jim was aboard, serving as a motor machinist's mate. The two boys were close companions, and in the 1930s the Navy encouraged brothers to serve on the same ship. Besides, their father, James R. Parks, had been a World War I pioneer in naval aviation; he had flown with an antisubmarine patrol squadron in

France, and when Tom and Jim were born, he was an aviation rigger first class attached to a patrol bomber squadron on North Island, off San Diego.

San Diego was an important naval base whose businessmen depended largely upon fleet revenue for survival, especially during the Great Depression. And unlike people inland, the coastal dwellers had many opportunities to see war clouds gathering. The docks were piled high with scrap iron being shipped to Japan to provide raw material for its steel industry. Tom heard his father express concern that this metal would come back in a bloody form, to take the lives of Americans one day. The United States was also selling the Japanese sophisticated sonar gear designed for antisubmarine warfare.

Jim enlisted in 1937, and on October 5, 1939, young Tom was sworn in as an apprentice seaman. He immediately applied for machinist's mate school in Norfolk, Virginia. He didn't make it. His first assignment was the USS *Rigel* at the destroyer base in San Diego, where he worked in an engine-room gang, putting machinery back into operating shape on World War I four-stack destroyers that were traded to Great Britain for operating bases in the Caribbean. The work was hard, the hours long, the pay scarcely royal. But even on $21 a month Tom could have enjoyed a couple of nickel beers and a free lunch—ham, cheese, potato salad, corned beef, and pickled eggs dyed red with beet juice—if he hadn't been only 18. The legal drinking age was 21 in California, and the sturdy, dark-haired Tom still had a little boy's round-cheeked face. There were compensations. It wasn't bad being in his hometown where he could see his girl, Corenne Ward.

But Tom didn't want to spend his whole hitch on home territory. Since Jim's ship was in Manila, Tom asked for a transfer to the Asiatic Fleet. From the Fort Mason docks in San Francisco Tom boarded the *Chaumont,* but it wasn't until the ship crossed the 180th meridian and was officially under Commander Asiatic Fleet that assignments were revealed. Sure that he would get the *Langley,* Tom was not happy to see his name listed with those ordered to the *Canopus*. He immediately applied for reassignment but was told that he would have to wait until he was received on board the *Canopus* before he could switch duty.

The golden sunlight, waving palms, and azure skies of Manila did not console this southern Californian who'd seen it all before. Unfortunately he could also see his mecca, the *Langley,* tied up at Sangley Point. Quick-tempered at times, Tom could only feel depressed as he was herded into a motor launch, but youthful optimism began to rise and he convinced himself that in another twenty-four hours he'd be on his way to the *Langley.* The euphoria didn't last long. As soon as he set foot aboard the *Canopus* he had a sneaking suspicion that she was making preparations to go to sea. He was right.

Tom was assigned to the boat shop but stood underway watches as an engine-room messenger. The huge steam engine was an old quadruple expansion type, one of the last of its kind on any Navy ship, and as far as Tom was concerned, the whole engine room was a one-of-a-kind Hades. After standing watches for two weeks in the bone-dissolving heat, he knew he didn't want to be a steam-power machinist's mate.

When the *Canopus* finally anchored in Manila again after six weeks at sea, Tom was in the first liberty party. But he found that the *Langley* didn't need another fireman third class and that *Canopus* wouldn't release him anyway unless he could arrange a swap. The Navy won; he gave up trying and decided it wasn't such bad duty after all. He became a messcook in the boat crew's mess.

Like many another, the 19-year-old sailor did a lot of staring down at the submarines alongside *Canopus*. He found out that sooner or later, if you were a messcook, you'd be asked if you wanted sub duty; it seemed that messcooks, always hoping for something better, provided a pool of non-rated men for the boats. Tom was asked. He didn't say no. In the fall of 1940, Parks was assigned to *S-39*.

Edmund Schab, radioman, also went aboard the *S-39* in 1940 from the *Canopus*. He was a seasoned man who had served on the tender for more than two years. By the time he switched to submarines, he was well aware that war was a very real probability, having witnessed an incident that was almost the start of one. Soon after Schab joined the *Canopus,* the tender went to Tsingtao, China, on the Shantung peninsula. Ed was in the radio shack when the submarine rescue vessel *Pigeon* notified *Canopus* that a torpedo had been accidentally dropped in the water. *Pigeon* requested permission to send divers for it. Commander Submarine Forces said, "Go ahead."

By this time—1938—the Japanese were engaged in a full-scale war with China and claimed the territory where the torpedo had been lost. Ed Schab knew that in 1937 the gunboat USS *Panay,* patrolling the Yangtze River to protect American commerce and nationals, had been dive-bombed by fifteen Japanese planes and strafed by nine fighters in the space of twenty minutes on a peaceful Sunday afternoon. Stunned and injured by the totally unprovoked but well-planned attack, the ship had fought back as best she could but had eventually gone down. Japanese planes continued to strafe the lifeboats as they headed for the shore. Three men were killed and 11 wounded, but prompt and profuse Japanese apologies for the "dreadful mistake" averted what had seemed like certain war.

Now, a year later, Schab and the rest of the gang in the radio shack were afraid that history was threatening to repeat itself. Nipponese army officers, binoculars trained on the scene from shore installations, noted the activities aboard the *Pigeon*. In no time at all, a chunky, self-important little Japanese tugboat steamed out and told the Americans flatly, "You can't dive."

But the orders from the *Canopus* remained, "Dive for that torpedo."

Pigeon resumed preparations. Shortly after, a Japanese cruiser appeared. The men in the radio shack began breathing a little faster. Things were getting hairy and the situation was reported to Admiral H.E. Yarnell. He replied, "Obey your last order; dive for that torpedo.

The crew of the *Pigeon,* who had been starting and stopping like wind-up toys, fell to again, fastening the divers into their bulky gear: canvas-covered rubber suits, bronze helmets, lead belts, and lead shoes. Another Japanese cruiser appeared. The quiet in the radio shack made the buzzing of the eternal mosquitoes sound like a dancehall on payday. But within the hour, all heads turned in another direction to find the flagship *Houston* present and in the process of training her eight-inch guns on the two Japanese cruisers—which responded in kind. Then the light cruiser *Marblehead* joined the *Houston.* While the two pairs of warships confronted each other with guns at the ready, the *Pigeon's* divers were cautiously lowered, and the slow process of bringing the torpedo aboard and then delivering it to the submarine was completed. No shots were fired. Ed Schab took a deep breath, his first in a long time.

Schab volunteered for sub duty because he had observed the informality and camaraderie—and the extra pay—that submarine sailors enjoyed. A happy type by nature, he liked the Philippines and the people liked him.

He had several girlfriends; scotch was only 75 cents a bottle; you could get along anywhere in the English language; and in the dancehalls the Filipino bands played the kind of swing music that a sailor could jitterbug and shag to. Besides, the local girls were small and slender, had rhythm, and could follow the intricate dance steps that sometimes became gymnastics. Confident and a little cocky, he was a 20-year-old who knew how to have a good time. He also knew how to stir up excitement when things got dull but was expert, most of the time, at staying out of trouble.

It hadn't been an easy life back in Massachusetts. His father had died when he was six, and his Polish mother, who couldn't speak English, was left with three children to support. In the depths of the Depression, when Ed was 16, he lied about his age, passed the tests, and joined the Navy.

Fresh out of training, he was ordered to the Asiatic Fleet. Although he'd reached 17 by then, beneath all the bravado he was a scared little boy when they told him he was going way out to China; the farthest he'd ever been from home didn't add up to 100 miles. But after he'd said goodbye to his family, the itch for adventure took over, and he began enjoying the life he'd chosen.

It took him almost nine months to make his way out. Ordered to several different ships for temporary duty while making various legs of the journey through Panama, he had deck duties all the way. When he reached San Diego he was put on the *Trenton* while awaiting transport to China. Another delay, and then fate stepped in. A pair of badly infected tonsils sent him to Mare Island Naval Hospital. With his usual bounce, and as soon as he was let loose, Schab explored San Francisco and went to the roller skating rinks that in sunny California replaced the ice skating in his home state of Massachusetts. At the roller rink he even met a girl he liked, Dorothy Reynolds, and left for Manila with her picture in his pocket. He didn't hear from her often, but even though he was no celibate, he didn't forget her.

Although there wasn't much difference in their ages, Schab had the jump on some of the other newcomers like Allyn Christopher, Ed Matthews, and Tom Parks because of his years of experience on the *Canopus*. When Schab actually came on board the *S-39*, he began to wonder why he'd requested sub duty. It was so small. It measured only 220 feet from stem to stern and carried just 42 men; machinery and torpedoes took up most of the space. He pictured it all closed up and submerged, realizing that they'd be shoulder to shoulder, all breathing the same limited amount of stale air. He knew that the two things that got you off a submarine fastest were (a) to have an offensive body odor and (b) to request it; any man who asked to leave was released immediately, no questions asked, because he might endanger the rest of the personnel. But Ed was an old China hand now, and asking out would be called losing face.

Was he scared? A little bit, but he hoped he wouldn't show it. It didn't occur to him that other people might feel the same way.

If Schab had told Pop Bridges how he felt, the understanding old chief of the boat, who lent an ear to everybody's troubles, would probably have given him a lot of reassurance. Bridges was everybody's favorite, from Captain Coe to the lowliest seaman, with few exceptions; one was the other chief, Dutch Mandekic.

Mandekic, much younger, looked upon himself and Pop as rivals. An intelligent man, the chief motor machinist's mate was German-born, had been a submariner on U-boats in the German navy, and still spoke with an accent so heavy that he was sometimes hard to understand. He was a tease by nature and, perhaps because he had difficulty verbalizing, loved to play practical jokes, most often choosing Pop as the butt. Bridges, like many of the crew, enjoyed a nap, after the noonday meal when the *39* was in port. Pop always chose the small control room, perhaps because he'd have it all to himself.

The control room contained two periscopes and three big wheels that opened the ballast tanks. One afternoon when Pop was dozing beneath the air manifold, his upper lip rhythmically poofing out with a zzzz that never quite turned into a full-fledged snore, his knobby, sun-browned hands folded across his chest, Mandekic decided to liven up the old fellow's siesta. Tiptoeing in, Dutch raised the periscope and called out in his best commanding voice, "Make all torpedoes ready for firing."

Pop's eyelids fluttered but didn't open, so Mandekic shouted, "Up periscope, stand by to fire." Pop's eyes were half open now, and Mandekic boomed out, "fire one, fire two, fire three, fire four," making as much commotion as though captain and crew were all present.

By this time Pop's bloodshot blue eyes, though dazed, were wide open, and when Mandekic yelled, "Down 'scope," up went Pop Bridges, bopping his balding head on the valve wheels of the air manifold overhead with enough force to keep him star-gazing for quite some time. He swore at the machinist's mate with all the fervor of an old parrot, signing off as he usually did by growling, "You damned Dutchman, why don't you learn to speak English!" Mandekic, doubled up with laughter, ran out of the control room, and crew members listening outside pretended not to know what had been going on. It was supposed to have been all in fun, but as always, there was an edge to the way Mandekic did it and an edge to the way Pop received it.

Bridges was a married man who took it seriously although his wife was in the States. He didn't go ashore often, but when he did, a lot of pent-up energy was released. His occasional toots didn't take place more than three or four times a year, but they lasted through several days. The scuttlebutt was that if Mandekic crossed his path during these sessions, there were fistfights. Perhaps the war already going on between England and Germany, as well as liquor, helped to unleash antagonisms between the two.

Pop's lapses from grace only endeared him to the men. As far as they were concerned, there wasn't another submarine in the Asiatic Fleet that had as good a chief of the boat. Bridges was father to the crew, even standing up to the executive officer and straightening him out if necessary. The captain was the most important man on any ship, but the men knew that the chief of the boat was next.

Bridges had been a submariner for many years, but despite his weather-worn face and drooping eyelids, he was probably not much more than 50. He liked to tell stories about the First World War, when he had made two patrols out of Ireland aboard the *L-10* as a torpedoman third class. And the men liked to hear them, again and again.

When the girl Ed Schab heard from now and then, petite, dark-haired Dorothy Reynolds, graduated from St. Elizabeth's Catholic High School for girls in Oakland, California, in 1940, the Depression had eased and the young woman found clerical work in the offices of Owens, Illinois Glass. Born in Oklahoma, she had moved with her parents to the Bay area when she was 16, just before she met Ed at the roller rink. Between working and dating she didn't have much time left for daydreams, but when she did, she thought of her brief encounter with the wavy-haired, reddish blond Schab.

She always went back to the beginning, remembering that night two years before when she had started talking to the young sailor as she sat on the sidelines and watched her girlfriend skate at the roller dome in San Francisco. She progressed to flirting with him discreetly as they discussed the relative merits of Artie Shaw, Harry James, and Benny Goodman. None of it was very heavy; they joked a lot, and Ed asked if he could see her home, which she had hoped he would do.

The Bay Bridge had opened that year, but they chose the ferry; it took longer, and besides, it was more romantic. When they got to downtown Oakland, though, Dorothy wouldn't let him take her the rest of the way home. Her parents were strict and considered servicemen the lowest of the low. She was afraid her dad would blow his stack and lock her up for months if he knew she'd gone out with a sailor. Ed had to report back to the hospital at Mare Island, but they made a date for the following weekend.

It was a movie date, as most of them were. They saw a double feature: jolly, big-mouthed Joe E. Brown in *The Gladiator*, which made them laugh, and *The Prisoner of Zenda* with Douglas Fairbanks, Jr., who couldn't quite equal the daring feats of his father. The 25-cent ticket also entitled them to the Pathé news, a Popeye cartoon, and a travelogue with the usual sunset fadeout leaving the beautiful isle of Fiji or some such. There was a sing-along, featuring an organist who ran through old favorites like "Down by the Old Mill Stream" and newer ones like "Tiptoe through the Tulips"; the words were flashed on the screen, and a little white ball bounced along the syllables in time to the tune. The only thing missing was Bank Night, when patrons could win dishes and other prizes, but that was held only on Monday or Tuesday when business was slower.

Dorothy and Ed didn't hold hands, and they didn't smoke, although they would have liked to do both. Holding hands on a first date wasn't mandatory, any more than a kiss was; it was strictly up to the girl. And you had to sit in the loge section of the movie house to smoke, and those seats cost more money.

They had another movie date the next week, winding up with a hamburger and a pineapple milkshake. Dorothy told her folks she was meeting a girlfriend. When the time came for Ed to go back to San Diego, Dorothy played hooky from school, riding the bus up to Vallejo in her school uniform, bobby socks, and saddle shoes. There were regrets on both sides, but they were too young to make long-range promises. Ed was also too poor, and a lowly seaman his age couldn't marry without permission anyway.

Dorothy and her family lived next door to her best girlfriend, Jerry Johnson. Jerry had an up-to-date mother who allowed her to smoke in the house, and Dorothy spent a lot of time over there, puffing away happily, knowing that if her parents ever saw her, there'd be hell to pay. Her Irish mother had been brought up hard-shell Baptist and disapproved of drinking and smoking, and although her English Catholic father did both, Dorothy was afraid he'd smack her and her brother, old as they were, if he ever caught them.

Dorothy and Jerry both liked servicemen and knew when the ships were coming in, even the Coast Guard cutters. They had a routine they followed when they wanted to cut loose and have some fun. Jerry's room was over the garage, a small detached building behind her house. When Dorothy went to spend the night, as she frequently did, the two girls waited until the families were asleep—never very late—and then over the fence they went.

Struggling against giggles and not daring to talk until they'd run a few blocks away, they'd stop and comb their hair, lay on a fresh coat of dark red lipstick, and head for downtown Oakland. There they'd haunt the places where the Navy hung out; Louis's Cafe, the Wunderbar, or the Silver Cafe. They'd dance and flirt, drink Cokes and fruit punch, and in their most sophisticated moments, accept a Camel, Old Gold, or Lucky and smoke it in short, quick puffs. If there wasn't a live band, the jukebox would blast out "And the Angels Sing," or "Chattanooga Choo-Choo," and the dance would be on. The extra wide, specially tailored bellbottoms that the sailors wore swirled as much as the girl's skirts. One of the best things about servicemen was that they didn't have cars. Without a car a girl couldn't be expected to neck, let alone pet, which meant that things progressed a little further anatomically. When Dorothy and Jerry said farewell, they rode the streetcar home by themselves and there were no unpleasant incidents. It was a nice safe life, and shinnying over the back fence in defiance of the older generation lent just that necessary element of excitement.

2. The Very Far East

For a young woman who had spent most of her childhood in mining camps high in the mountains of Idaho, Colorado, and California, the Philippines were a breathtaking experience even at sea level. The Boulevard Hotel, where Caroline and Larry Bernard took a room upon arrival, was both comfortable and convenient. But the heat defied the high ceilings; the flies and mosquitoes defied the netting over the bed; and the lizards defied control of any kind, scuttling in and out of sandals left on the floor. It was a combination that didn't go well with a first pregnancy. Caroline, having survived 28 days of almost continuous seasickness—and its humiliations—on an army transport from San Francisco, had hoped for a chance to settle down for a while when they disembarked at Manila. Instead, Larry left immediately for Olongapo where the *S-39* was in overhaul and sent for her a few days later. Longing to see him and no longer nauseated (even though tomatoes seemed to be about the only food she wanted to eat), she had hired a taxi and headed for the joyous reunion—they hadn't been married a year yet—only to find their accommodation was a nipa (palm leaf fiber) hut.

Surrounded by swaying palms whose trunks were encircled by metal guards to prevent rats from stealing the coconuts, shacks of this kind—home of the average Filipino—had fiber roofs and walls of woven palm secured by split bamboo lashed with vines; no nails were used. When it rained, the openings were covered by sliding horizontal windows made from many little panes of thin-sliced translucent shell, widely used in even the most elaborate homes and hotels. The one-room hut was set up on stilts to avoid flooding during the torrential rains and to insure the circulation of air. The toilet and shower emptied directly below without benefit of pipes, and the only running water was from heaven. Drinking water was pumped by hand from nearby artesian wells and brought to the huts in five-gallon cans. (Well-drilling, promoted by the United

States government, had improved island sanitation immeasurably.) It was not the bridal suite at the Manila Hotel, but it was certainly a test of true love and, for Caroline, a test of true grit. Returning to Manila after ten days in the nipa shack made her appreciate the Boulevard Hotel much, much more.

The Bernards had come to the Philippines with two of Larry's submarine school classmates and their wives. Caroline was glad to have these ready-made companions to share her triumphs and troubles. Although at first she seemed to have more of the latter. One of Larry's first social obligations when the 39 returned to Manila from overhaul was to pay a call on the skipper and his wife. It was a rigid ritual. Caroline dressed as carefully as if she were going to a funeral, tucking her freshly coiffed brown hair into a wide-brimmed straw hat and feeling her girdle cling tighter and tighter as perspiration seeped through the talcum powder. She glanced down the backs of her legs to make sure her stocking seams ran in a straight line from the heels of the brown and white spectator sports pumps to the hem of her brown linen shirtmaker dress.

"You look swell," Larry said.

Frowning over her shoulder at him, she said, "Don't use that word."

"Why not?"

She ran her hands over the barely perceptible bulge beneath the belt of her dress. "Because that's just what I'm starting to do, swell."

"Come on, you look great. Let's get going." Larry tried to take her arm but missed as she reached back to scoop up white gloves, a must for call-paying.

The Navy didn't ship private cars to the Philippines, so everyone took taxis or two-wheeled, horse-drawn gigs called *calesas* or *carromatas*. These conveyances were so cheap even the Bernards could afford them. An ensign and his wife, living on $229 a month (including 25 percent extra submarine pay) barely had enough to stretch from payday to payday back in the States, but out here many things cost less—especially help in the form of houseworkers, gardeners, and *amahs* (children's nurses).

The Army provided quarters for its officers and their families, but the Navy almost never did, so Captain and Mrs. Coe lived in a new suburb called Pasay, not far from the Polo Club. Both Caroline and Larry were all eyes as they swung down Dewey Boulevard, past the famous Manila Hotel facing the bay, the Army-Navy Club where much of their social life would center, the High Commissioner's palace, and beautiful homes surrounded by lush and extensive gardens. They glimpsed the partly exposed hulls of two Spanish vessels sunk long ago, little dreaming that in less than two years Manila Bay would contain the pitiful remains of ships marked USS.

A little farther on, the driver pointed out an old fort named San Antonio Abad, which had been captured early in the American attack on Manila in 1898. But the biggest eye-popper of all was the sight of a little man toting a long, pale brown reptile whose thick body was marked with the darker crossbars that identified it as a boa constrictor. A dozen bare-footed, raggle-taggle children followed behind, munching lantanas (a fruit that resembled a large yellow grape) and giggling as they threw the peelings at the indifferent boa, which—though nonpoisonous—could crush a person to death.

As they turned into the suburbs, Larry explained that there wasn't much point in their trying to find an apartment just now, since the real heat and rain would start soon and in two weeks, on March 31, the Asiatic Fleet would leave for Shanghai and Tsingtao.

"What does that mean?" Carolyn asked with a tremor in her voice as she visualized spending months in Manila without Larry.

"It means relief from the heat. Wives and children go, too, so there'll be plenty of you catching whatever commercial transportation you can find. We'll be away about three months, you'll have a chance to see interesting places, we'll all cool off, and the Navy will operate in a change of waters."

It sounded much better than Caroline had thought at first. She had no way of knowing that it would be the last time for what had been a longstanding yearly event. An era was coming to an end.

Rachel and Red Coe greeted the Bernards warmly as they all sat down in a pleasant living room with Chinese rugs and the rattan furniture that almost everybody used in Manila because it was cool, well made, and inexpensive. A ceiling fan revolved overhead, creating a breeze that chased the flies and mosquitoes to the far corners of the room. Caroline commented on how attractive the two-story house was, and the Coes explained that the new single-family dwellings were still being built on stilts because of the damp rice fields and carabao (water buffalo) close by.

Caroline noticed at once that Mrs. Coe was well along in her second pregnancy. The Coes' daughter Jean, two and a half years old, joined them briefly before her *amah* led her away with the typical gentleness displayed by Filipinos and Chinese toward children. Little Jean, clutching her rag doll by its yellow yarn hair, went without a whimper. Caroline, who had only recently begun accumulating small talk after a childhood in the mountains, where she and her sisters had been tutored for lack of enough children to form a school, found Rachel Coe friendly but not the gregarious sort that her husband was. There were no embarrassing lulls in the conversation, though, because Coe stepped in frequently, telling amusing incidents about his experiences in teaching navigation to midshipmen at the Naval Academy, his last duty before coming to the China Station.

The tall captain had the complexion of a true carrottop. Tall and fair as fair could be, he found it impossible to enjoy the beach without blistering and took care to wear hats and long-sleeved shirts to shield him from the scorching tropical sun when he played golf. He was outgoing, witty, and a shrewd judge of human nature. In contrast, his tall and slender wife had dark hair and eyes and a skin that tanned effortlessly during the many hours she spent playing tennis at the Army-Navy Club or riding horseback at Clark Field. Carolyn found out that Rachel Coe was not following the boats to Shanghai and Tsingtao this year because her pregnancy was too advanced. Instead, she would take her doctor's advice and go to Baguio, the cool summer resort in the mountains, accompanied by little Jean and her nurse. As the Bernards left, Larry discreetly placed three calling cards on the silver tray by the front door, an integral part of the etiquette of the occasion. One of the cards had Caroline's name alone; the others said "Ensign & Mrs." Mrs. Lawrence G. Bernard had called only upon Mrs. James W. Coe because a lady never calls upon a gentleman.

When the Bernards' taxi pulled away, Rachel Coe went out for a short stint of gardening in the cooler twilight hours. It was one of her favorite occupations now that she was too bulky for riding or tennis. Born and raised a Quaker in Wilmington, Delaware, she had gone to Bucknell University, then secretarial school. Interested in merchandising and textiles, she had also attended a course for prospective buyers given by Macy's, but that was 1931, and the management told her honestly, after about a year and a half in New York, that there were no jobs for anyone, let alone someone new in the field. This Depression frustration was the only one the young woman had experienced; her father, Frederic Gowthrop, had his own business and as a plumbing and heating contractor worked constantly and exclusively for the Du Ponts, Depression or not. Although straitlaced in many ways, her mother had been Phi Beta Kappa at Swarthmore College, graduating in 1894 when most girls barely made it through grade school. Consequently, Mrs. Gowthrop did not automatically think that woman's place was in the home. When Rachel said she really wanted to strike out on her own and chose Honolulu, Mrs. Gowthrop did not protest. Ten years before, Rachel's sister Helen had done the same, utlimately traveling around the world.

Rachel was offered a job shortly after she arrived in Hawaii. Considering the paucity of any kind of work at the time—for males, let alone females—she jumped at the chance, despite the eyebrow-raising business she would be involved in. As a secretary for the Von Hamm, Young company in Honolulu, she was responsible for making out lists of wines and whiskeys that the firm was ordering in large quantities now that Prohibition had ended (she did not let her Quaker parents know what the company imported). Then she met Jim Coe of Richmond, Indiana, a 1930 Naval Academy graduate. They married in Honolulu in 1935, later returned to Annapolis for shore duty, and—when it came time for a change—both agreed that Asiatic duty sounded fascinating. For Rachel, it meant taking another step in the round-the-world trip she had never completed.

Submarines were a mystery to Rachel, as they were to most Navy wives. After Jim took her aboard the *S-39* for dinner when they first came to the Philippines, she begged off further visits because of her pregnancy. The heat of the tiny wardroom, the the odor of turkey mixed with diesel and sweat, made a gymnasium seem a rose garden by comparison. Though she never told him so, Jim sometimes brought the peculiar aroma home with him. The submarine smell, she called it.

Like her sister, who had married into the Army, Rachel had to face one of the basic principles of her Quaker upbringing when she married a naval officer: "Thou shalt not kill." When asked about having military men in a family whose religion stressed nonviolence, her father said loyally, "If I had a third daughter, I'd marry her off to a Marine," but no one knew how he really felt. Rachel was aware that war was possible and that submarines were not mechanical dolphins playing games for their own amusement, though it was hard for her to understand how anyone could deliberately kill. Before the Second World War ended, Rachel Coe, brought up in gentleness, would know what it meant to have murder in her heart.

Rachel enjoyed playing bridge at the Army-Navy Club in Manila, but her background had not prepared her for the amount of drinking among some of the wives. The Navy kept tropical working hours, going out to sea at 0700 (7 A.M.) and returning at 1500 (3:00 P.M.). Rachel, a nondrinker by choice as well as upbringing, looked askance upon the imbibing that started before lunch and seemed to go on into the night. She knew that Jim was no teetotaler, but somehow it was easier to accept in the male. Still, she was not preachy so she kept her opinions to herself and stuck to her iced tea and fruit punch. Part of the drinking could be blamed upon the women having too little to do, what with nurses, houseboys, laundresses, and cooks (who even did the marketing) so easy to hire. The problem was not peculiar to the armed services; it existed among wives of American businessmen in the community, too, many of whom had never known such affluence at home.

Living in the Far East had already taught Rachel some new realities. Although she regretted not being able to join Jim for the next few months in Shanghai and Tsingtao, there had been grim experiences there the year before, and she had been forced to turn away in her helplessness as had many another Westerner.

Back in 1863 the United States and Great Britain had consolidated areas conceded to them in Shanghai, China's largest city, and had possessed them ever since. The French had operated their sector separately, but it was all part of the territory known as the International Settlement, frequented by Europeans of diverse backgrounds. Many of the Russians were refugees from the revolution of 1918. Rachel found the architecture in this part of Shanghai indistinguishable from that of any modern city. She enjoyed the conveniences of the Park Hotel, with its guests from all over the world and the extensive parks nearby that had no doubt given it its name. But Rachel wanted to see more than this and she ventured forth frequently with sometimes frightening results. Outside the Inter-

national Settlement the sick, dying, and hungry among the awesome prolifera-
tion of the Chinese population were facts of life it was hard to ignore.

One day she emerged from the hotel, slip of paper in hand upon which the
multilingual desk clerk had written in Chinese characters, as he always did, the
destination she had selected for the morning's excursion. Her particular ricksha
boy trotted up bowing and smiling what Rachel called his death's head grin—all
teeth, cheekbones, and skull with no flesh beneath the taut, grayish skin. She
dropped the instructions into his outstretched palm, careful not to touch him. At
first, the young woman had shuddered at the thought of letting the cadaverous
body haul the weight of a person her size; this man looked incapable of pulling a
child the age of her daughter. In addition he was being used as a human dray
horse, and her ancestors had fought hard to change conditions like these. But her
friends at the hotel had said, "You've got to close your eyes. There's absolutely
nothing you can do. There are millions upon millions of them, and if you don't
hire him, you're taking the rice out of his mouth." So she did, but she never got
used to it. There were hordes of ricksha boys crowding the entrance to the hotel,
even though one in particular had established himself as "hers." Competition
was so great for the privilege of hauling foreign bodies that the emaciated mass
never stopped trying. The backdrop of the beautifully kept green parks, fashion-
able couples dressed in finest silks and tweeds with jewels to match, and the
rosy cheeks of well-fed Caucasian children heightened the contrast between
East and West.

On this particular day, Rachel tried not to look at the convolutions of the
bent back between the shafts as the frail coolie struggled to get the ride
underway. The wheeze of his heaving chest was smothered by the sound of
scurrying people, screaming vendors, and squalling children as they left the
international sector. Rachel had learned to ignore the pauses when the ricksha
boy stopped by the side of the road to urinate, but she never learned to ignore the
sick and dying that passersby casually stepped over to go on about their
business. She never managed to relax until she finally stepped off at her
destination. First, there was the fear that a sudden stop might throw her against
the ricksha boy; the *amah* she had engaged for Jean at the hotel had warned her
never to touch these men for fear of disease which she could bring home to her
child. Second, she always seemed to be holding her breath in an effort to make
herself lighter—a totally irrational impulse, as she well knew. Last of all, no
matter how many people she saw riding the same conveyances, there was a
feeling of guilt.

Suddenly the ricksha *did* stop abruptly. Only her agility in leaning sideways
prevented her being thrown on top of the crumpled scarecrow body that lay face
down, a thin stream of blood trickling from the nose smashed against the filthy
pavement. A hundred hands reached toward the pitiful figure, but not to help; as
though he were merely a traffic obstruction, fingers clawed him off to one side,

the head thumping against the cobbles. Her ricksha boy was dead. In a second, a dozen others were pushing and shoving for the privilege of pulling her the rest of the way, crying out, "Missy, I take you, I take you," desperate for the few pennies involved. Later, Rachel found it hard to talk about what had happened. The people at the hotel were right. You simply had to put it out of your mind.

Although less traumatic, other customs were equally strange. Even in the finest shops along Bund Avenue or Nanking Road, after Rachel had been offered and had accepted the ceremonial cup of tea that preceded commerce, she would often notice an ancient, gray-bearded Chinese sitting quietly in the corner smoking his opium pipe. It was an accepted part of the culture. The sleepy-eyed elder, father of one of the shop's proprietors, had earned his right to sit peacefully, easing his arthritic twinges and other discomforts of age with the soothing juice of the poppy. His children considered it their duty to provide him with the facilities.

Rachel found the routine at the Park Hotel perfect for anyone with children (although she and Jim sometimes dined elsewhere to sample the many varieties of Chinese food). Three European-style meals a day were provided in the hotel dining hall, or you could have food brought to your room. Inexpensively hired *amahs* guarded the children like dragons, sleeping outside the door so that if a child cried in the night, or if you needed anything, they were right there to help. These nurses also saw to it that little ones were shielded from the constant caughing and spitting of the sick poor; they washed the children's hands dozens of times a day.

When Rachel was told about the knitting *amahs,* she was eager to hire one of those also. The knitting *amah* did not socialize with the other help; she simply sat working, day after day. Rachel had only to buy the wool, point out what she wanted in old copies of Vogue and Harper's Bazaar, and indicate for whom the article was to be made. Without taking measurements, the *amah*—who spoke no English—would fashion dresses, sweaters, jackets, socks, and caps that fit perfectly. Even clothing ordered for friends or family in the States was no problem.

Rachel's knitting *amah* was about 50 years old with threads of gray beginning to show in her smooth black hair. It didn't seem to bother her to sit cross-legged all day in her drab jacket and pantaloons, nor did the bad light in the corner she had selected hinder the rapid and precise click-clack as she knitted German style with no pause to throw the yarn around the needle. She kept this up from eight o'clock in the morning until six at night for a dollar a day plus one bowl of rice placed on the floor beside her at noontime. Rachel thought it a cruel and killing life but was warned again, "Don't interfere; that's the way it's done."

Being a young woman who had always been fascinated by textiles, Rachel could not resist having some dresses made, as well. For $5 worth of labor and $5 worth of the finest brocade, she could have a magnificent evening gown; a pair of shoes handmade from the same material cost another dollar for the cobbler. The Far East was the most extreme example of extremes that Rachel Coe would ever encounter—luxury and poverty, haves and have-nots, with no in-between. In some ways, she was relieved not to be going back to Shanghai this year.

Ed Schab would never forget his baptismal dive. The first thing he became aware of was that all the usual sounds—the snuffling, throat-clearing, slap-slap of sandals, occasional raucous laughter and four-letter words—had stopped completely. Quiet was necessary so that the diving officer's orders could be heard. Then a heavier vibration set in because the screws were turning at full speed, and Ed figured that his own quivers would be hidden by the quivering old pigboat. Captain Coe had come into the control room to stand by the periscope; the shoosh of escaping air could be heard from the tanks being vented. Suddenly awash in perspiration, Ed felt a stream of it run down his forehead and land on his bare chest as they submerged, but to his astonishment his stomach stayed below his ribs. He had imagined it might be like the drop in a fast elevator, but in fact it was easy; he liked it, and he could feel the corners of his mouth turning up in a smile of relief. Daring to look around him now, he saw that some of the other "virgins" were looking around, too. He caught Ed Matthews's eye and heard him whisper, "It's a lot better than patrol bombers."

Edward (Zeke) Matthews, determined to get into the Navy, had made it on the third try and, after training at Great Lakes, Illinois, was sent to the Naval Air Station in Seattle, Washington. It was good duty but he didn't like it. He had always wanted to be a sailor who went to sea. When the Navy asked for volunteers for the Asiatic Fleet, the short, dark-haired, dark-eyed Matthews was first in line, and after being in Cavite for a couple of weeks, he volunteered again—this time for submarines.

Zeke had been orphaned at age nine and raised by foster parents. One of the things he liked best about the *39* was that its crew was like a big family. When he first reported on board, he'd missed out on supper all around and guessed he'd better shut up and forget it. But right away someone asked the hungry 20-year-old, "Had any chow?" and, when he shook his head, went back to the galley and fixed him some. When he finished and went topside, J.S. Browning, who was about to go ashore, asked, "Got any money?" Pay records were always a couple of months behind, so Matthews shook his head again and was told, "We'll lend you some." Then Browning said, "Know anything about Manila?" For the third time Ed had to say no. "Don't go there alone at first," the gunner's mate advised. "Ask anybody who's going ashore and they'll take you so's you can learn the ropes. I'm going now—I'll show you around if you want." But Matthews had had enough new experiences for one day. "I'll take a raincheck," he said, then added softly, "but thanks, thanks a lot."

Matthews was a slight but high-energy type whose well-being depended heavily upon the availability of food. He soon discovered the never-ending pot of delicious soup simmering in the galley 24 hours a day; it was great for hangovers, colds, insomnia, and just plain hunger. Nobody ever knew whether Schoenrock, the ship's cook, who had all the temperament of a French chef, started the soup from scratch now and then or just kept adding seasonings and scraps as they came along. And nobody ever dared ask. Matthews didn't care; he was contented for the first time in a long time and liked the feel of the whole experience.

As part of the communication gang, Schab's duties when surfaced were radio receiving and transmitting; after submerging he moved into the torpedo room as a sonarman. The first time he went in there he noticed the artwork mounted on top of the gyro setters: grinning down on him were two chrome Buddhas, one Japanese and the other Chinese. Both had been mounted on the tubes by Torpedoman Third Class Leonard Johnson. Johnson had bought them in Tsingtao on a bum boat, a small vessel used for collecting garbage and for peddling various wares to ships. The Buddhas had become fixtures, good-luck symbols for the torpedomen and the crew in general.

When the *39* was asked to give the chaplain from the *Canopus* a ride back from Tsingtao to Manila, the good man decided that the officers and crew needed a spiritual workout after so much carnal activity ashore. The padre was a Catholic priest with red hair and a face to match. Leonard Johnson knew that the color suffusing the chaplain's cheeks and nose came from bar exposure, not sun exposure; the Father had been asked to leave several pubs, but not because he'd been trying to make converts. In other words, he was a very human man of the cloth who might have been expected to be tolerant of the foibles of others.

Captain Coe requested that officers and men attend church services in the torpedo room, where a makeshift altar had been set up in front of the tubes. Solemnly the crew filed in wanting to do something for their captain and their souls as well. Some of them were a little dark under the eyes and heavy-lidded above from the joys of Slick's Bar and Grill near the waterfront in Tsingtao, but all were eager to be made new again. The chaplain had their full attention, but when he turned to pray, he found himself looking right into the faces of the grinning Buddhas. He stopped abruptly, and the crew began to laugh; even the captain had to press his lips firmly together.

The chaplain folded his hands and asked without a glimmer of humor in his bloodshot blue eyes, "Who put these statues here?" Johnson, sensing a holier-than-thou attitude, said, "I did, sir." He paused briefly, then added, "We always chin-chin to the Buddhas when we fire torpedoes." There was no mistaking the padre's disapproval, and the service ended abruptly. The man of the cloth also complained about the records that the crew enjoyed playing over and over again on an old, hand-cranked gramophone. Leonard found it hard to see the harm in "Caviar Comes from Virgin Sturgeon," "She had to Go and Lose It at the Astor," and "Peter Grew"—although they did get a little tiresome, since these three selections were the only ones on board.

As soon as they got back to Manila, Browning was transferred to the USS *Perch*. It was an Asiatic Station fleet boat, considered by some to be a step up in the world, but the gunner's mate did not leave without regrets.

Leonard Johnson hailed from Eau Claire, Wisconsin. Tall and heavyset, with a mop of unruly brown hair, he was one of the rare enlisted men on board the *39* who had gone to submarine school in New London, Connecticut. He was a transfer from a bigger, newer, faster, more comfortable fleet boat, and he'd taken a kidding at first about his ability to cope with the rigors of an S-boat after a life of ease on the USS *Pike*. A dynamic Scandinavian who sometimes stepped in where angels feared to tread, Johnson's favorite exercise was called Battle Surface Action, and when the call came, "Take stations for Battle Surface," he was the first to head for the control room. He enjoyed the luxury of feeling a little sorry for Earl Nave, the well-aware-of-it, very competent, torpedoman first class who had to stay in the torpedo room because he was top man and couldn't be spared.

By the time Johnson reached the ladder, Captain Coe had given the order, "Down periscope, 100 feet," and the diving officer had followed with "One hundred feet, shift to series, 1,000 aside," which was high speed. Johnson clambered up the ladder into the conning tower. As first loader he was always first in line. The ammunition handlers of the gun crew were lined up from the magazine, in the forward part of the forward battery room, back to the after part where a scuttle, a long tube, projected through the hull for the purpose of passing ammunition after the boat had surfaced. The next order from the skipper, "Battle Surface" was the most important, followed by "Blow all main ballast, maintain 100 feet" from the diving officer.

As the water in the main ballast tanks was blown out, Johnson knew that the bow and stern planesmen could no longer hold her down to depth because she had become so light. Tensed and ready for the coming action, the best part, he heard the diving officer say, "Full rise on the planes, pressure in the boat." The submarine started up at a steep angle. The captain watched the depth gage, and as they reached the point where the conning tower hatch was almost out of the water he ordered, "Open the hatch." With that, the first couple of men were smacked with a deluge of salt water from the bathtub-shaped bridge as they flew out of the conning tower like bullets from the pressure within, landing with a thud.

Now the gun crew scrambled over the bridge side onto the deck as fast as they could go to unlimber the gun. Johnson took out the muzzle tompion, a plug that kept the barrel of the gun dry, and snatched off the pressureproof breech cover. It was good to smell fresh air and feel moisture on his skin that wasn't his own sweat. The ammunition scuttle was opened, and the crew down below in the forward battery room began passing up ammunition. The gunnery officer and captain were on the bridge by this time, and as the first shell was loaded and the gun trained on the target, Captain Coe ordered, "Commence firing."

The whole operation took 60 seconds from the "Battle Surface" order to the first shot. The object was speed, accuracy, and to surprise the enemy. Although Johnson, along with many others aboard the old S-boat, felt the creeping sickness called war coming on and knew that his life and that of others could depend upon his competency, he was young enough to enjoy Battle Surface Action, primarily because it worked off pent-up energy accumulated in the close quarters of the submarine. He didn't mind the bruises at all. It was a kind of game and a lot of fun.

The torpedo and gunnery officer, Leonard Johnson's boss, was First Lieu-tenand Roy Klinker, the only bachelor among the four officers. He was tall, dark, narrow-boned, the smile on his face often satirical. Klinker was a Naval Acade-my graduate, as were most of the officers in the fleet in 1940, but his background differed in one important respect: he had gone to sea at age 15 and had been a quartermaster in the merchant marine for two and a half years. His Danish grandfather had been a master mariner, and Roy had decided to follow in his footsteps. Besides, he was the oldest in a large family with not much money for extras; it was time to go on his own.

Roy's dad had not followed the family tradition. He managed the Henry Hess lumberyards in Sebastopol and Guerneville, California. On Roy's eigh-teenth birthday his father, who was only 17 years his son's senior, took him into one of Sebastopol's speakeasies on Ellis Street for a coming-of-age drink. As they clicked glasses, Mr. Klinker asked the bartender, "What'll we do with this boy now?" The barkeep replied, "Send him to Annapolis." Roy entered in 1931.

Admiral Thomas Hart was superintendent of the Naval Academy during Roy's first two years. It wasn't all a bed of roses for a headstrong young fellow. The discipline irritated Roy at times, especially in things he'd learned years before as a merchant mariner. Since he'd been on his own so long, there was sometimes a touch of superiority in his attitude when ordered to do basic chores.

One of the dullest aspects of plebe summer was being taught how to tie knots by a chief boatswain's mate whom Roy considered less expert than himself. As the lesson progressed, Roy tended to glance out more and more often at the sailboats on the Severn River, now and then gnawing at a hangnail just to break the monotony.

Suddenly he heard the chief say, "Klinker, you're not very interested."

Hoping to liven up the session, Roy replied eagerly, "Mr. Jones, I can tie knots that you don't know anything about. Would you like to see a sheepshank with a square knot?"

With a glint in his eye that Roy should have realized was not solely admiration, the chief said, "How do you do that?"

Enjoying the opportunity to show off, Klinker gave a performance worthy of vaudeville. After nodding his appreciation, the chief, with a smile, promptly put Klinker on report. Roy had been unaware that a midshipman could be junior to a chief petty officer and had intended no disrespect, but now he knew that almost everybody is "sir," not "mister," when you're a lowly plebe.

Shortly after arriving in Manila, Klinker was invited to a bienvenida (welcoming) reception for newcomers at the Army-Navy Club. When the receiving line broke up, the Commodore's wife ordered a chair to be placed on the lush green lawn under the shade of a molave tree. Whether by accident or intent, the white wicker chair with its big fan-shaped back had a thronelike appearance, and when the Commodore's lady sat down in it, the newcomers knew they were expected to visit with her and make small talk as part of their social obligation. Roy, his starched white collar already chafing a neck red with prickly heat, lined up to do his duty.

He had been told that taking a wife to the China station was like taking a ham sandwich to a banquet, and while he waited, he ran a practiced eye over the young women present. Most of them were daughters of service officers, said to have nothing on their minds but husband-hooking. Whether this was true or not he didn't care. He already had a girlfriend. Lili Torres came from the proud Spanish segment of the local society, a group that often had Chinese or Malay blood as well.

When Roy's turn in the line came, he plunged right into the small talk— "Yes, ma'am, I certainly do like Manila," and "This is my first Asiatic duty"— while anticipating the moment when he could politely break away. The Commodore's wife, in a flowered chiffon dress and a feathered hat that sat atop her salt-and-pepper curls like a miniature crown, ran the gamut of tired clichés while looking over Klinker's shoulder to see what else was going on. Then Roy, his mental time clock set, became aware that he'd been there a good ten minutes, and at the next pause in the chitchat, he thanked the lady for her company and bade her farewell.

Placing a kid-gloved hand on his arm, she exclaimed, "Wait a minute, young man. You stay right here. I'll pick out a nice Army or Navy junior for you, and then you may go."

This was a red flag to nonconformist Klinker, who said loudly and firmly, "Pardon me, ma'am, but no thanks. I asked your permission to leave, and I'm going," which he did.

The next day Roy was called to the flagship *Houston*. "Klinker," the

Commodore said, "you insulted my wife." "I did no such thing," Roy replied, and he went right back to the *S-39* to write a letter of resignation—which was rejected. It was one of a long series of resignations; the letters forced officialdom to listen to his complaints (many of them valid) and often got him what he wanted, but seldom increased his popularity with the powers-that-be.

Roy and classmate Ty Shepard often closed the bars of Manila. They never had to worry about drinking and driving because they used the same taxi driver every time. He would pick them up at La Ronda, the Magic Bar, or the Winter Garden and see to it that they got safely back to the boat. When Roy tired of Manila night life or ran out of money, he played cards at the Army-Navy Club. He played bridge instead of poker because he felt that it was more scientific and that he had a better chance to win. It was not unusual for a game to go on for days at a stretch, and he could often pick up $400 or $500 between cards and playing pool.

As a former enlisted man himself, Roy felt strongly about the rights of the crew. He made it a policy that his torpedo gang could vote on any new striker who wanted in, and if they turned thumbs down, that was that. A striker was a non-rated man, an apprentice seaman or seaman first class who was in training (striking) for a specific rate: torpedoman, gunner, quartermaster, a machinist's mate engineer.

Earl Nave, torpedoman first class, who worked with Klinker, was a good friend. If Roy ran into him on the beach, he always bought him a drink and sat down for a bull session. About the same age, late twenties, they were similar in other respects. They were both assertive people who enjoyed each other's boasting and sea stories and respected each other's ability. Nave had gone from third-class to first-class torpedoman in record time.

One man for whom Roy had respect, although they had a run-in almost every time they met, was Hyman Rickover. He knew that Rickover, class of 1922, had had a rough time at the Naval Academy because of his religion and that his naturally cantankerous personality had developed an even more abrasive shell as a result. Jews were no longer a novelty, however, and one black had been admitted to the academy in the 1930s, though he didn't graduate. Times were changing. But even after graduation Rickover's career had been peppered with pitfalls, and his first request for submarine school was turned down because he was over age, a 29-year-old full lieutenant. He was also, in a sense, overqualified, since he had earned a master's degree in electrical engineering from Columbia University in 1929. But a friendly rear admiral under whom he had done battleship duty put in a word for him, and in January 1930 Rickover entered the submarine school in New London, Connecticut.

Upon graduation, his first assignment was aboard the *S-48* as engineer and electrical officer. Although he became her navigator and executive officer in

1931 and qualified for command soon after, the *S-48* turned out to be his last submarine assignment; he was relieved as exec in June 1933 and reported to the office of Naval Materiel in Philadelphia. Nobody knew why Rickover had not received a submarine command. Rumor had it that, with his advanced knowledge of engineering, he'd been given to telling his skipper what to do instead of waiting to be told—and skippers write fitness reports.

In 1935 Lieutenant Rickover was assigned to the battleship *New Mexico,* home port Long Beach, California. So was Roy Klinker, fledgling ensign. Rickover's working schedule was said to be 24 hours a day; his penny-pinching in the interest of Uncle Sam's Navy had made him famous. Whatever his eccentricities, the year after Rickover became her engineering officer, the *New Mexico* won the coveted E Award for engineering efficiency (which she had not done before) and repeated it for the next two years while Rickover was still aboard.

Klinker cut his engineering teeth under the tutelage of Rickover. A maverick himself, Roy liked the snarly lieutenant from the start, although he had been immediately warned by more seasoned ensigns, "Be sure you look hot and sweaty and are wearing dungarees, like you just stopped work, before you ask permission to go ashore. And don't ever do it before the dot of 1630 [4:30 P.M.] when shore leave starts, because if he thinks you've shorted your duties by one second, you've had it."

Klinker took the advice but observed for himself that though Rickover's demands were as tough as the shell of a black walnut, he was basically fair, especially if you didn't let him push you around. Cursing the lieutenant at times, Roy often couldn't help grinning at some of his hammer-fisted ways. For example, new ensigns were required to go into the actual machinery spaces of the battleship and trace out the piping systems in their qualification-for-promotion notebooks. It was the time-honored custom to fudge a bit and take shortcuts like copying from the ship's blueprints—but not under Rickover: he locked up the plans and nobody dared pry them loose.

The time finally came when Klinker's itch to go ashore threatened to spread throughout his whole body. He'd worked hard, done everything he should and deserved a break, he told himself as he walked down the passageway to the engineering office. Properly clad in smelly dungarees, and not an instant too early, he greeted his superior politely but had not yet stated his actual purpose when he was treated to one of Rickover's blank, disconcerting stares. This went on for so long that Klinker finally exploded and was astonished when Rickover said, "Klinker, if you really wanted to go ashore why didn't you say so at once? Permission granted." From then on, Roy was convinced that when Rickover played games with you, you could win his respect only by being as aggressive as he was.

Rickover and Klinker were fated to meet at intervals through the years.

When Roy was ordered to the *S-39*, he heard that his former boss, now Lieutenant Commander Rickover, had become an Engineering Duty Officer, a specialist in construction, repair, and ship design. Rickover's first duty in this capacity was at Cavite in the Philippines. It was a small navy yard, but the U.S. Asiatic Fleet depended upon it. Before the advent of Red Coe as commanding officer, the *39* was scheduled to go into the yard for overhaul. One day the chief engineer came back to the boat so wrought up that Klinker swore he had tears in his eyes. When Roy asked, "What's the problem?" the reply was, "That goddamned assistant planning officer over there turned down every one of my work requests."

"What's his name?" Klinker asked.

"Rickover."

"Ah ha," Roy said, "Tell you what; I'll put your requests into a letter that I think will bring results if you can get the captain to sign it." Then he sat down and worked up the kind of blistering message to the master martinet that experience had taught him was the only way to bring Rickover around. It took a few beers and a little ruminating on the part of the captain before he was willing to sign the letter and let it go, but he did—and Rickover, though nitpicking and squawking as usual, finally honored the requests.

Klinker considered an S-boat the best training a submariner could have because it was a basic piece of machinery, but he frequently lost patience with the patchwork pigboat and cursed it out because it was so primitive. When old batteries were removed for overhaul or replacement, always a dangerous operation, the acid fumes were so strong that the men's clothing was eaten up faster than a thousand moths could have done it. Everybody had to have a new uniform. Then when the boat came out of the navy yard after overhaul, ready to make her deep dive to see if her hull was tight, the skipper and the inspection officer were concerned because leaks were reported all over the boat. Pop Bridges, whose experience nobody could question, smiled his wise little smile and said, "Don't worry sir. They all leak at first. Give her time to rust up. It's a riveted hull, and after she shakes down for about a month there'll be no more leaks." As usual, Pop was right. But the question still remained: how would *39* react if she had to go farther down than the regulation 200 feet, as could easily happen in wartime? Klinker was due for a change of duty within the year, and he fervently hoped it would come before bombs started falling and the U.S. Asiatic Fleet collapsed like a child's celluloid bathtub flotilla.

Jim Pennell, machinist's mate, was another man who landed on the *39* via the *Canopus*. He was 25 years old, thin-skinned when it came to lack of appreciation of his work, and highly intelligent but almost uneducated. His father had thought book learning an unnecessary frill and preferred to see his son at 14 go off with the circus, where Jim worked for four years before joining the Navy. Pop Bridges ordered Pennell to messcook duty for one month after coming aboard. He obeyed because he wanted to be a submariner, but he resented having to do it. In the midst of the stint, insult was added to injury when Pennell made machinist's mate second class, and old Pop, unimpressed, insisted that he finish out his month of dishwashing and -toting anyway, At that point, Pennell considered Bridges an insensitive old man who, like his father, gave him neither credit nor consideration. Goaded into proving himself, Pennell qualified in less than four months—then had further cause for resentment when he was made to wait until he had completed six months of submarine duty before drawing the additional pay. He thought Division Commander R.B. Vanzant was responsible for this decision, but that didn't make it any easier to take. At times he wondered if submarines were what he wanted after all. He devoted himself to his work, not mixing much with the crew. When he went ashore it was usually with Danny Tella, a rough, tough engineer who'd been aboard the *Canopus* with him and had joined the *39* on the same day.

Not everybody fell in love at first sight with submarine duty, and it sometimes took years before a marriage occurred—but there were few divorces.

3. Last Times

Caroline Bernard and Dottie Lautrup, along with many other Navy wives, arrived in Shanghai before their husbands did. They had been fortunate enough to catch a small but luxurious Italian liner, the *Conte Verde*. The first glimpses and fresh breezes of Shanghai were exhilarating, and Caroline knew she was about to live the good life she'd been hearing about. Dottie suggested that she and Caroline share a room at the Metropole Hotel until the men arrived, and Caroline, glad of experienced company and always eager to save a few pennies, happily agreed.

That first night, Caroline reveled in the luxury of it all. For a mere pittance by U.S. standards, they enjoyed a magnificent dinner in an elegant dining room where white-gloved waiters stationed themselves discreetly behind potted palms whose leaves bore not a trace of dust. The food, artistically garnished, was displayed by the *maître d' hôtel,* who whipped off silver covers and placed the dishes at the ladies' eye level for approval. Caroline's conversation consisted largely of oh's and ah's.

Later, when she climbed into bed between linen sheets, she shivered with delight as a cool breeze, so different from Manila, wafted through an open window, but was startled by a rasping noise outside, followed by low-pitched but penetrating groans. The lights were already out, and the strange sounds elicited no comment from Dottie. Caroline turned over and closed her eyes. Again the groans began, like a creature in dreadful pain who had given up hope. The groans were punctuated by a choking cough ending in gasps that made Caroline sit upright, then drove her out of bed to the window. The room was on the third floor in the rear of the hotel. Enough light streamed from laundry and service rooms for her to see figures lying, one behind the other, in the narrow alleyway. The sounds were coming from one of the bodies down below.

"All right, Caroline." It was Dottie's voice. "This doesn't happen every night but it does happen fairly often. It's China, I'm afraid. Those are ricksha boys out there. It's the only place they have to sleep—no homes, no beds, nothing. Most of them have tuberculosis or worse, and they don't live long. One of them is dying, that's what you hear. I'm a registered nurse—I know what it sounds like."

Caroline ran to the door. "I'll go down to the lobby and tell the people at the desk. I'll tell them to get a doctor, an ambulance. We have to do something. Where's my robe?"

Dottie was out of bed in a flash to put a detaining hand on Caroline's arm. "The people at the desk won't do anything, because, if the man dies, it's traditional that his survivors be supported for the rest of their lives by the Good Samaritans who stuck their necks out and tried to help. Besides, there aren't enough hospitals. The only ones around are British or U.S. church-sponsored, and they're crowded to the hilt. Come on, get back in bed. I'll shut the window— you shut your ears."

As Caroline reluctantly climbed back into bed, she couldn't help picturing the dying man outside, coughing his life away, choking on his own blood, his head propped against the unyielding frame of the ricksha whose wheels had ground out his life. Suddenly she felt sick. She would learn that millions of Chinese were conceived, born, lived, and died in the alleys and that nobody thought much about it.

When the 39 boat came in and the Bernards were reunited, they moved into another room at the Metropole at a monthly cost of $60. This included three meals a day plus a lavish English tiffin, or tea. For $5 a month more, Caroline hired an *amah* to wash, iron, mend, and make up the room. The British, with their long history of holdings around the globe, were accustomed to such luxury, but most of the Americans were not. They would never experience anything like it again. And although Caroline was as human as the next in enjoying this life that so little resembled a mining camp in the Rockies, she never ceased to be appalled at the grim realities so close to the plush surface.

After dinner she and Larry often strolled down the avenue to window-shop, especially enjoying the exquisite handmade children's clothes featured in one of the stores. One evening, while Larry declared again that he wanted a girl and admired the tiny, beruffled dresses, several urchins sneaked out from between the buildings, holding out bony little hands and crying, "*kumshaw, kumshaw,*" the street word for money. The Bernards had been told never to succumb to these waifs or they'd regret it, but Larry, defenses down from contemplating the approaching birth of his own child, could not resist the skeletal mites with the sad black eyes.

Reaching into his pocket he dropped coins into three or four palms, then gasped in amazement as the sidewalk blackened instantaneously with a tatterdemalion army of children all screaming "*kumshaw*" at the top of their lungs as they pressed in. Larry and Caroline likened it to being caught in a stampede, but the "cattle" of Shanghai were scores of crippled and diseased children, some of whom had been deliberately maimed at birth to incite sympathy as beggars. The Bernards had to fight their way back the several blocks to the hotel, and only the sight of the glaring uniformed doorman dispersed the crowd.

But there were happy experiences on the streets of Shanghai, too. Walking down Bubbling Well Road one day, Caroline and Evelyn Mehlhop were accosted by a beggar of indeterminate age with a look of Confucian wisdom in his eye. The hand he held out was cleaner than usual, and there were no obvious deformities to be glimpsed through his rags. Beggar or not, he was a practicing psychologist, and singling out Caroline, he plunged into his spiel: "Missy, you no like worry, I can see. You have happy face. I got bargain for you, deal like American say. You give me five dollah and I do your worrying for you all the rest your life."

The whole idea was so preposterous and the price so outrageous for a struggling naval officer's wife that Caroline couldn't resist. With the spirit of the Old West, she decided to gamble for high stakes. Digging into her purse, she dropped the money into the palm of the astonished man without even trying to haggle him down. No less astounded was her companion Evelyn, who put out a protesting hand, but Caroline said firmly, "No, that's it. I'll never worry again. Every time I start, I'll think of my friend here and know he's doing it for me."

During the *39*'s 1,000-mile trip from Manila to Shanghai, Captain Coe kept the crew hopping with various exercises. They ran through all the emergency drills several times: man overboard, fire, collision, and chlorine. They had realized the importance of the last not long before when sea water had seeped through loosened rivets in the hull and into a battery well, creating deadly chlorine. The sharp, acrid, cough-producing gas demanded instant surfacing and immediate ventilation. The newcomers to submarines were surprised to see that the chlorine had eaten the tarnish off the brasswork, making it shine as though it had been worked on for years. It wasn't hard to imagine what it could do to human lungs.

During the four-day run to Shanghai the *39* also exercised at battle stations, submerged and surfaced, and made a daily trim dive. For Engineer Larry Bernard, still learning the ropes, the trim dive was a delicate balancing operation, it could have serious consequences in wartime if not done accurately. A submarine on the surface is buoyant and to submerge must have negative buoyancy. After the boat is submerged, to reach the desired depth it must achieve the same weight as the water it displaces, or neutral buoyancy.

To maintain balanced neutral buoyancy requires compensation. Sea water is flooded in or pumped out of the variable ballast tanks, of which there are three:

forward and after trim tanks and the auxiliary tank in the center of the boat. Since the weight of the submarine changes from day to day; depending upon the amount of fuel, food, and ammunition used, the diving officer must calculate the compensation needed and pump out or flood in the proper amount of sea water in the three tanks. If all 42 men on board the boat were to go forward or aft at the same time, immediate compensation would be required to maintain the trim.

Another dramatic change could come from water temperature. A vessel constantly passes in and out of variable currents, and hot currents are less dense. In addition, the deeper a submarine goes, the heavier it becomes from compression of the hull, necessitating the pumping out of water. All of these factors are constantly monitored, but to make sure the compensation is correct, a trim dive is made, allowing the diving officer to order water shifted around among the three tanks if necessary. When a trim dive showed perfect calculation, Larry felt good for the rest of the day. He knew that in wartime, an enemy trying to locate a submarine would be alert for the telltale signs of a poor compensation, such as the noise of pumping or blowing water, or an increase in speed.

Each spring the men looked forward to the cool climate and liberty in Shanghai, China's largest city, and later on in Tsingtao. Shanghai is located on the Huang-p'u river, a tributary of the Yangtze, whose muddy waters carry out many miles to sea. If the *39* approached the area in daylight, word would travel fast the moment the water clouded up, the sight of which made the crew as happy as though they were panning for gold and had found it. If the *39* came in at night, as they were doing in 1940, the engine-room watch personnel periodically opened a vent valve to see if the water was muddy yet. Old China hand Earl Nave, called "the honker" by the crew, yelled out in his foghorn voice, "Tell Gibbons to move his lazy ass and see if we've hit muddy water yet."

John Gibbons, who wasn't intimidated by Nave's blowhard manner, ran some water into a can, then held it out for everyone to see. "Mud," he said triumphantly. Bob Bixler, torpedoman, wiped the sweat off his brow with a hairy forearm as he proclaimed, "Lafayette, we are here. Hot damn, cool at last." When whoops of joy were heard throughout the old pigboat, even Pop Bridges woke up long enough to smile. He'd soon be going back to the States and the wife he hadn't seen for years, so he planned to do a lot of shopping in China. He wanted to take the missus some of the monogrammed satin undies that were so popular with the younger men. She wasn't too old for such things by a long shot, and neither was he. He'd saved up his money so he could afford the best.

There were many reasons for the men to enjoy China. Upon arrival, the *39* would have open gangway in Shanghai for several weeks. This meant, "Come back only when you have the duty." Also, the exchange rate had jumped to 19

Chinese dollars to one U.S. dollar, so that an enlisted man could make a good liberty on $3 or so. There was another advantage: at certain bars you could sign chits when you ran out of money, then square away the bill on payday. And then there were the girls. Most of the cabarets in Blood Alley had orchestras for dancing, with Chinese hostesses lined up on one side of the room and White Russians on the other. Take your choice.

The street called Blood Alley, a part of the International Settlement, was a focal point for night life for sailors and marines from all parts of the world. It had earned its name because of the large amounts of vital fluid spilled in ferocious battles among seafaring men of different nations. In 1940, since the U.S. was not the world power it became later, it was well enough liked, nor did the Americans have any particular hates. Not so other countries.

When the evening was well advanced and the crowd had settled down to serious drinking, Schab would tell his friends, "Watch the fun you guys," and he'd slip the waiter some change to ask the orchestra to play the French or German national anthem. As soon as the music began, the Schab party always jumped to their feet, no matter which country was being honored, and stood at attention with innocent looks on their flushed faces. If it was "Marseillaise" being played, the Germans sat stolidly in their chairs while the French sailors stood glaring at the Teutons, hardly able to wait until the anthem was over to avenge the insult.

The moment the last note sounded, the battle began, with Schab and friends cheering it on at ringside, having the time of their lives without giving up a drop of their own blood. When the fight died down Ed Schab would wait a decent interval. Then, if things were getting dull again, he'd pick out another country for pot-stirring purposes. Not that the *39* boat people didn't get into fights, Schab among them, but they were apt to be within-the-ballpark feuds, not with other nations.

It was customary to vary operating conditions, so shortly before the *39* was ready to move on, the wives started haunting ticket offices to obtain a ride north to Tsingtao, a city held by the Japanese. It was catch-as-catch-can, and after long hours of waiting in line, the women signed on for anything they could get because ships to that port on the Yellow Sea were carefully controlled. Although it was about the size of Manila (some 600,000 people), Tsingtao, with its red-roofed two-story buildings and quiet beaches, seemed a sleepy town in contrast to teeming Shanghai, whose waters were filled with ferryboats, sampans, and merchant and fighting ships from all over the world, set against a backdrop of skyscrapers. But Tsingtao, established as an administrative center around the turn of the century by the Germans, who then held the territory of Kiaochow, was an important entry for foreign goods.

Caroline Bernard managed to get a ticket on a British ship for the 36-hour run. (The ships' blackout at night was her first taste of wartime conditions.) She had been told that Tsingtao, built around the bay, was the Riviera of China with its lush green hills and majestic trees, and she was not disappointed. She and Larry found a comfortable and inexpensive room in a German boardinghouse run by a Herr Mahler, reputed to be the No. 1 Nazi in the Orient, and his wife. The Mahlers were very cordial, and Frau Mahler did not shy away from political discussion, but her husband did not express his opinions.

Herr Mahler and his wife had left Germany after World War I because of the dreadful economic conditions. He was much respected in Tsingtao, and though he formed and drilled youth groups who swore allegiance to Hitler and flew the Nazi flag outside his house, he had been away from Germany so long that there was room to doubt that he knew the full extent of what was taking place in his native land. Nor did the Bernards, and others like them, understand all the implicatons of German doctrine and the scope of Nazi territorial ambitions.

Herr Mahler's humane gesture in defending the gates of the Catholic cathedral, where French nuns had sought refuge when the Japanese army invaded, impressed Caroline greatly. It was told that he had stood alone and unarmed, refusing to let the soldiers enter; to the credit of both sides, the rules of sanctuary had been observed and the sisters were safe.

Frau Mahler, a physical culturist, was full of advice for Caroline regarding her now obvious pregnancy: "You should walk more, strengthen the legs and body. It's better for the *puppchen*." Anything good for the child appealed to Caroline, so she took the advice to heart, persuading Evelyn Mehlhop to accompany her.

One day they walked and walked until Caroline suddenly realized they had gone so far that the verdant, hilly landscape had changed into barren, desertlike flatland and that a walled village loomed up in front of them. They were within a few hundred yards of it when three Oriental men with shaven heads appeared and walked toward them. Two looked like priests, but the third wore the habit of a monk with a sort of rosary around his neck that ended in a golden symbol not unlike a cross.

When they were close enough, Caroline said, "Catholic?" and, putting out her hand, touched the monk's beads. The effect was electric. The man jumped back as though desecrated, and too late Caroline realized that the walled enclave was not a village but a monastery. She had overstepped the bounds. Smiling placatingly, the two women backed off, then turned around and started back the way they'd come, going as quickly as they could without actually running.

"Caroline," Evelyn murmured between shivers, "you're not in Peoria, Illinois, or Eureka, California. Not everybody wants to be friendly here."

On the way back they hiked to the top of a grassy knoll and sat down to cool off. There was a splendid view of rolling green hills, and in the distance sunshine struck golden lights from the waters of the harbor. The turquoise sky overhead was flocked with tiny puffs of cloud. Then the women fell silent and Caroline became aware that the gentle trilling of birds in a nearby tree was periodically obliterated with booms and then, much closer, sharp zings like rifle shots. They *were* rifle shots. A spill of dark figures in the valley caught Caroline's eye, dropping back and advancing exactly as soldiers would do in battle. She and Evelyn headed for town fast. Later on they heard that units of the Japanese army had been out practicing with live ammunition.

When George Lautrup told his wife that Dr. Michaud, who ran the U.S. Navy dispensary in Tsingtao, had no nurse, Dottie Lautrup volunteered to help out several hours each day. She enjoyed the nursing profession and had just about had her fill of shopping, sightseeing, and tea-drinking. The dispensary boasted a beat-up examining table long rusted into one position, a glass-doored cabinet containing medical instruments that looked like implements of torture from the Middle Ages, and a plump German stove decorated with chipped tiles.

At times, buying the delicious peaches, pears, strawberries, and other cold-climate produce, Dottie felt as though she were at home in Connecticut. But many Tsingtao street signs were in German, as were the music and the menus in the generous sprinkling of beer gardens. There were also squadrons of little boys in uniform, marching to school in perfect formation with packs on their backs and serious expressions on their faces. And the only real hospital in the city was German, staffed with nurses from the Fatherland.

For the men aboard the *39*, liberty in Tsingtao was a constant reminder of Japanese aggression. When the crew came ashore, money jingling in their pockets, they always used rickshas for transportation. The status of the coolie in Tsingtao was no better than anywhere else in China, so the innumerable ricksha boys would dash out in a mad scramble for the American fares. But there were armed Japanese sentries throughout the city and an especially heavy guard at the waterfront. These soldiers beat the coolies back with weighted canvas clubs, and the downtrodden ricksha boys stood mute beneath the blows until their passengers were seated. The soldiers eventually solved the problem of the rush for the pier by the simple expedient of throwing ricksha seat cushions over the seawall. Since replacements were out of the question for the impoverished coolies, from then on they stayed in their designated area until the sailors came to them.

Cholera broke out in Tsingtao; the Americans were safe because they had all had shots, but not so the Chinese. In a fervid program of inoculation, the Japanese army set up stations at intersections, where they stopped each ricksha and forced the coolie to pull the vehicle over a medicated mat. He was then ordered to a nearby dispensing area to be shot in the arm—while his fare, if any, waited—and given a slip of paper attesting to the fact that he'd received his injection. Most of the ricksha boys promptly lost the chits and so got shots again and again. Those strong enough to survive the overdoses of serum were unlikely to die of the disease. The sailors speculated on what the medicated mat was supposed to do but never came up with an answer.

The usual windup of China maneuvers for the *39* crew was a gala ship's party with dancing, drinking, and dinner at a restaurant called the Sea Pavilion. The officers were invited to attend, and all personnel, with their girlfriends and wives, enjoyed the early part of the evening together. But protocol demanded that captain and officers leave before the dividing lines blurred to the point where someone overstepped the bounds. It was basically the crew's big celebration, and no officer had either the right or the desire to drink too much or be involved in a brouhaha at a ship's party. It was common sense for morale and discipline, and the men respected the unwritten rule. Sensational sea stories were another matter. Everybody from the old man down was supposed to lie a little, and guys who could lie a lot, like Earl Nave, were generally bought the most free drinks.

But Coe, Lautrup, Klinker, and Bernard were also required to attend a formal dinner given for the officers, and their ladies, of Submarine Division 201. At this affair Larry enjoyed himself so much that he passed out, and Red Coe insisted on helping Caroline get him home. He and George Lautrup managed to get Larry up the stairs and neatly stretched out like a corpse on the sofa in the sitting room.

"Thank you, thank you so much," Caroline said, almost as flushed with embarrassment as Larry was with drink. She was praying that the skipper and exec would leave. "He'll be fine now, thanks again, captain."

Coe did not take the hint. Contemplating the laid-out Larry and remembering his own occasional indiscretions, he decided that Bernard did not look comfortable. No, not at all. Having had one or two himself helped the captain to judge, as he squinted at the hapless man, that what Larry needed was to have his tie loosened and his shoes removed. Caroline feared that Larry might wake up any minute and toss his cookies, but all she could say in the face of such camaraderie from the commanding officer—who, after all, was the one to write fitness reports—was, "Yes sir, I mean, he'll really be all right. I mean, don't bother, you've taken too much time and trouble already."

"No trouble at all," Coe replied. As fate would have it, the captain motioned Lautrup to the end where Larry's tie was located, while he went to the other. Carefully untying the knotted lace, which seemed to Caroline to take forever, Coe slipped off the shoe and was suddenly confronting Larry's big toe sticking out through an enormous hole in the black silk sock.

He didn't bat an eyelash. Bowing solemnly to the gasping Caroline, a sensitive bride who saw her reputation as a housewife shattered, Coe motioned to Lautrup with a twinkle, and the two departed, leaving the Bernards to mend their fences, along with their socks, at dawn's early light. Long after Larry's snores had subsided to the stillness of a deep, inebriate sleep, Caroline lay awake. Keyed up by the evening, she tried to induce slumber by concentrating on what sounded like woeful chants in the distance. She had originally thought they were of religious significance but had found out that they were marching songs sung by the Japanese army. Between those sounds and the harsh slap-thunk made by the goose-stepping Nazi youth groups, the speck on the map that was Tsingtao presented a sight and sound preview of the enemies the United States would soon be facing.

The two most important men aboard ship were glad to be leaving China, but for different reasons. The stateside transfer for Pop Bridges was getting closer every day. The monogrammed nightgowns and stepins had been bought and paid for and were stowed away where no one could see them, especially Mandekic. Though he seldom went ashore, Pop was weary of the Navy Club in Tsingtao. And though he could never be tired of submarines, he knew he was getting a little old for them. He didn't have to leave if he didn't want to, but he'd been considering the comforts of a surface craft, especially one of the new destroyers, which he certainly rated by seniority. He'd also begun to feel that young men should fight wars; they had the foolhardiness of it, as he'd had in 1918. Age brought common sense, and common sense brought caution, too much of it for you to want to stick your neck out and get killed. He sighed for all the young crew members on the *39* that he'd "fathered." The way things were going here in the Far East, they might be fighting for their lives any minute.

Red Coe's impatience to leave Tsingtao had to do with wife and child, and the imminence of child number two, back in the Philippines. He was thoroughly enjoying his first command and liked everything about being boss, but he missed Rachel and Jean and was a little worried about the advent of the new baby. Rachel had assured him that she had confidence in the Navy doctors and hospital, but suppose she went into labor in Baguio? The road back to Manila was long and tortuous, and he pictured his wife stopping off to give birth in the midst of a landslide, an ever-present danger in the high wooded Benguet Hills with their tons of loose rock. If that didn't happen, Rachel or Jean could be swept away in one of the famous cloudbursts or even more destructive Baguíos (typhoons) that had destroyed portions of the road a number of times.

The captain's worries about his wife were not without foundation. It was the beginning of July and the baby was due soon. Rachel had enjoyed the cool weather and homelike greenery of pines and firs, and thought that the change had helped Jean. The child was exceptionally thin, but her appetite seemed to have improved in the bracing air.

Jean was also very happy with her new *amah*, Lottie Antipolo, a young Filipina Chinese who had come to the Coes' Manila household in a curious way. Rachel had been digging in the garden early one hot afternoon. Jim was out to sea, the servants were taking their siesta; even the gardener wouldn't work at that hour. Rachel was sure the household help thought the American Mo'm, as they called her, was crazy, but she enjoyed the green outdoors so much that a siesta, inside under mosquito netting, held no lure. Troweling around a hibiscus bush, she suddenly drew back as she caught a flick of motion. By the time she got to her feet, she realized that the small snake she had seen must be the seldom encountered but deadly *dahon palay,* the arrow-headed rice leaf snake.

Dropping the trowel, she ran to the house crying out, "Clemente, Clemente, come here, hurry up." Just last week she had read that a boy riding his carabao through a muddy field of green rice had been bitten on the leg and died shortly after. She also knew that the nursemaids of Manila watched the children like hawks because of the *dahon palay,* taking them to a special park that was being continuously swept out in what amounted to a sort of snake-watch.

By the time Rachel ran inside, the *lavandera* (laundress) had come in from the kitchen along with Clemente, the cook, and Jean's *amah* had reached the foot of the stairs. Rachel described what she had seen, while the dark eyes watching her grew larger and larger. When she had finished, Clemente said quickly, "Mo'm, we go," and started for the kitchen, the *lavandera* close behind, and the *amah,* without so much as a glance upstairs where her charge lay napping, following the pair.

"Where are you going?" Rachel cried, bewildered.

"No stay no more," Clemente called back.

"But you can't go," Rachel protested, "I can't pay you until the captain comes home at the end of the week. You won't get the money that's coming to you."

But none of them seemed to care. They were out of the house one-two-three and never came back to collect their salaries, nor was Rachel able to locate them later. That was why friendly Lottie Antipolo had been hired as Jean's new *amah,* her last name the same as that of a village a few miles east of Manila which housed a miraculous image of Our Lady of Peace brought from Mexico in 1826.

One morning in Baguio, when Rachel was avoiding her image in the mirror because she had gained 60 pounds, she became aware that the baby had suddenly dropped into birth position. For the last week she'd been urging herself to leave but delayed each time she inhaled the cool, piny air. Now, delay was impossible. The night before, she had been informed by a tearful Lottie that hers was not the only pregnancy in the Coe household. The *amah* had fallen in love with one of the waiters at the resort in Baguio, and morning sickness had already set in. Rachel assured her that as long as the Coes were in the Philippines, Lottie and her child had a home. Rachel decided not to risk the 130 miles of threadlike road and the unpredictable storms. Instead, she booked passage on a private plane. It was a first flight and almost a last. The Coe party were the only passengers in the tiny six-seater, and Rachel had not anticipated the fearful buffeting from rain and wind that had Lottie telling her beads between bouts of nausea, and made Jean's small face pucker with tears as she cried out, "No, Mommie. It isn't fun like a merry-go-round." The Filipino pilot spoke Spanish and Tagalog, no English, but Rachel figured that it didn't really matter, since she was speechless all the way. When they landed in Manila in the midst of more rain, she was already plotting transportation for the 22-mile drive to the Cañacao Naval Hospital at Cavite—where nine-pound Henry Coe was born shortly after.

It had sounded like a great idea at first. Parties for young folks sponsored by Mrs. Field Marshal Douglas MacArthur, wife of the bigshot himself. Allyn Christopher, still needing an ego boost after being relegated to the galley again, had even thought he was chosen because of his intelligence, looks, and ability to wear skintight bellbottoms, of which he now had a specially tailored pair. With his snowy white hat tilted at just the right angle over one brow, he fancied himself a match for the hep, snappy-looking sailor on the recruiting posters with a caption that read, "The Navy Needs You."

But he began to suspect he was a fall guy the moment he arrived at the dance. There were half a dozen sailors in dress whites standing against the wall like wax dummies while the dance floor filled up with young U.S. civilians. The boys wore black ties, the girls were in long dresses with full skirts that swirled in the Fred Astaire–Ginger Rogers dips and twirls popular with the private school crowd. Not one of the girls ever glanced at the servicemen, nor did anyone introduce them. Allyn wondered if these couples could cope with a fast shag or a lindy, but if he only got the chance, he'd dip and twirl like the rest of them. It wasn't that he was hard up for female company; he had a Filipina girlfriend he liked very much. It was the principle of the thing: the monotony, the boredom— the insult, if you wanted it straight—of being invited to a party that you not only got slicked up for but were inspected for, and then you were treated like a piece of furniture.

The enlisted personnel, no more than a dozen by the time they all arrived, had been ordered to appear from various ships, and since the whole thing smacked of officialdom, none of the sailors felt free to break loose and do something to pass the time, like shooting craps in one of the reception rooms. Most of them were trying to qualify for submarines and didn't want to risk being put on report. They kept standing there, arms dangling anthropoid style, not knowing what to do with their hands. A sailor's best bellbottoms were so tight across his middle and rear that he had to hook his wallet over the waistband of his pants underneath his jumper and tuck his cigarettes and matches into his sock. He couldn't even slide a handkerchief into his pockets, let alone his hands.

Allyn discovered that if the most recent man aboard the *S-39* was also the most junior, he was the patsy designated to attend Mrs. MacArthur's dances until a new arrival fit the qualifications. Christopher attended quite a few of these nonmemorable affairs. And then one evening when Allyn was, as usual, plastered against the wall, eyes riveted on the floor as the frills and black ties whirled by, a bejeweled grande dame with a kindly face approached him and murmured, "I've been watching you and I can tell you're miserable. Come and sit with me."

She was an American widow in her seventies whose husband had made a fortune in the Benguet gold mine in the hills of Baguio. She regaled a wide-eyed Christopher with tales of the old days and saw to it that platters of delicacies—including caviar and smoked fish, food to gladden the heart of a Scandinavian—were constantly replenished, along with bottles of chilled champagne. From then on, Christopher looked forward to Mrs. MacArthur's entertainments, although he still resented extensive newspaper accounts that appeared after each party referring to these galas as "rankless."

Christopher never did warm up to what he considered the MacArthur philosophy of where the little guys belonged who manned boats or toted guns. Retired from the U.S. Army in 1939, the general had been hired in 1940 by Manuel Quezon, first president of the Commonwealth of the Philippines. Given the title of Field Marshal, MacArthur's primary jobs were to establish a military academy and a well-trained Philippine army. In addition to a salary, reputed to be large, his expenses were paid and he and his family were given the penthouse apartment atop the Manila Hotel.

The Manila Hotel had the reputation of being one of the most beautiful in the Far East, and Allyn Christopher thought that visiting it would allow him to enliven his letters to his mother with a description of something a little classier than the Santa Ana Dance Hall. The idea was to walk around the lobby, peek in at the bar and the dining room, glimpse the swimming pool and other sports facilities, maybe take a couple of snapshots—what any tourist would do. But although he was stubborn enough to try it half a dozen times, he never got inside the entrance. On each occasion the doorman blocked his way, saying, "Enlisted not allowed." And the last time, when he added, "I don't give the orders around here," Allyn figured that he knew who did—the elderly gent who lived in the penthouse.

When the *39* boat was in overhaul in Cavite Navy Yard, three kinds of work were done on her: yard work, contractor's work, and ship's force work, the last by her own crew. Ed Schab and Allyn Christopher, who had girls in Manila, had both been on liberty from Friday to Monday morning, and the lightheaded, heavy-eyed pair teamed up to hire a taxi back to Cavite. While the boat was in drydock and uninhabitable, with a stripped galley and bunks ripped out, the crew were sleeping on a barge. After a weekend in the city enjoying the comforts of female companionship, this form of accommodation held little appeal for either man, but Christopher, who hadn't been around as long as Schab, had no plans but to obediently return as scheduled and do his share of the chores allotted to the ship's work force.

"Jeez, we ought to be able to figure out some gimmick to get off duty for a few more days," Schab said, rubbing his aching brow between the eyes where it hurt the most. "First off, I could use a good night's sleep; second off, I'd light out again for Manila and my girl. Even if I didn't have enough time to go to Manila, Dreamland Ballroom's right here in Cavite. Dancing the night away beats painting the old radio shack on the 39-boat anytime."

"You said it," Allyn agreed, "but the exec is tough."

"Bah," Schab dismissed Lautrup with a wave of the hand. "A smart sailor can outsmart a tough exec. We just need a gimmick, that's all."

They pondered for a few minutes while the taxi dodged pony-drawn *carromatos* and short, square Filipinas who trudged along, balancing on their heads five-gallon gasoline cans—almost as big as they were—filled with the family's daily supply of water pumped from nearby artesian wells.

"We need some sort of medical thing for an excuse, but neither of us looks sick," Schab said.

"Somebody told me they make smallpox vaccine here from carabaos instead of cows like we do in the States and that Americans get real sick from it with high fevers and everything."

"Uh, uh," Schab shook his head disgustedly. "We already got one small-pox vaccination. Why would we get another?"

It was a rhetorical question that Christopher didn't even bother to answer as he braced himself for the screeching two-wheeled half-circle made by the taxi to avoid a pig, a rooster, and a diaperless child in that order. As the driver thumped the cab down on all fours and resumed the right direction, Schab's eyes suddenly gleamed with the light of inspiration. "Hey, hey, hey, I've got it. You ever been circumcised?"

Christopher blinked but answered, "No."

"Me either, but the docs all recommend it. So does Pop Bridges."

"Yeah?" Christopher didn't sound convinced.

Schab laughed, then dug Allyn in the ribs. "I don't really mean to do it. I just mean to go right in as soon as we get to the yard and tell the exec I'm gonna do it. Then I'll request a few days off for the purpose, and instead I'll whip on down to Manila. What do you say? You game? What have we got to lose?"

Christopher hedged. "Tell you what, I got to make a phone call first, then I'll meet you at the office."

Schab did just what he'd said. Too bad the exec wasn't Mr. Klinker or Mr. Bernard; they weren't easy, but they were more friendly types. Lautrup was really military, with a straight-up Prussian bearing and cool gray eyes that turned steely at times. Even so, circumcision was supposed to be the right thing to do, and Mr.

Lautrup was certainly concerned with that. The more Schab thought about it, the better he liked the idea.

Lautrup was in the office, parade-ground bearing obvious even behind a desk. Schab removed his cap and suddenly found he was having to make a real effort to summon up his usual aplomb.

"Yes sir," he began, "I'm all caught up with my work, and I'd like to request a few days off to go over to the dispensary and be circumcised. Last exam I had, the doc recommended it."

George Lautrup stopped writing, then fixed Schab with a cool stare. Finally, he said, "I think it's an excellent idea," and turning to the yeoman, added, "Escort Schab to the dispensary and back."

Schab's spirits plummeted as he caught the expression on the yeoman's face. There was no way out for either of them; the yeoman would have to see to it that Schab got where he had said he was going and did what he said he was going to do. Lautrup turned to his work, and Ed followed the yeoman out the door, thinking, I had to open my big mouth and where's my buddy Christopher, that S.O.B. I'm in it all alone.

At the dispensary Schab's last hope faded when the doctor assured him that, yes, he'd have time. He motioned to the operating table and informed Schab that newborn babies didn't get anesthetic for a simple peel-off, and neither would he. Nor did he get transportation afterward; he had to hobble all the way back to the barge. When he couldn't even visit Dreamland for the next few days—let alone Manila—because he hurt too much, he realized that sometimes an exec could be as much of a wisenheimer as a radioman second class.

When Tom Parks was assigned to the engine room, he found Dutch Mandekic a man who knew the Nelseco diesels from A to Z but didn't indulge in much chitchat with the lowly. However, Parks knew that everybody likes to give advice, and he found that if he made a real effort to draw Mandekic out, the chief could be helpful. But it was Ralph Scalia, machinist's mate first class, who became Parks's mentor. Scalia, as his name implied, had an Italian background and was a dark-haired, dark-eyed, fast-talking type who was a camera bug in his spare time, a joker all the time, and one of the few who rivaled Earl Nave in boasting of enough experiences for ten lives.

Taken under Scalia's wing for training purposes, Parks understood that he would become the machinist's mate's oiler, coffee kid, and general "gopher," which translated into a striker who ran around at his mentor's request doing all the peon jobs, such as reading and recording temperatures and pressures. Lubricating machinery in a constant maintenance routine was part of his act, as well as running back and forth for endless cups of coffee, and being quick and willing to do whatever else was requested of him.

In return, Scalia helped Parks with his notebook and taught him everything he needed to know about the engines. Some of the training required the kind of faith that one acrobat has to have in the ability of another when trading trapezes in midair. The eight-cylinder engines were big, about 20 feet long, and the first time Scalia asked Parks to help him take out a connecting rod bearing, Tom was unaware of what he was getting into.

"Okay, okay, lie down there in the bilges, Parks," Scalia ordered. "I tried prying this damn nut off but I can't, so we'll have to work on it with a slugging wrench and a hammer." Scalia straddled his supine helper and directed Tom's hands so that he held the 20-pound, two-foot-long wrench correctly on the nut with the handle extending out over his face. "I'm gonna swing at it to loosen it with this sledgehammer. Steady on. I advise you to shut your eyes. Okay, okay, here we go."

Tom felt the breeze from the weighty sledgehammer as it passed over his face and a slight constriction in his gut at the mental picture of what could happen if Scalia missed. But by the third time he lost the flutters and even kept his eyes open, so great was his respect for his teacher.

The most important thing in a submariner's life was to qualify. Parks, who had wanted more than anything to be an airman, had done a complete turn-around. Now, his prime ambition was to wear the dolphins, insignia of the submarine service, then maybe have them hand-embroidered on the lower right-hand sleeve of his dress jumper. A sailor or an officer had to be aboard six months before requesting qualification. The idea was that every man know how to do every job on the boat. Even cooks and steward's mates had to meet these requirements. Schoenrock, galley ace, had excelled so that at Battle Stations he was also gun captain. But qualifying was not just glory. The men drew $15, $20, and $25 dollars extra per month, depending on their ratings. Sub pay bought a lot of beers.

Tom wrote his mother, "You should see what I have to do to qualify. I don't have to tell you that I didn't take school too seriously, but I'm willing to bet that nobody will have a better logbook than mine." In his qualifying logbook, Tom had to describe the various systems necessary to operate the submarine, and supplement the descriptions with drawings of the mechanisms. The book also showed a check-off list by compartment under "Rig for Dive," "Rig for Collision," "Rig for Depth Charge," and other emergencies. While underway, there were "School of the Boat" sessions for candidates for qualification. Tom and others also took advantage of in-port duty days to go over some of the areas with senior petty officers. Even guys like Schab who made a joke out of everything else took qualifying seriously.

The moment came when Tom Parks thought he was ready to take the next to last step and have the chief of the boat review his logbook, then take him through compartment by compartment and question him. He wanted Pop Bridges, whom he highly respected and who would be leaving soon, to pass on his work instead of a new chief, as yet unknown. There was an element of superstition involved, too. Pop represented stability; somehow it would mean more.

Bridges told Tom that he had reviewed his logbook and that it was very good, but as he stepped through the watertight door into the control room and ordered, "Rig for dive," the lined, friendly face suddenly became noncommittal, the concerned father replaced by the neutral judge. For a minute the change of role disconcerted Tom and he prayed that he wouldn't boob himself, but he recouped and went into action. He checked the main ballast tank vent valve operating gear in the overhead to make sure it was rigged for remote operation. Then he showed Pop that the pin was disengaged from the operating handle. He followed up fast by checking the operation of the periscope and the trim pump, and got the necessary permission to rig out the bow planes. He checked the bow and stern planes operation and the proper position of the ventilation flappers— all with such speed that the corners of Pop's mouth raised an eighth of an inch before he caught himself. The rest of the examination went well even though, like a distance runner who'd set himself too fast a pace in the beginning, Tom faltered a couple of times. He was actually out of breath, heart pounding, by the time he finished.

For the final examination by one of the officers, Tom felt calm by comparison. He did notice though that he couldn't eat his usual eight or ten of Schoenrock's special pancakes, and got threatening looks from the temperamental cook when his plate went back half full. That evening, after taking Larry Bernard in his stride, Tom celebrated being a full-fledged submariner by buying Scalia and others a drink at Whitey Smith's bar in Manila.

"Bottoms up, pal." Scalia drank and placed the shot glass firmly on the mahogany bar, then smiled at his pupil. "You sure look a lot better now than when Mr. Bernard started taking you around."

"I thought I looked cool as a cucumber," Tom said.

"You was the same color."

Caroline Bernard and the others finally obtained passage out of Tsingtao on a Japanese ship that was so dirty the women inspected every mouthful of food before they ate it to make sure it didn't crawl. In addition, the wind began shoving the ship around and the bosom of the sea heaved until it seemed as though it was trying to toss the vessel entirely off its chest. Dottie Lautrup lay face down on her bunk with fingers hooked under the top and toes under the bottom edge of the mattress in an effort to stay off the deck. As the storm approached typhoon status, Caroline, whose baby bulge did not permit lying on her stomach, was grateful for being one of the few passengers who could have eaten if there'd been anything decent to eat.

The typhoon was still building up when the women arrived in Manila. After going through customs, they went straight to the Army-Navy Club for messages. The *39* was out to sea, but Larry had left the cheering information that the Bernards had a home at last. He had found a two-bedroom apartment and rented some rattan furniture, including a seven-by-seven-foot bed, a kingsize in the days before the Western world had heard of them.

When Caroline unlocked the door her joy was somewhat abated. In the middle of the living room were a half dozen large crates containing personal possessions—sheets, towels and so forth. Only a month away from giving birth, Caroline could not pry open the sturdy containers made of thick lumber and since she had neither husband nor servants to call on, she ran next door to the Boulevard Hotel to borrow a strong man with a hatchet. But by the time she located linen and got the bed draped with mosquito netting, she was almost too tired to fall into it.

The storms continued while the Bernards were getting settled, and there was one that Caroline and her friend Kay Putnam would never forget. The two women, both pregnant, had decided to combine a routine trip to the doctor at Cavite with a visit to the tiny commissary, where a few staples and canned goods could be purchased. (Fresh meat and vegetables were bought daily by their cooks in town.) On the way back, it started to pour.

A Philippine taxi was an adventure at any time, but during the monsoon season it often became a test of courage as well, since most of the rackety old vehicles would have been junk-heap fodder anywhere else. At first, the women were able to see the sights along the road through the slanting rain: the old adobe church that was famous for having an organ with pipes made of bamboo, and the moldy little general stores, mostly run by Chinese merchants, whose sagging shelves often contained imported U.S. canned goods including tuna, used by Filipinos during the rainy season when fresh fish was hard to obtain. This was preferable to eating perishable items held without refrigeration, still standard outside the big cities. Although American medicine had greatly improved the water supply, controlled rat infestation, and instituted a program of inoculation against plagues which had decimated the island population in the past, there was still a long way to go.

They passed rice fields flooded with water. They glimpsed fishing rafts with bamboo derricks for hoisting nets, and groves of coconut and breadfruit trees, barely identifiable now as the storm intensified, making the rain look like sheets of water flapping in the wind. The road became so inundated that moisture oozed up between the floorboards, and they were still out in the country when water started sloshing around their ankles and dissolving the paper bags holding the groceries. Then the engine sputtered, gurgled, and stopped completely. From out of the mangrove trees in the swamps along the roadside came a troop of squat, muscular, backcountry natives dressed only in G-strings, with big bolo knives thrust through the material twisted over one hip. Snakes writhed in the flood water, which had risen to crotch height, and a bloated rat's body swept by, its staring eyes lashed by swirling twigs. But the sturdy peasants, chattering among themselves, paid no attention; some pointed to the stalled taxi and others came forward to press their noses against the window and stare at the strange creatures inside.

"Dear God," Caroline breathed, "I know they're headhunters."

"Don't do anything to make them mad," Kay muttered, smiling weakly and blinking back tears.

Suddenly the flattened noses straightened out and the faces turned in another direction. The girls' alarm grew; Caroline feared that reinforcements had arrived, and prepared to do battle if the headhunters pried open the door. The taxi driver ignored them; he was outside with the hood up, trying to start the engine while sluices of water ran through the machinery.

Suddenly the door to the taxi was flung open and a head was thrust inside. "Looks like you ladies need help. Horses do better than taxis when the water's running high." It was an American sailor, and behind him was another with a horse-drawn gig. They stowed the groceries for Caroline and Kay while the natives watched the transfer with interest. As soon as the women were driven away, the black eyes switched their gaze with equal intensity to the taxi driver and sailors, who were all in confab now over the engine.

When the Bernards' baby Lance was born, both parents were in the hospital. While on maneuvers, Larry had developed severe stomach cramps that turned out to be ulcers rather than sympathetic labor, and he was still confined when Caroline's two-week stay was over. The 15 pounds Caroline had gained during her pregnancy had dropped away like magic, plus a few more, and though she was trying to nurse Lance, she couldn't seem to take the interest in food that she needed to regain strength. The doctors told her she wasn't used to the heat and mosquitoes. Even when she developed an infection, they kept on telling her she was okay, until she started blaming herself for being a poor sport and a hypochondriac in the bargain.

When it came time for her to go home, she really got scared. She hadn't yet hired an *amah* for the baby. Lance was her first and she had wanted to keep him to herself for a while, but she hadn't counted on Larry's being sick and unable to help, nor on feeling that every step she took required as much effort as climbing a hill. Even the thought of the ride home tired her out. So it was with mixed feelings that she received the message that Roy Klinker would escort her and the baby back to Manila. She was glad of any kind of help but considered Roy a typical pleasure-seeking, nondomesticated bachelor who probably thought diapers were dishtowels and rattles were instruments used in a rhumba band. It would be hard to make conversation when she scarcely felt able to hold her head up.

When the nurse handed her the baby, Caroline's arms shook so that she was afraid she might drop him, and her heart sank when she saw Klinker. But the tall, lean lieutenant, making a quick appraisal of the situation, gently took the baby from her and summoned a taxi. As Caroline climbed gratefully into the cab, she watched Roy maneuver his long legs in sideways without letting go of Lance or waking him up. "Where in the world did you learn to handle a baby like that? You act like you've been doing it for years."

"I have," Roy said. "I was the oldest in a big family, and we didn't have much money. I learned how to diaper a baby when I was still in diapers myself. Every time I got a new kid in training pants, another one came along."

Roy proved he wasn't boasting. He escorted mother and child to their apartment at the old Sequia without so much as a squeak from the two-week-old. He made formula, arranged the bassinet, changed the baby, and put him in it. He also came back regularly to check on things until Caroline found an *amah* and Larry was released from the hospital.

Nothing flies as fast as rumor, and the U.S. Navy wives could no longer ignore the one they disliked the most. At every cocktail and dinner party, the ominous words were spoken with a quick glance over the shoulder: "I hear we're going to be evacuated." The rumors intensified with the advent of Admiral Thomas C. Hart as Commander-in-Chief, Asiatic Fleet, in late October 1940. Hart started off with a shake-up in the high command (its most senior officer, the Commandant of the 16th Naval District, would be replaced five times during the following year). Hart saw clearly that the Japanese were not getting the raw materials they needed so badly, especially oil, and that the time was drawing close when they would make their move to expand. The Philippines would not be a good place for dependents; besides the consideration of their safety, there was the problem of extracting greatest efficiency from the inadequate forces at hand to defend the islands, and men concerned about their families could not give full attention to their jobs.

By November rumor became fact and evacuation was an order. Army wives were still untouched, as were the dependents of federal officials and businessmen. Resentment was heavy: "Why pick on us? Why aren't all women and children ordered home?" the Navy wives asked. A year later, they would have to concede that Admiral Hart had been more foresighted than others.

Jo Triebel, whose husband Chuck commanded the *S-41*, heard a number of Navy wives say, "It's my husband who's in the Navy, not me. I'm a civilian; I'm not going." When word of the rebellion filtered through to Admiral Hart, that stiff, teetotalling, regulation-conscious officer let it be known that every one of the officers whose wives remained would be confined to their ships indefinitely with no leaves granted.

Caroline was bewildered by the rapid turn of events. In the space of a few short months she had settled into her apartment, given birth, found help, and finally welcomed Larry home from the hospital. When Larry could pry his son loose from the possessive Chinese *amah,* he was able at last to inspect the child long enough to make the usual remarks, such as, "Caroline, he has your eyes but his chin looks more like my father's." When the evacuation order came, father and son were scarcely acquainted.

The sorrow of separation was kept at bay by the number of things that had to be done in the short amount of time before departure. There was the dilemma of deciding what to take back. A harried Commander Ben Gantz, from Admiral Hart's staff, had given the women a briefing at the Army-Navy Club, explaining that space would be very limited because of the large number of dependents to be squeezed into one ship. Each woman would only rate a few feet of storage in the hold and one small suitcase in the crowded stateroom. There was no question in Caroline's mind as to the most important items. Two-month-old Lance had recently been christened in the Catholic Church across the street from the Bernards' apartment. He had worn a handmade silk robe for the occasion, and his mother was going to make sure it went along. The second item, a Chinese nest of tables, was also the last, since it filled the storage space and settled the issue. Small preoccupations helped keep big worries at bay—the lonely months ahead, the difficulties of raising a child alone, the memory of Japanese soldiers in Tsingtao and the thought that soon they might appear in the Philippines.

As the month flew by, the Bernards tried joking to keep their spirits up. Larry said, "Watch your language when you're home in the States. I don't want your folks to think you picked up street talk from me." They laughed, remembering Caroline's words when Captain and Mrs. Coe had come to call: "Larry's asleep, but I'll wake him. He said he was all crapped out when he came back from the ship." Larry had told his bride later that the term "crapped out" was not used during formal calls. But finally they ran out of amusing remembrances; then came the long pauses when they looked at each other wordlessly because the only subject they could think of was separation.

Rachel Coe had loved every minute of her life in the islands and was glad for everything she had done. Her recent visit to a new factory where brightly patterned cambray cloth was manufactured from abacá, the hemp used in Manila rope, was part of her continuing interest in textiles. In Baguio she had enjoyed the wood carvings of the Igorot people displayed at the teeming Sunday market, and, in Manila, the sightseeing trips to the walled city, where she had explored ancient buildings such as Santo Tomás University, founded by Dominicans in 1611—25 years before Harvard. She would remember nostalgically the broad Pasig River that flowed through the city, spanned by the modern Jones Bridge. Automobiles, trucks, streetcars, and buses zoomed by in the inner lanes, but the lane nearest the river was reserved for horse-drawn *carromatos.* Rachel liked riding in the sleepy little carriages because they permitted sightseers to imagine that they were still traversing the picturesque old "Bridge of

Spain", with its moss-covered stones, that had preceded the modern structure.

Rachel would also miss her early morning horseback rides at Clark Field and the occasional opportunities she had had to test her skill at jitterbugging. When Jim, himself an excellent dancer, took her to a ship's party, a partner trade always ensued. Inevitably Rachel was put through her paces by the shortest sailor and wildest jitterbugger on the *39*. She was proud that she had managed to stay on her feet but her ambition had been to equal one of them.

There were a few things she wouldn't miss. One was the powdered milk called Klim (milk spelled backwards) that they used for lack of fresh. Then there were the flit-gun sessions at the Army-Navy Club, when the boy responsible for keeping down the insect population always chose a moment when everyone was seated to make his rounds under the table, dispersing spray all over trousers and long dresses. Also, she felt it would be best for the children if they did not stay too long in the islands. The fuss the servants made over the boy child, Henry, left no doubt as to the status of women in the Far East. Even Lottie Antiopolo was no longer as concerned with little Jean; the young "master" was always attended to first. And last but most important of the things she would be glad to relinquish was the maddening sight of barge after barge leaving Manila loaded with scrap iron sold by the United States to the Japanese.

Parting came too soon. The pier on Manila Bay where the SS *United States* awaited her passengers looked like a street in Shanghai, so great was the crowd and confusion. The murmured words of distraught men and women trying to say goodbye, without privacy, in these last bittersweet moments were erased by the cacaphony of a brass military band playing lively, inappropriate John Philip Sousa numbers. In counterpoint to the band were the squalls of children who, if they didn't cry for other reasons, cried because their mothers cried and because their fathers kept saying, "Don't cry, I'll be all right. Don't worry about me."

For many, the wait to go aboard ship was the worst part because, when a dreaded thing has to be done, it's best to do it quickly. But when the ship's whistle added its strident voice to the whirlpool of sound, those present felt a chill that did not go with the tropical climate. No husbands were allowed aboard. When Caroline Bernard held out her arms for the baby, Larry shook his head and hugged the child closer. The women were starting up the gangplank now, wishing the line would move faster because each time they waved back the parting grew sadder.

"Larry, give me the baby," Caroline implored. But Larry still held on to his son. In the crowd Caroline caught sight of Rachel and Jim Coe in one of the long, silent, sorrowful farewells that were taking place all over the crowded dock.

The ship's whistle blasted three times for departure, and military police began urging the women on, rounding up the stragglers. The band chose that moment to play its most tactless selection of the day, "The Old Gray Mare, She

Ain't What She Used to Be." Caroline tried to turn grief into anger at this stupidity so she wouldn't cry again. Now the woman behind her was urging her on. She had no choice but to reach out and pull the baby out of Larry's arms, not daring to look back as she walked up the gangplank.

As the *United States* steamed out of Manila Bay, she passed the fortress of Corregidor, the Gibraltar-like stronghold with its beehive tunnels and vast underground chambers that held an arsenal of guns, ammunition, and medical equipment for the U.S. Army. Women preoccupied with trying to find their way aboard ship and keep track of their young were unaware that in the spring of 1940 extensive underground facilities for the Navy had also been built there, providing radio communications and storage for spare parts and general supplies. None of it would prevent the islands from being taken, but it would help some of the vessels of the Asiatic Fleet to get away.

4. War Games

The crew of the *39* were little affected by the departure of the Navy women; their female companionship was still around in the form of Filipina girlfriends. The most notable sign of things to come for enlisted men was the bolstering of the Asiatic Fleet by eight of the modern submarines whose number during the fateful year 1941 would reach 23, pushing the six original S-boats into the background. Fleet-boat skippers outranked S-boat skippers, being Lieutenant Commanders. You could hardly expect a two-and-a-half striper to live as Captain Coe had to live at sea, sharing a portside stateroom with his first officer. Only eight by eight feet, it contained upper and lower bunks, lockers, and a washbasin. When two six-footers like Lautrup and Coe were in it at the same time, even cockroaches had a hard time squeezing by.

S-boat personnel found out early that most fleet-boat sailors pitied them, but true Asiatic pigboat sailors had all the feisty pride of a cadre of hard-living, tough professionals who, by the very fact that they'd been able to survive S-boat existence, considered themselves superior. A wise skipper did everything in his power to keep this feeling alive, especially with the threat of war in the offing, and Red Coe was a very wise skipper indeed. There would be no deployment this year to Shanghai and Tsingtao, and since the men had considered these recreation centers one of the big advantages of Asiatic duty, substitute diversions would have to be found if he was to maintain a happy, efficient ship.

Coe had a close friend and classmate from the Naval Academy who was captain of the *S-38*, Lieutenant Wreford G. (Moon) Chapple. With the departure of their wives, the two skippers banded together even more than they had before. Chapple, about the same height as Coe, was a bigger-boned, more robust man with a craggy, amiable face, who had been a football player and heavyweight boxer. In appearance he was the exact opposite of the natty officer of film and fiction. It was said that Chapple could put on a brand-new outfit made by the best tailor in Hongkong, and ten minutes later it would look as if he'd slept in it.

When Chapple had attended the Naval Academy, plebes had still been expected to entertain first classmen at mealtimes. Born and raised in Montana, Chapple told cowboy yarns and sang ribald range songs until he had milked his connection with the Old West dry. Then, knowing he had to come up with something fast, he seized on comics and put together a series of Moon Mullins cartoon skits. They were so successful that Chapple earned the nickname of Moon forever; considering that a first name like Wreford didn't break down to anything very catchy, it wasn't too bad.

Moon was a seasoned China hand; with one interruption he'd been stationed in the Philippines since 1933. Many a submariner in the Asiatic Fleet was known as a hellraiser and Moon ranked with the best of them. When Coe arrived, Chapple immediately took him under his wing, introducing him to the Nutshell Cafe in Cavite with its sawdust and peanut shells on the floor and its half liters of San Miguel beer served in chilled mugs. Another hangout was Tom Dixie's Kitchen in Manila. Dixie was a tall American black man who had spent an untold number of years in the Philippines. His place was especially popular for late night snacks after cockfights, jai alai, or the many other diversions, good and bad, that Manila offered, and was patronized by both officers and men. It was known as not only a good place to pick up a bite but a good place to pick up a fight.

Coe and Chapple were drinking companions ashore and had been known, when things were dull, to compete with each other if no one else was available. One morning when Allyn Christopher was on the handling lines, Coe came on the bridge with a shiner that made everyone wince. Christopher's "G'morning, Captain" barely elicited a grunt, and Chief of the Boat Bridges carefully kept his eyes trained on the captain's ear or chin, avoiding the shiner as he discussed the day's events—or rather, related them, because Coe was still not making comments.

The *39* was tied up side by side with the *38* and at this point Moon Chapple lumbered on deck on the *38* and called over, "Hey Red, where'd you get the black eye?"

Coe answered gruffly, "Fell out of bed."

And Moon responded, straight-faced, "Sure you did." The scuttlebutt was that they'd gone out together to raise a little hell, and when they didn't find any, they raised it with each other in a for-fun brawl.

Coe had a flair for words, humor, and music. Typical of his creative side was his enjoyment of costume parties at the Army-Navy Club, at one of which he had appeared dressed as a native from an outlying village, complete with a live fighting cock tucked under his arm. The waiting period put Coe's inventive ability to the test, and he used it for the welfare of his men. In addition, the *38* and *39* had been friendly competitors at many a softball game. And now Chapple and Coe fostered more athletic events, adding variations as they went along.

In February 1941 there was some shifting of personnel aboard the *S-39*. George Lautrup left; Roy Klinker moved into the slot of exec; and a new officer, Guy Gugliotta, arrived to complete the complement. Gugliotta, fresh out of sub school, had to leave behind his bride of seven months, Bobette, because of Admiral Hart's evacuation order. Guy had had a rough time at sub school in New London after getting off to a bad start. Along with classmates Luke McDonald and Jim Andrews, he had been assigned transportation from Hawaii to the States aboard a Navy tender. The three men were a day late reporting in because the ship was late, but it was made plain to the culprits by Lieutenant Commanders George C. Crawford, known far and wide as a clenched-jaw student-cruncher, and Karl G. Hensel, acid second in command, that the school accepted no excuses. Both seemed to take a particular dislike to Gugliotta, who further compounded his errors by calling Mrs. Hensel Mrs. Crawford and vice versa. Then, after a drink or two, Gugliotta took a pratfall while dancing at an officers' club Halloween party to which sub school ensigns had been invited but which they were not expected to attend. Neither Guy nor Bobette had experience or sense enough to realize this and they were the only young couple present.

When orders came just before graduation, Gugliotta found he'd been handed the now doubly undesirable Asiatic Station, where he could not take his young bride. Rightly or wrongly, he felt it was a sort of punishment for his sins, because many other newlyweds and even bachelors were ordered to coed places like Panama and Key West. Guy did not bring a chip on his shoulder to the *S-39*, but he did bring a bruised ego and lacked the kind of faith he'd had in himself before the submarine school experience.

When Gugliotta arrived in Manila, he was met on the dock by squadron personnel, who took care of his baggage and got him steered in the right direction. By evening he had met all the other officers on the *39* except the captain, and was rerouted in the direction of the Army-Navy Club for dinner, drinks, and his introduction to Red Coe. Slightly wrinkled but properly dressed in fresh khaki complete with tie, Guy's curiosity about his new commanding officer was equaled only by his trepidation that Coe might have some of the characteristics of the sub school officials.

The club was enhanced by the aroma of gardenias and frangipani and the sight of pastel organdy and chiffon skirts whirling around the dance floor. Gugliotta's guide said resentfully, "The damned Army still has its women here. It's not fair." Then he pointed to a redhead at the bar: "That's your skipper."

Red Coe was playing liar's dice. As soon as he heard the words, "Ensign Gugliotta reporting for duty, sir," he shook the hand of the new officer, motioned him to a chair, passed him the whiskey bottle, and pantomimed removing the tie. The Coe technique was tried and true, and in ten minutes Gugliotta knew he had never felt more at home in his life.

Being the most recent to arrive, Guy inherited the jobs of gunnery, communications, and commissary—in other words, he was "George." This was the name given to the most junior officer on board, who became an assistant to other officers and had many collateral jobs. On a submarine, however, "George" had more responsible duties than elsewhere, since there were so few officers. Almost immediately after Guy reported in, the 39 went to sea. A little nervous, like any novice on trial, Gugliotta wanted to impress his captain favorably, and as the week progressed he began to breathe more easily. He felt that his watch-standing as officer of the deck was good, his diving officer's technique above average, and, when he functioned as torpedo officer, his two fish ran hot, straight, and normal and got two hits, which had to be called a perfect showing. His ego was not completely restored, but he was getting there. It was a very good week for Gugliotta until he stood his final midday watch in a pair of shorts. Between sunburn and prickly heat, he not only found it hard to sit down but learned respect for the tropical sun the hard way. But it didn't matter, because the old man had given him the same responsibility as the other officers.

A few weeks later Guy experienced the Coe Complete Confidence Course. The boat was anchored in Manila Bay, and Gugliotta had the duty when word came that a typhoon was on its way. He sent an immediate message to Coe at the Army-Navy Club, who messaged back, "Get underway." Gugliotta did so with only the duty section on board, but he couldn't seem to get up any speed; it turned out he'd forgotten that the anchor was still down. When he finally got going, the 39 stayed at sea a couple of days, riding out the storm, with one green officer and a third of a crew. Typhoon over, they came back in. Gugliotta felt great. He loved the 39 boat and thanked the Lord he was lucky enough to have Coe for a skipper.

Right at the start, Guy had several more samples of Coe's style. Admiral Hart's security measures had included a clampdown on submarine movements so that the boats never actually knew where they were going until they shoved off. Coe devised a "Where Are We Going?" pool—slips of paper with possible destinations sold at one peso each. Then he added a "What Time Do We Anchor?" pool, with slips numbered from 0 to 60 and the winner decided by the minute of anchoring. The sum of 60 pesos, or $30, was an amount worth winning for any sailor; the men couldn't wait to buy up the slips, some taking three and four.

One day while steering in column, Gugliotta had the deck and noticed Coe sending an odd-looking signal to the 38 just astern. As communications officer, Guy silently asked himself, what the hell is Coe trying to do, then ventured to say aloud, "Sir, that signal looks screwy to me."

"No sweat, don't worry about it," Coe said soothingly. His cap was jammed tight on his forehead, his eyes were closed, and his thumb and forefinger moved up and down as though taking measure.

A few minutes later a similar cryptic message was received from the *38*, and this went on for half an hour, with messages like P-K4, KT-KB3, P-Q3. Gugliotta began to fear that they would be called down by the division commander for using some bastard code.

Finally Coe opened his eyes, stopped measuring the air, and trained a pair of binoculars on the bridge of the *38*. Guy was further confounded. The two boats were close enough to toss a baseball back and forth, so why the binoculars?

Suddenly the redhead broke his silence. "The dirty crook," he said. Then, noticing the expression on Gugliotta's face, he added, "We're playing chess, and Chapple is cheating."

Roy Klinker, a chess expert, had just come on the bridge and asked, "How is Captain Chapple cheating, sir?"

"We're both new at the game, but we agreed not to get any help. That dog has Fletcher with him right up on the bridge," Coe said in disgust. Bob Fletcher was a recognized expert.

"Let me give you a hand," Klinker said.

Coe hemmed and hawed for a minute, then drawled, "Well, as a matter of fact, our yeoman's pretty good, and he's been helping me. But not in such a boldfaced way. He sends the moves up from below but only now and then. Tell him to come to the bridge and bring his chessboard with him. If Chapple can do it so can we."

The moment of parting had come for Pop Bridges. The quartermaster had passed the word over the 1 MC, "All hands to quarters, main deck." It was an impressive group that assembled to pay their respects to the departing chief of the boat. Captain, officers, and crew were in spotless dress whites so highly starched that they forced a man to stand at attention. The most impressive of them all, though, was the elderly gentleman with the nutcracker face and the blue eyes that had taken on the depth of the sea he had looked at so intently for so many years. Bridges' right sleeve was covered with hash marks from shoulder to wrist.

The new chief of the boat stepped forward, box in hand, to present the fine gold pocketwatch inscribed, "From the Officers and Crew of the S-39." The captain spoke briefly, with the grace for which he was noted, of Pop's long years of service. It was a solemn occasion. Lumpy throats were the order of the day. And then everybody was lining up at the prow to shake Pop's hand, and the good wishes were repeated and repeated. Zeke Matthews, who had been orphaned at an early age and had appreciated Bridges more because of it, did not find it easy to express himself. Among the last to shake Pop's hand, he got as far as "I want to . . ." then gripped the gnarled fingers harder and couldn't get any more words out but was reassured, as always, when Pop said, "I got you, son." And then at last there was no one left to say goodbye.

The new chief of the boat had been chosen before Pop's departure. The captain had called a wardroom session with his officers, and they sat down to kick around likely candidates. The most senior was Chief Machinist's Mate Mandekic, and seniority was a factor that had to weigh heavily. But the age and weakened condition of the temperamental pigboat required that her engineers be the best and available at all times; there was the question of where Mandekic was needed most.

"There's another factor here," Roy Klinker said. "Mandekic is due for orders soon."

The captain nodded, "It would be good to have a chief who's had a little seasoning if there's a war coming on. Somebody the men are used to working with." Drops of perspiration rolled down Coe's high forehead and dropped unnoticed on his khaki shorts.

"There's a war coming on, you can bet on that for sure," Bernard mumbled.

Gugliotta said nothing; he was too recent an arrival to know the personnel, and he wisely kept his opinions to himself.

"What about Earl Nave?" Klinker asked.

Coe shifted in his seat. "Bridges is a hard act to follow."

"Nave is one of the best torpedomen around. The men respect him," Klinker said.

Coe's and Klinker's glances met, locked for a moment, then sheered off. They didn't always see eye to eye. A few months back, Klinker had urged Coe to recommend Nave for the rank of warrant officer, but Coe refused; Nave was a very good man, and the *39* would have lost him if he had become a warrant. Now, with Mandekic out of the running, Nave was a natural second selection. The captain was well aware of it but might have preferred making the selection himself. Roy Klinker was not the diplomatic type. He had proved that when he had called Coe "Red" one day aboard ship and had been brought up short by his superior. Coe's camaraderie with his officers did not extend to a nickname basis. Klinker had again run afoul of Coe when he had given him unsolicited advice on a navigational matter, a subject Coe had taught at the Naval Academy.

"How would Nave's personality stand up on patrol?" Larry questioned. "He can be very funny, but he's loud as a foghorn and his profanity gets tiresome."

"Yes, it tends to double every sentence he speaks," Coe chuckled, "but to tell you the truth, he would probably be a diversion if the going got rough."

Klinker looked pleased, Bernard relaxed, and Gugliotta made mental notes of the insights he'd obtained. Roy Klinker's orders, too, were due in the not-so-distant future. It wasn't hard to imagine that he'd be ready to go and that the old man would be ready to let him.

"I'll have to see Mandekic and Nave together and explain the reasons for our choice," Coe said, "but since we all agree, that's it."

Earl Nave took to his new status with a blast of profanity, a sheepish look, and an attempt to control his language that lasted two or three days. He was not Pop Bridges—nobody ever would be—but he knew his business, and he'd demonstrated his ability. A boaster by nature, he found it almost impossible not to top any stories told, including places visited, women slept with, and sassbacks given to officers. The men respected his professional ability, but many saw him as a bull mouth who could really get under your skin if you tried to compete with him. His out-and-out lies were commonplace but always sworn to as the truth, and "the honker" validated his nickname by the sheer force and volume with which he faced down anybody who dared try to equal his feats, let alone surpass them. On the other hand, he was rarely out of sorts and always good for a laugh.

In his early thirties, Nave had none of the fatherly qualities or dignity the men had been accustomed to but nevertheless was good for morale, because if you couldn't top him, you could hate him. He made an excellent whipping boy for frustrations, disappointments, pent-up energy, and grudges against the system in general. After Mandekic received orders a few months later, the *39* had only a few men aboard in their early thirties. And it was a good thing. Wartime conditions would prove young organisms better able to stand the strain of the old S-boats.

There were a couple of people aboard that Nave didn't try to outdo. One was Chief Cook Walter Schoenrock. Few people dared to cross Rocky. Initially a baker, Schoenrock had needed galley experience to make chief commissary steward, so he applied for submarines—and quickly developed all the temperamental qualities associated with those who practice *haute cuisine*. In addition, his IQ and leadership ability were high, and he doubled as gun captain. His build was muscular, not rotund; Rocky did not overindulge in his own pastries. He was not a man to be taken lightly.

Aboard the *S-39* everyone ate the same food, but the officers paid by the meal and the crew ate free of charge. When the submarines were alongside the *Canopus*, they could eat there, enjoying the change to more ample quarters and the chitchat of people from other ships. But everyone agreed that *Canopus* food was the worst anywhere in the world; few men, even the most penurious, had ever been able to forcefeed themselves a 24-hour ration of *Canopus* crud. Submarines in general and S-boats in particular, as compensation for other lacks, prided themselves on having the best food in the Navy. Schoenrock held forth in a galley area six feet wide by twelve feet long, a sectioned-off part of the crew's mess with a passthrough counter. Here he was god and played the role to the hilt. The striker who helped him didn't dare move a toothpick without his consent, and any newcomer, officer or enlisted, found out quickly where he stood if he overstepped the bounds in Rocky's territory. Rocky enjoyed turning out special-occasion cakes, and baked several fancy ones in celebration of Nave's advancement to chief of the boat. Gugliotta, who had the duty, had been enticed by the aroma, and his nose led him to the galley. The cook had just finished swirling pink rosebuds over dark chocolate icing.

"Boy, that looks good," Gugliotta exclaimed. "What's underneath?"

"Angel food."

"Um, um." Guy's hand reached out for a swipe at the icing, but he never completed the action because Schoenrock grabbed up a nearby cleaver and held it an inch above Gugliotta's wrist. The ensign retreated.

Two Filipino steward's mates served meals to the officers and took care of their quarters, and also stood lookout watches. Amador Tayco had a wife and six children in Manila and, despite being senior to Cecilio Fabricante, was the younger of the two. In the way of every new generation, he smart-alecked the shorter, slower Fabricante, who barely cleared five feet and got his words so scrambled that at times he seemed to be talking a new language. Fabricante, though, had the advantage of being a barber and, by cutting the crew's hair, picked up almost enough in tips to bring his income up to Tayco's. It was a give-and-take situation too mild to be called a rivalry; nevertheless, Tayco chose not to sleep with Fabricante and the rest of the crew in the forward battery compartment, but rigged his bunk nightly on top of an ammunition locker near the wardroom. This was his territory. He used it during the day to assemble tableware and food for the officers, and of course he was responsible for having the surface free and clear when it was necessary to remove ammunition. One day Roy Klinker asked Tayco, "Do you understand Fabricante's English?" Tayco answered, "No, sair." "Do you understand his Tagalog?" Roy queried. The reply came as promptly as before: "No, sair." Somewhat exasperated, Roy persisted, "Then how do you understand Fabricante?" Tayco replied, "I no understand him, I tell him, Mr. Klinker." The crew liked them both and got a kick out of the banter that took place between the Filipinos and themselves. So did the officers.

Both Tayco and Fabricante loved to play the lottery. They were not alone. Most of the men liked gambling in any form and would bet on acey-deucy (which was played a great deal on the boat), the World Series, a Coe-Chapple chess game, or how many seconds Nave could go without saying son of a bitch or any of a dozen other favorite swear words. The jai alai courts were a popular spot in Manila for gambling, although most U.S. sailors had never run into the game before unless they lived near the Mexican border. Betting on jai alai was a favorite diversion for Tom and Jim Parks, who had grown up in San Diego, 17 miles from Tijuana. Usually when the evening ended, neither man had a peso in his pocket. But happily for Tom, he was able to borrow from the ship's fund, a brainchild of Red Coe's.

Everybody knew that when a man was broke but needed to go ashore, he'd pay any amount of interest to the loan sharks in Manila. The crew were sometimes in hock so deeply that they couldn't leave the ship without being jailed by the civil authorities. After a few such incidents, Coe called in Gugliotta, who—as "George"—was handling recreation. "Guy, I think we need a slush fund that the crew can borrow from without signing away their lives or getting in trouble with the law. It'll be a nice way to build up some money for the recreation fund, too. We can have bigger and better ship's parties and beer busts, and that's good for morale right now."

"How'll we get it started, sir?" Gugliotta asked.

"With this," and Coe wrote out a personal check for $100. "Anybody who wants to go ashore and is broke can borrow a maximum of $10 for starters and pay 10 percent interest when payday comes. I bet I'll have my money back pronto, and the recreation fund will soon have more than it knows what to do with. You can decide, according to the amount on hand, the limits each man can borrow."

The men went for the whole idea. It was their money. They earned it, they blew it, they borrowed it, and they paid it back to their own, not to some usurer in town. Officially it was called the "Ship's Recreation Fund"; unofficially, it was known as the Screwing Fund. In no time at all it was up to $2,000.

In the spring of 1941, the annual military inspection took on added importance. Most of the Asiatic Fleet spent the greater part of April and May in the southern islands, stopping at Zamboanga and Tawitawi, and operating in the Sulu Sea for scheduled exercises. Although all the officers had been to submarine school, many of the crew had not, so those men were sent to the USS *Pigeon*, to be qualified in the use of the Momsen Lung prior to departure. At school in Connecticut and Pearl Harbor, closed diving towers were used. During *Pigeon* instruction the men climbed into a diving bell, were lowered 100 feet or so, then turned loose in the open sea. The vicious moray eels, sharks, and sea snakes of many varieties provoked remarks like, "Cri'sake. So I escape, so what, so something worse kills me." But bitching was standard procedure. To put the lung in use aboard a submarine, it was strapped around the diver's chest and inflated from a compressed airline in the escape hatch. A face mask was held in place by gripping the mouthpiece with the teeth. Although the lung later proved of dubious value, this kind of training made the threat of war take on reality. Qualification notebooks were required for both officers and men, and Gugliotta

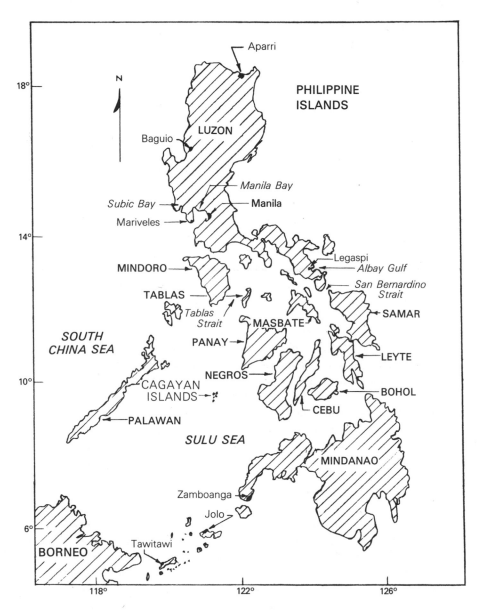

immediately set to work on his, eager to wear the dolphins as soon as possible. On the way south, much time was spent diving the submarine for speed and accuracy because it could be the most important lifesaving operation of all. Good diving could mean the difference between damaging the enemy or having him damage you, and it required split-second timing.

During the course of a 24-hour period, three dives were made, including a night dive. Each morning the first dive was to establish the trim of the boat. For all dives the procedure started on the surface with the watch, which was composed of the officer of the deck (who assumed diving-officer duties), the quartermaster of the watch, and two or more lookouts, all on the bridge. The helmsman was in the conning tower.

When the officer of the deck called out, "Dive, dive, clear the bridge," he gave two blasts on the diving alarm. The lookouts dropped down into the control room, where they rigged out the bow planes, then put the bow and stern planes on hard dive. Simultaneously, the quartermaster dropped down into the conning tower. The officer of the deck, always last to go, quickly counted noses as the others left the bridge to be sure he was not stranding a man topside; then, as he scooted through the bridge hatch, he pulled it down tight and spun the wheel that secured it. The quartermaster double-checked the bridge hatch and, dropping into the control room, did the same with the conning-tower hatch. The engine-room watch stopped the engines and shut the engine induction valve; the electrician watch came into the control room and took charge of the electrical controls of the main motor speeds.

In the control room, the chief of the watch opened the Kingston (flood) valves of the main ballast tanks and bled some high-pressure air into the boat. Because the galley was close to the main switchboard, it was usually the cook on watch who threw the battery circuit breakers, putting them in series to achieve greatest power. At this point the interior of the boat was sealed, but the main ballast tanks were open to the sea and filling. To speed up diving in a situation where every instant counted, the Kingston valves on the bottom of the main ballast tanks were usually kept open, allowing the tanks to flood to the point where the pressure inside them was the same as the outside sea pressure. This was called "riding the vents"; in this condition it took less time for the main ballast tanks to fill when the vent valves at the top of the tanks were opened.

The radioman on watch secured the antenna trunk against flooding. The diving officer reported to the conning officer (normally the commanding officer), "Green board, pressure in the boat." The green board, called the Christmas tree by submariners, was a box with green and red lights that showed, by electrical contacts, the open or shut positions of hatches, valves, and other openings. When all lights were green, they gave the right indication for submerging. The "Pressure in the boat" report confirmed that the boat was tight.

The commanding officer ordered the depth that he wanted and the diving officer repeated this depth to the planesmen. At high speed the boat would find ordered depth readily. The diving officer then ordered the electrician on the controllers to "shift to parallel" and would slow down to check his trim. He might order pumping (or blowing) water—either method used for transferring weight—among the variable ballast tanks; similarly he might order pumping or blowing to sea from, or flooding from sea into, any of them to achieve a good trim. Air was used for blowing tanks as sparingly as possible, not only because the noise it made could alert the enemy but because there was a limited supply in the high-pressure air flasks. During this period the diving officer ordered, "Shut the vents," which the chief of the watch did, so that the main ballast tanks could be blown dry when desired. Submerging was then complete, but technically the dive was not completed until the submarine surfaced once more.

Following standard submarine procedure, all orders were repeated three times. For example, if the diving officer ordered the stern planesman, "Three degree down bubble," meaning the down angle he wanted put on the boat, the stern planesman repeated immediately, "Three degree down bubble, aye, aye, sir," and as soon as it was done, he reported, "Three degree down bubble." This triple repetition made it almost impossible to misunderstand an order or to claim not to have heard one.

As Gugliotta checked through his notes, he wished he could write the procedure down as fast as the men could do it. If all went well, submerging took no more than 45 to 50 seconds.

Zamboanga had one definite advantage. Although the latitude was only about 8 degrees above the equator, the climate was much cooler than in Manila. The men didn't have much time, though, to enjoy the refreshing breezes and pleasant sight of innumerable lush, green islands dotting turquoise waters. Coe began working everybody hard in preparation for the inspection due within the week. They went out early and drilled long and late at emergencies, attacks submerged, and gun drills. As the least experienced officer, Gugliotta was put through his paces over and over again. His redheaded skipper frequently sneaked up behind him when he had the deck and yelled, "Collision port side," or "Man overboard," taking the new officer by surprise deliberately to see how quickly and efficiently he handled the drills. Zeke Matthews, who was also in the process of qualifying and wanted practice, volunteered for many of the drills. At "Man overboard," he would station himself quickly at the bow with a boathook and grapnel to pick up the dummy thrown into the water. On surface craft the man was always picked up by a motorboat, but on a submarine the officer of the deck had to maneuver the ship itself alongside so that the victim could be rescued from the bow. The operation required speedy, accurate handling on the part of the officer and deft manipulation by the sailor with the grapnel. When the skipper boomed out "Well done," a phrase used sparingly in the Navy, Matthews and Gugliotta exchanged looks of satisfaction.

There was some recreation. Larry Bernard, seeing a chance to indulge in his favorite sport, broke out the wherry and went fishing; the *39* feasted that night on tuna. Gugliotta took several groups hiking, going far enough on one occasion to find a village where the inhabitants put on a dance. The old headman beat out the rhythm on bamboo castanets while a young boy and girl, dressed in baggy white cotton pantaloons, shuffled and postured with symbolic hand gestures. The villagers, male and female, wore much the same outfit except that the more prosperous men sported wide money belts and carried the traditional bolo, a beautiful and vicious knife, sometimes double-edged and weighing several pounds. Unlike the Moros, these natives were friendly—including an accepted member of village culture called the Bini Boy, who danced with a pink comb in his oiled and wavy hair, gesturing more gracefully than the women.

Coe called on his inventive powers and dreamed up maritime relays in competition with the *38* boat. (Losers, of course, to buy beer.) One man rowed ashore, another man ran up the mountain, another man ran down, and a fourth rowed back to the submarine; then a new team started all over again. A lot of people got a lot of exercise and blew off a lot of steam with this simple diversion. But when liberty was granted to the crew in Jolo, a tiny town on a tiny island south of Zamboanga, there were a few casualties. One optimist tried to smuggle a bottle of whiskey aboard; another imbibed so much that he called the shore patrol officer a no-good bastard—several times. A third man fell ten feet through a hatch, breaking only his nose and gashing his scalp. The count was not bad, considering the length of maneuvers and the dearth of entertainment.

Whenever the *39* was anchored in Manila Bay, Subic, or Mariveles, the "laundry boats" would come rowing out to pick up dirty linens and clothes from officers and crew. It was part of a division of labor that enabled the greatest number of Filipinos to make some small amount of money they could count on. In a perverse kind of rationale, the man who could afford the most was charged the least: the captain got special low rates, and each successive officer paid on a rising scale. Nobody understood why—it was the custom. When the submarine nested beside the *Canopus,* laundry was done aboard her free of charge, but when they were anchored where no service was available (which was true most of the time during the six-week maneuvers), each man was responsible for his own clean clothes.

Larry Bernard cued newcomer Gugliotta into the routine. Handing him a bucket and saltwater soap, he said, "Soak the clothes overnight in the bucket. In the morning I'll demonstrate the cleaning method."

Came the dawn, and Guy was ready for a shower on deck. Since fresh water could never be used casually on the primitive little submarine, except in port, where more was readily available, sea water was it. The only shower the boat boasted, on the after end of the superstructure, was used by both officers and men. But even the salty stuff that sprayed from it, and the saltwater soap that stripped off skin along with dirt, felt good after torrid temperatures submerged.

"Where's your bucket?" Bernard called. Guy held it up. "Okay, spread your gear out beneath the shower." Guy did. "Now turn on the shower, scrub yourself, and tramp hard on the clothes while you're doing it. Presto, clean clothes." It was a variation on the ancient method, still used in primitive spots around the globe, where women beat clothing on rocks.

"Get a move on, Gugliotta," Red Coe called out as he came on deck toting his own bucket, and Guy's tramping turned into a tribal dance to hasten the process. An old S-boat was a great experience in democracy, but nobody wanted to keep the captain waiting, especially when he'd grown a little testy as the annual inspection loomed closer.

There was a lot of last-minute work to be done the night before the inspection, and everybody was nervous, although nobody wanted to admit it. The officers were busy with paperwork, and the men were spit-and-polishing everything twice over, egged on by newly-hatched Chief of the Boat Nave, whose well-developed proboscis sniffed out dirt with all the zeal of an anteater.

"I'll be damned if the honker didn't find a wad of gum that's been stuck under a locker for at least 50 years," Bob Bixler exclaimed, with a trace of reluctant admiration in his voice.

Schab, who was not Nave's greatest admirer, drawled, "Yeah, he's part bloodhound all right; his shnoz shows it."

"And he ain't above using it for brown-nosing, neither," Stowaway Johnson sang out. Everybody laughed. Nave was coming in handy for relieving tension, and Stowaway Johnson was always good, if only because of his tattoos. Not many young sailors coming into the Navy in the late thirties indulged in the art anymore. Aboard the *39* nobody else had to bother; they could all enjoy Stowaway's graphics. Front view, starting at the shoulders, the big man had a smiling baby's face over one breast labeled "sweet," and a frowning baby's face over the other labeled "sour." The legend on Johnson's stomach read, "Man O War, USS Constitution" with a clipper ship boldly riding the waves. The knuckles of one hand bore the word "hold" and the other "fast." Because of a superstition that land animals bring good luck to sailors, one ankle had been engraved with a pig, the other with a rooster. All pictures in full color, of course.

When Stowaway turned around, his rear view was even more amazing. A large, craggy boulder was tattooed across his spine with "Rock of Ages" written above it. In the small of the back, the legend "Twin screws, keep clear," was easily discernible. And in a final burst of craftsmanship, bluebirds, in full color and full flight, soared across each cheek. Stowaway had the reputation of either working like a madman or being completely smashed. The crew figured that the tattoos had probably been as complete a surprise to him, after a few days' blotto ashore, as they were to every new sailor who came aboard and got his first glimpse of Stowaway naked under the deck shower.

On inspection eve, the only sailor who was really relaxed was Allyn Christopher. From messcook he had gone to the engine room, where the temperatures averaged 120 degrees around the clock and hands got blistered and bloody no matter how many layers of cloth were used to handle anything. For Allyn, it had been almost literally out of the frying pan and into the fire. He borrowed an icepick from Schoenrock's galley to punch out another notch on his belt. Then, by a stroke of luck that Allyn attributed to the officers being fellow Scandinavians, Klinker had asked if Christopher could be in his deck force, and Bernard consented. The change was so welcome that at the moment Allyn felt as though he could take anything in his stride.

As in most inspections, they all boobed a little, from the captain on down, but nobody boobed too much. Gugliotta thought he was getting off easy when it looked as if the only role he had to play was O.D. during a "Collision and Abandon Ship" drill. But when the *39* returned, Division Commander R.B. Vanzant picked Guy to make the landing. The current in the area was shifty and strong, and the *Canopus* usually complicated things by starting a fast swing around her anchor just as the boat was about to come alongside. Fortunately, it didn't happen this time, and the only criticism Guy received was that he had used "a little too much speed." The pigboat sailors got the word that their exercise record compared very favorably with the record of fleet boats in Pearl Harbor. They were not surprised.

The submarines and destroyers participated in joint exercises, one of which resulted in a sub colliding with an old four-stack destroyer. Always looking for signs of superiority on the part of their frail craft, the submariners enjoyed hearing that, although the boat's periscope was bent over at a 45-degree angle, the tin can had a big gash ripped in its bottom. They grabbed ego-builders wherever they found them.

And then it was the end of May 1941, time to return to Manila after six weeks' rehearsal for war. Nobody was sorry to leave the southern islands. In many areas the Navy had not been allowed shore leave because headhunting still existed. Also, the rains had begun, and American hides, even those of old China hands, were not as impervious as the hides of the Moros, who ignored the deluges and kept right on sailing around in their *vintas*, narrow dugout canoes with colorful rainbow-hued sails.

Maneuvers were to conclude with the submarines traveling back to Manila under simulated war patrol conditions. When the word was passed, "All hands to quarters," Red Coe appeared on deck, squinting in the fierce sun which, in the way of the tropics, had almost instantly burst forth after an equally fierce rain.

With sweat stains spreading across the back of his shirt and under the armpits, the old man was brief: "We'll be cruising submerged all day. As we leave the anchorage, a destroyer will drop depth charges nearby so that we can get an idea of what a depth charge sounds like." Coe then turned to the duty officer and said, "Set the special sea detail." That was it. The officers and crew of the *39* went about their business.

In a short time Submarine Division 201 was ready to leave with the exception of the *37* boat which was outboard in the nest alongside the *Canopus*. The *37* should have been first to depart. But her captain was holding forth to his crew, still at quarters, on the perils, importance, and obscure details of the simulated war patrol conditions coming up. Awnings had been struck on board the *37* as they had on all the other boats, and his crew, listening to the interminable explanation in the blazing sun, looked more hot, flushed, and miserable with each passing moment.

Suddenly rescue came in the form of a loud voice booming down from the heights of the *Canopus*, "Hey, Bligh, how about getting the *Bounty* underway." Nobody loved to see pomposity deflated more than an S-boat sailor. The horse laughs that echoed through all the boats (except the *37*, of course) stilled the flapping jaw of the skipper, and the division got moving.

Both officers and men found the return trip to Manila a new experience in discomfort and a portent of things to come. The interior temperature of the boat started at 80 degrees, the same as the sea water, and by the time she had been submerged for eight hours or more, the air was so thick you could ice a cake with it. Another important change brought about by the simulated war conditions was to institute section dives. It was peacetime practice to summon all hands to dive the boat, though only a third of the crew was on watch at any one time. Now, the section on watch made the dive, providing utmost speed and efficiency. As Tom Parks wrote his girlfriend Corenne, "Section dives are a radical departure and give us the feeling that we're really preparing for war."

Corenne Ward was more aware of war preparation than most young women in the United States. San Diego, where she had gone to work for the telephone company, had become a boomtown; jobs, so hard to find just a few years before, were going begging. On payday the once sleepy little city could hardly contain the soldiers from Fort Rosecrans and Camp Callan and the avalanche of sailors that swarmed in. Even a 5,000-couple-capacity dance floor and ten bars at Sherman's Cafe couldn't accommodate the pounding feet and elbow bending of Uncle Sam's finest.

In addition, at the Consolidated Aircraft plant where Corenne's uncle worked, production of the "Catalina" flying boat was steadily increasing month by month. Many planes built there were bought by the British, who sent crews of young air corpsmen to San Diego to ferry them home. The British flyers were eagerly welcomed, comfortably housed at the San Diego Hotel, and much entertained by the local population—including Corenne's uncle who met many airmen at Consolidated and brought them to his home. In this way Corenne was introduced to John Bellamy from Sheffield, England.

Bellamy was a new experience for her. He was foreign enough to intrigue a 19-year-old whose travels had not yet extended far from home. And their friendship was without the language barrier that often existed between Amer-

icans and other Europeans. England was already in the midst of a war, fighting
with great courage against great odds, and airmen of whatever nationality had a
special glamor. There was mutual attraction between John Bellamy and Corenne. They found much to discuss, and he told her of his war experiences and his
home and family. His description of his mother made Corenne think of a grande
dame in the style of Queen Mary, complete with toque. And there were little
hints here and there, unwittingly revealed by the airman, that an American girl
might find it rough being accepted by the matriarch of the family. Nothing
definite was said about marriage or even a formal engagement, but there was
preliminary skirmishing around both subjects.

Tom was far away and would be for some time, but Corenne didn't have a
guilty conscience and she didn't stop writing to him or thinking about him.
Knowing how long packages took to travel by surface craft, Corenne began
planning Christmas gifts well in advance. During her lunch hour she haunted the
record department of the Marston Department Store, listening to the latest
releases as they came out so that she could choose those she thought Tom would
like best. She ended up with Glen Miller's, "Moonlight Cocktail," "Sunrise
Serenade," and "String of Pearls," all tops on radio's *Lucky Strike Hit Parade*.
She also made an appointment with a photographer to have a portrait of herself
made. It seemed strange to be planning Christmas gifts in June, but the package
could be three to four months en route. She kept in touch with Tom's parents,
too. Corenne knew they liked her because gardenia corsages were delivered
through Mrs. Parks on special occasions like birthdays and holidays. In the
United States, it was still an innocent world.

In another part of California, to the north, a woman had been fighting for
her life in a little hospital in a little town called Bishop, population 2,000.
Caroline Bernard had a lot of time to think between doses of sulfanilamide. It
was a new drug, and although swallowing tablets big enough for a horse wasn't
easy for a person with a sky-high fever and a bone-dry throat, Caroline knew that
her cooperation might mean the difference between making it and not making it.

In her waking moments she often went back in her mind over the leave-
taking in Manila and the trip that followed. It had been a rough journey. The ship
was jampacked, and each woman with a babe in arms was responsible for
bringing with her, and caring for, her own supply of formula, diapers, and
bottles in an era when disposables were virtually unknown. The harassed staff
had all they could do to provide meals and linens. Most of the cabins had been
stripped so that cots could be installed to supplement the built-in beds. Caroline
was one of seven women and a baby assigned to two rooms. Five of the women
volunteered to sleep in one room so that Caroline would have enough space in
the other to run a clothesline, which was constantly filled with baby clothes
washed in the small lavatory basin. Even so, it was a tight squeeze for Caroline

and the other woman to share the small cabin with the baby and his bassinet. They were forever ducking the wet diapers and flannel nightgowns that
flapped themselves dry in the eternal pitch and toss of the stormy voyage.

As the SS *United States* neared the Aleutians on the great-circle route, the
already heavy seas became mountainous. Caroline was not seasick, but the lack
of energy that had plagued her since the birth of her son became an intense
fatigue. The only thing that kept her going was knowing that her mother would
be there to meet her when the ship docked in San Francisco.

Caroline was sure that the bracing air and high altitude of the mining camp
where her father was chief engineer would make her feel better—but it didn't
work that way. Her feet seemed to be dragging 50-pound weights, and everything was an ordeal, even the nightly letter to Larry. Suddenly came a raging
fever, severe pain, delirium. Her parents were frantic with worry. Despite heavy
snows, they were able to make it to Bishop, the closest town with medical
facilities, and just in time. Peritonitis had set in.

Caroline was suffering from a quaint-sounding ailment that had killed
scores of young mothers in the past. It was called childbed fever; her grand-
mother had died of it. The doctor in Bishop said she'd had the infection since the
birth of her child, but it had taken a long time for the healthy young woman to
succumb. Caroline recalled seeing hordes of mouse-size cockroaches crawling
in and out of open hampers containing clean sanitary napkins in the Cañacao
Hospital and wondered if that had anything to do with it. She would never know.
The tropics often played games with constitutions unused to them, no matter
how young and healthy. Her doctor advised her not to go back to the mining
camp; it was too high, and too remote from medical facilities for a woman who
had been so ill. It was decided that she would recuperate faster if she and the
baby went to Deadwood, South Dakota, to stay with the Bernard family for the
remaining months before Larry got orders back to the States.

Rachel Coe fared better than Caroline in the matter of accommodations
during the rough voyage home. Perhaps because she was a skipper's wife, she
was allotted a two-room suite for herself and the children. She had been warned
by the Navy doctor, though, to stop nursing her son before she left Manila.
Knowing what conditions would be like aboard the crowded, stripped-down
luxury liner, the physician had no illusions that mother's milk would continue to
flow in sufficient quantity for a baby the size of Henry. Rachel was glad she had
taken the doctor's advice. She found herself spending most of her time, with an
infant slung under her arm, chasing a four-year-old and washing out clothing for
all during naptime, if the children could be persuaded to sleep. After a day or
two, though, even the young were not moving around much. When the sea's
anger turned to fury, a grand piano broke loose, caromed across the salon,
knocked down a stewardess, and broke her leg. Mothers locked the doors to

their staterooms and holed up for the duration. Jean grew thinner during the course of the journey; she would eat nothing but lettuce, and that didn't stay with her long.

The pitching of the liner was so severe that carpenters, for safety's sake, went around ruthlessly nailing down the beautiful French furniture. Cribs and bassinets ran out, so an orange crate was nailed to the foot of Rachel's bed for the baby. Since each woman had been allowed so little baggage, Rachel had frequent ironing to do and found it a feat of engineering to bring the iron in contact with the cloth between rolls of the ship.

On this return journey, American women were still experiencing the contrast between the sublime and the ridiculous that had been such a large part of the China experience. Most of them had left multiservanted households in Manila. New mothers who had never done without an *amah* knew little of what it meant to care for a child 24 hours a day. They were forced to find out amid all the cramped discomforts of a troop transport.

In Malba, Long Island, Bobette Gugliotta tried to struggle out of the shock engendered by being a bride of six months who faced two long years ahead with no hope of catching sight of her husband, short of a miracle. A trip to the Far East on her own was out of the question for several reasons. First and foremost was money. When Guy had been ordered from Honolulu to sub school in New London, the course had just been cut from six to three months; that put it in the category of "temporary duty," for which travel funds were unavailable for dependents. For Bobette to join her young husband in Connecticut, the pair had had to scrounge. An ensign's meager pay did not cover a ten-day hospital bill, engendered by Bobette's strep throat, plus passage on the Lurline and train fare across country. Uncle Sam did not give many benefits to his armed forces, which was why so many of them were eager to take the "hazardous duty" risks for the few bucks more that went with being a flyer or submariner.

When Guy was sent to the Philippines, Bobette went to live with her mother, where food and shelter were free. She had worked briefly between semesters at college in Los Angeles before marriage. But she was loathe to tie herself to a job when there was even a remote possibility that the miracle might occur and Guy might come home soon. Common sense told her it was impossible, but a 21-year-old with her head in the clouds, whose interests were art and literature, did not want to listen to reason. Besides, Guy had written that the latest scuttlebutt said more fleet boats were scheduled to join the Asiatic Fleet, so it was only logical that the aging, underqualified, obsolescent little S-boats, designed for peacetime coastal patrol, would be sent home. The only trouble was that the same rumor had been circulating for at least five years.

After drooping through the winter months like the heroine of a Victorian novel, Bobette visited her husband's large family in New Jersey and found great compatibility with her librarian sister-in-law, Anne. Anne frequently spent weekends in New York with Bobette, where the two women shared some great moments at the theatre, seeing plays such as Lillian Hellman's *Watch on The Rhine*, starring Paul Muni. It was the era of pageboy hairdo's, cashmere sweaters with pearls, Robin Red nail polish, and inflexible fashion rules dictating that well-dressed women wore hats (except at dinner parties and dances), print dresses from Easter to Labor Day, and navy blue clothing only in springtime.

The young and not too affluent who lived in a cold climate often bought something called a skunk chubby for winter wear. This boxy jacket could hardly pass for mink, but when dyed brown, as it usually was, it was attractive enough. Bobette had one. Ankle-strap shoes had just come in for dress wear, and saddle shoes were still in favor with young males and females for everyday.

An inveterate reader, Bobette combed local bookstores in Flushing and College Point and sent Guy *Damon Runyon's Best, That Day Alone* by Pierre Van Paasen, Robert Benchley's *After 1903 What?* (which made a big hit with skipper Red Coe), and *Delilah* by Marcus Goodrich. This last, a sea story involving a destroyer in the Philippines, was popular with everybody. All books were passed around among officers and crew, since most submariners were avid readers.

The Navy women Bobette had known in Hawaii when she and Guy were married in 1940 were still there, or had moved on with their husbands to other duty. The women returning from the Philippines were strangers, and none that she knew of lived close by. Lacking fellow sufferers, the young bride was in the perfect situation for feeling sorry for herself. She did.

Roy Klinker had been fighting a short-timer's attitude. It happened to everybody in line for a change of duty, generally starting about six months before the event. Help in combatting the ailment came to Roy from an unexpected quarter. The *38* boat had a battery explosion, a serious affair involving a casualty, and Admiral Hart summoned all the submarine officers to the flagship *Augusta* following the incident. It was the first time Klinker had seen the sharp-featured officer since graduating from the Naval Academy when Hart had been superintendent there. It was only because of the seriousness of the situation that he was seeing him now. Known as a disciplinarian, Hart was also a realist.

When all the officers were assembled, he rose to his feet from behind his desk and without preamble plunged in. "Gentlemen, I want to say one thing about getting ahead in the Navy. There are two kinds of luck, good luck and bad luck. The officers involved in the explosion on the *S-38* had bad luck. We can't pin down any responsibility. But there is an air of irresponsibility about the fact that the accident happened at all, and we cannot tolerate that in submarines." Roy divested himself of his short-timer's attitude in a hurry. There was too much at stake for himself and others, and not much room for doping off unnoticed on a submarine.

The China Station was noted for eccentric characters, both civilian and military. The testy, uncompromising admiral qualified as one of them. So did equally testy and uncompromising Lieutenant Commander Hyman Rickover; as planning officer at the navy yard, he had told Chuck Triebel, the skipper of the *S-41*, that the $7,000 allotted for overhaul of the rickety vessel was far too much and that he was working hard to see where it could be cut down. Since Uncle Sam was not noted for lavish expenditures on bringing its old pigboats up to scratch, it was hard to figure how or why anybody would want to shorten the already short allowance. Klinker was happy to be going home to the relative peace and quiet of new construction at the Mare Island Navy Yard in California.

Roy received his orders to put the new submarine *Seadog* in commission. Ironically, he would continue to run into, and have run-ins with, the man with the face of a fox and the brain of a genius. Rickover would turn up at Mare Island in the propulsion business, come on board *Seadog* in workman's uniform as an inspector, and raise hell with everybody about waste, cost—you name it. Roy, in equally fighting trim, would chase him off and be rewarded with the grudging words, "Klinker, you haven't changed a bit." But that was future tense.

Suddenly it was June and time to leave the Philippines. Roy had a number of reasons for being eager to go, but one was supreme—he didn't share the frequently expressed opinion that the Japanese could be wiped out in a few weeks. In the spring, when the *39* was at sea, he had spotted a Japanese flotilla and exclaimed to himself, I've never seen that many ships together at one time. It was a chilling sight. After a *despedida* at the Army-Navy Club, Roy took off with the usual enormous hangover. It was the height of the typhoon season, but after two and a half years in Asia, Klinker knew what it was to ride out a killer wind, and was shoving off before the most vicious storm of all was unleashed, that man-made blast that would do far more damage than nature had ever done.

Shortly after Roy's departure, Dutch Mandekic left. Larry Bernard, engineering officer, moved up a slot and became exec. Gugliotta, in gunnery, ceased being George because a new George came on board: Ensign Charles (Monk) Hendrix, Naval Academy '39. With the advent of Hendrix, Coe now had a complete complement of officers who admired him wholeheartedly. With Monk it amounted to hero worship. Coe had been his navigation instructor at the Naval Academy and remembered the eager young student. Wanting to see if his teaching had made an impression, he gave Monk, in addition to his other chores, the navigator's job. Hendrix answered the description of the All-American boy in ways that most submariners did not. He neither smoked nor drank except for an occasional beer. He had been a fine athlete at the academy, excelling at lacrosse and baseball, and continued to maintain an exercise ritual. Traditionally, submariners on the China Station had taken the motto "No strain in Asia" to heart. Coe was a golfer, rode a bike, and after a few drinks at the Army-Navy Club had been known to play something called bicycle polo, which usually left him limping. Others rode horseback, bowled, played tennis and billiards, or swam—but casually, between typhoons. Although the relaxed atmosphere had changed by the time Hendrix arrived in June 1941, Keeping Fit, especially with open zest and enthusiasm, was not usual.

So when Ensign Hendrix, in his bright-eyed way, instituted early morning exercises on deck—pushups, kneebends, running in place, headstands—his not-so-eager converts took care to control their groans when they couldn't escape. The guys who had been ashore and were just returning with blurry eyes and limp appendages tried to sneak past the jolly group and scurry below to find aspirin for their aching heads.

But Jim Pennell was impressed with Hendrix's athletic skill because it took so many different forms. Along with his other accomplishments, Hendrix not only swam and dove like a champion, but rowed like one. When Pennell asked how he'd learned to use oars so well, Hendrix replied, "I'm the son of a doctor and grew up in Port Deposit, Maryland, on Chesapeake Bay. It was second nature to learn to do anything connected with water." Pennell, who'd settled down after his initial discontent, also admired the new officer because Hendrix always had a smile and an encouraging word, and was eager to learn every working part of the vessel. Their good relationship was quickly put to the test when Pennell caught sight of the agile ensign climbing into a ballast tank one day shortly after reporting on board.

"Sir, Mr. Hendrix," Pennell called out, sputtering a little as he tried to find a diplomatic way to say it, "I mean, sir, do you have permission from the captain to go into the tank like that, without a lifeline?"

Hendrix shook his head. Bolstering himself with the thought that he was several years senior in age and many years senior in Navy experience, Pennell said earnestly, "Well, sir, the general safety rule is that nobody ever goes into a ballast tank, or any other kind, without someone tending the lifeline at the manhole entry. A person could be knocked out by poison gases or a lack of oxygen, and nobody would know the difference."

Hendrix's smile was a little shamefaced. "Get a lifeline, Pennell. We'll do it right."

It was the first time Pennell had advised an officer, but he had heard Pop Bridges do it, even to the point of contradicting the captain—politely, of course, but firmly. Freedom of speech was a good part of submarines.

Another Hendrix crusade was to convince Allyn Christopher and his friend John Mattingly that they would benefit by regular workouts at the YMCA in Manila. Monk didn't realize that among crew members attendance at the Y was tantamount to an admission of faulty virility.

"We'd never live it down," Christopher whispered to Mattingly. "Let's get hold of Jack Neighbors and go drink a few beers. The whole thing is making me nervous. I'll tell Mr. Hendrix we're scheduled to go on a hike or something healthy he'd approve of."

The truth was that Christopher did sneak into the Y now and then, but not for exercise. Many of the crew were farm boys scarcely out of the growing stage, accustomed to fresh dairy products, as Allyn had been. At sea, the *39* didn't have room or refrigeration for frills but stocked up on basics such as boned meats, cereals, fresh fruits and vegetables. When the boat was in port and the opportunity arose, Allyn could easily tuck away three or four banana splits laced with chocolate and marshmallow sauce, and the Y had the best sundaes even though Christopher ate them with furtive glances at the door to be sure that nobody he knew saw him there.

The captain had another reason for welcoming Hendrix aboard. With Monk's athletic record, the *39* stood a much better chance of beating the *38* boat at softball. One of their periodic contests was coming up, a field meet complete with barbecue beer bust, special sporting events, and a poetry-reciting contest— a sort of Olympics in the spirit of the old Greek games, where an agile tongue won as many laurels as an agile body.

The *38-39* get-togethers were usually held at Mariveles. Some of the events were sugar-coated learning exercises for newcomers. In bilge diving, the contestant zipped down the torpedo room hatch of his own boat and recorded the reading on the forward trim tank gage, ran aft into the control room for a reading on the auxiliary tank in the waist of the ship, then raced back to the motor room to take a reading on the after trim tank. After each reading, he was also required to eat crackers and whistle a tune. That was the zany part. The educational part lay in learning how to read the tanks fast and accurately.

With the advent of Hendrix, the softball contests took on new life. He hit hard, ran fast, and caught well from start to finish because he never took advantage of the plentiful beer available. Chapple, skipper of the *38*, played outfield or first base, wherever he was needed most. Coe did the same, being of equal height though not of equal ability. But this day the *39* boat players, inspired by Hendrix, scampered around the bases like pros and ended up winners, which they had not done nearly so often in the past as they would have liked. Coe pounded congratulations on the backs of his players and was pounded in return. In the distance two Filipinos appeared carrying a 40-pound roast pig stuffed with rice for the feast that would follow shortly. The crisp brown skin glistened in the sunlight, and the tantalizing odor wafted clear across the field. Filipinos called it *lechón asado*.

"Drink lots of beer, boys," Coe sang out as he pulled his jersey over his head. "The *38* boat's paying for it at last, and they can afford it."

Across the way, Chapple retorted, "The rich get rich and the poor get scrozzled. But we'll show the skipper of the *39* who's boss in the field events."

Coe just smiled. He had a surprise for Moon Chapple. By accident, he had discovered that Radioman Rice could not merely walk on his hands, but walk and walk and walk—indefinitely. Coe was sure that the points made in a walking-on-the-hands contest would secure first place for Coe and company, and he planned to lay a bet on Rice that would make profits in Philippine gold stocks look like peanuts.

Rice had been in cold storage across the field during the softball game, sitting on a bench staying cool and relaxed under an awning so that he would be at his hand-walking best. Coe glanced at him, saw him leaning back with cap pulled down over his eyes against the glare of the sun, perfect. Maybe the best idea was to get the contest underway right now before tricky Chapple had a chance to beg, borrow, or steal somebody who was also good at the gymnastic feat.

"Hey, Moon," Coe called out, "are you really a sporting man or do you just pay lip service to it?"

Chapple's attention was caught by the note of elation in Coe's voice that didn't go with the deliberately casual expression on the redhead's sunburned face.

"Depends upon what you have in mind," Moon said tentatively.

"Weee'll, I reckon," Coe summoned up his Indiana drawl, "the whole idea's no good. The *38* couldn't possibly have a contestant who could beat ours in a Walking on the Hands contest."

"Hell's fire, is that all?" Chapple exploded. "What's so great about that? I can do it myself if nobody else'll volunteer." But several *38* boat people stepped forward from the slew of men milling around after the ball game.

"Hiland," Coe said to the man nearest him, "tell Rice we're about ready to start."

Betting began; the two skippers were head to head, and clusters of crew from both boats broke out money. Across the field, Bill Hiland could be seen talking earnestly to Radioman Rice, still at ease on the bench. After a few minutes Hiland cupped his hands around his mouth and shouted, "Mr. Bernard, will you come here a minute?"

Bernard detached himself from the group and walked over to the bench where Radioman Rice reposed. Two of Chapple's crew were practicing hand-walking now. Coe smiled silently; Rice could outdo them blindfolded and on broken glass besides.

Coe turned and looked across the field, beckoning to Bernard and Hiland. Suddenly Jim Pennell said self-righteously, "I knew somebody shoulda sat with Rice during the game. I offered to, remember?" Peterson, who didn't drink and couldn't understand why anybody did, glanced at the skipper. Coe's sunburned face was unreadable as he watched Bernard and Hiland putting Rice's limp arms around their shoulders, then letting go to see if he could stand alone. He couldn't. He looked as boneless as a straw scarecrow. Schab tried a feeble joke: "And I thought we were gonna win hands down."

There was silence. Then Coe's face cracked into a sheepish grin. Chapple grinned too but he didn't laugh, not just then. He could afford to be gracious.

The roast pig had been reduced to greasy bones, beer was low in the keg, and a theatrical Philippine sunset was staining the sky when the intellectual portion of the day's events was announced. First came a liar's contest. The 39 entry was new Chief of the Boat Earl Nave. As he jumped to his feet and began his fast-paced, loud-mouthed spiel of incredible achievements laced with profanity and scatalogical spew, Zeke Matthews said in his mild, noncritical way, "He's always himself. Nobody can beat our minister of propaganda." (This was Nave's latest nickname; he had a new one every week.) It was a no-contest contest; the 38 couldn't begin to match the honker. Sheer volume, if nothing else, won the day.

The poetry competition was another matter. The men wrote and recited their own creations, and several of them took it very seriously. Tom Parks numbered Robert Service, Rudyard Kipling, and Walt Whitman among his favorite poets, and had worked hard on his entry entitled, "The Pigboat Sailor's Lament." The first stanza kicked off, "The submarine is an infernal machine, conceived in a madman's brain to sail over or under the billows green and drive guys like me insane." Delivery had a lot to do with success, the more comic or dramatic, the better. Many chose to rhyme the tried and true, such as tropic breeze and bamboo knees. The last-mentioned affliction had been around for as long as Filipinas had reclined on grass mats, but the severity of the abrasions when a guy returned from liberty ashore had been visible only in the last year, since enlisted men had been issued tropical working shorts.

Finally, the meet ground to a halt. Mike Kutscherowski, the 39's middleweight champ, was called on to settle a fight in which several teeth had been lost and blood flowed copiously from smashed noses; the Philippine sun went down in a blaze of crimson that rivaled the gore spilling on the grass. Tayco and Fabricante, after packing up the picnic gear, neatly divided the hog's head between them to take home. It was the most succulent part of the roast pig, but Americans didn't have the sense to know it.

Coe and Chapple drove off together to take the day's celebration a bit further. So did others. It was the last field meet they would have, although they didn't know that yet. Crew members lucky enough to have liberty, but not lucky enough to have a regular full-time girlfriend, took off for what was considered a typical, good to excellent Manila weekend. With a fifth of 20-year-old "King's Ransom" from the Washington grocery store (costing $3.12) tucked under an arm, they'd head for a nipa shack in Mapahan known as Mopy's and Joe's and spend a couple of days in the company of two or three different hostesses. It was a well-run place, clean, safe, and quiet, although sometimes enlivened by the fisticuffs of hard-drinking types like Danny Tella, who was hard to handle even when his light-drinking friend Jim Pennell tried to calm him down. Pennell and Tella, both *Canopus* graduates who had stood boiler-room auxiliary watches together on the tender, had gone on board *39* the same day. Pennell felt a sense of responsibility for the free-swinging, happy-go-lucky Tella, a contrast to his own personality in every way.

There was some contact among Army and Navy officers, but by and large it was perfunctory and mostly at social events at the club or at athletic contests. Gugliotta's oldest sister Anne had written him to look up her college friend Thelma and husband Steve Mellnik. The Mellniks and daughters were living on Corregidor and invited Guy to spend a weekend. Steve, a West Point graduate, was an Army captain who had command of a coastal defense unit. After a two-and-a-half-hour trip by ferry from Manila, Guy arrived at the fabled rock considered the bastion of Philippine defense. Densely forested by army engineers for camouflage purposes, it looked like an innocent tropical island inhabited only by wildlife. Actually, there was a population of 8,000, making it larger than many U.S. cities of the era. At night huge searchlights might suddenly flood down upon vessels passing below in the water—nipping many a flowering passenger-line romance.

Enjoying a weekend of family life with the Mellniks, Guy was happy to hear of the imminent return of Thelma and daughters to the States along with other Army wives. Misery loves company, and people without partners can't help resenting people who have them. Saturday passed pleasantly with reminiscences of home, drinks, dinner, and the diversion of small children. On Sunday, Steve took Guy for a tour of the island, showing him its defenses with great pride. Gugliotta was surprised to see that the fire control equipment was antiquated compared to what he had been accustomed to when attached to the relatively new destroyer *Bagley* before attending sub school. But he didn't comment. Mellnik also expressed the current Army opinion that "the big guns will blast the bastards out of existence." Guy noticed that the six-inch guns, instead of having stereoscopic range finders, were still using a triangulation method old as the Egyptians. The Army seemed to be anticipating a Japanese surface attack rather than the air attack from high-level bombers that would render the defense on Corregidor, and elsewhere, impotent.

The basic simplicity of an S-boat did not extend to its head. The tricky toilet required 13 steps for proper flushing or it would backfire. Air pressure was used to empty the bowl, so no flight of fancy could picture anything worse than the actuality of turning the wrong valve. Since there was only one head on the old pig for its forty crew members, men peed over the side when that was possible, in the bilges when it wasn't, or held it as long as they could. Bouts of dysentery, common in the tropics, sometimes ran through the crew and were dreaded by the non-rated firemen or seamen usually assigned the job called captain of the head. But to distribute the nasty chore as fairly as possible, the title changed hands weekly. On the bright side, S-boat temperatures of 115 degrees dried urine to a minimum and kept most people in a state of constipation. Everybody's nightmare was the possibility of leaving out, or mixing up, any of the steps necessary to successfully flush the cantankerous can. The unthinkable was to have the ancient mechanism break down completely.

Nobody was too exalted to catch hell from a captain of the head. One day when Gugliotta had the duty, he was amused to see that week's "captain" come huffing and puffing topside complete with bucket, brush, rubber gloves, and a face red with rage. This captain of the head was only a seaman, but he shouted out the order: "Everybody line up and go through the motions of using the head. Some goddamn fool turned the wrong valve and then beat it, and left me to clean up the whole shitty mess." The seaman checked them off one by one, chiefs and all, scrutinizing each pantomime performance. Nobody laughed. He didn't pinpoint the culprit, but he had the satisfaction of seeing ratings far above him obeying his orders, for a change.

And then the unthinkable happened. With the perversity of things mechanical when operated by people under tension, the flapper valve in the crew's head collapsed completely shortly after operations were stepped up because of the war threat. It was Jim Pennell's job to repair it. The toilets at that time were an unsuitable porcelain, subject to infinite cracks and leaks (as the war progressed, these would be replaced by metal ones). Pennell immediately broke out blueprints and traced the broken part of the boat's anatomy to the A.B. Sands Company in Brooklyn, New York. After more sleuthing he found that the firm had been out of business for 20 years.

Given both the demands of nature and her demanding schedule, the *39* boat couldn't take the time to find another source as far away as Brooklyn. But this was exactly the kind of mechanical challenge that Pennell loved. Hotfooting it over to the Cavite Navy Yard, he told them the sad tale and they poured him a valve. It turned out way oversize and rougher than a grater, and Pennell bitched like hell about it, but he didn't really mind the job of making it workable. He took it on board and machined it, filing and scraping and honing until it fit just right.

5. First Blood

Several attempts to better living conditions in port had been made by August of 1941, although there would not be much time left to enjoy the changes. At long last, enlisted men were given a club of their own, where they could have a drink without paying more than it was worth and without having a hostess sent over to double the costs. The club was in a new building on the Manila waterfront, constructed by the Philippine Commonwealth and rented by the U.S. If a man took on a load, or grew belligerent, he was less likely to end up in hot water than if he'd thrown a punch in a bar in town. No officer could use the facility unless invited by an enlisted man.

Submarine officers were allotted quarters in Manila free of charge. Each large, three-man room at the University Apartments came equipped with a bath, refrigerator, writing desk, couch, and Chinese maintenance help. The officers couldn't believe their luck—which lasted for a couple of months. Then, while the submarines were out to sea, the rooms were taken over by newly arrived reserve officers, and the disgruntled submariners traipsed back to the *Canopus*. Their quarters ashore were restored just in time for them to deposit their civilian clothes, golf clubs, and other gear and leave it all for the enemy.

Endless practice for warfare without actuality kept nerves on edge. The dives were long and tiring, watch-standing and workload had reached the reversed proportion of 16 hours on and 8 off. The submarines were now going to sea with torpedoes prepared as war shots, making realistic practice patrols with a full load in the torpedo tubes. There had been a few lemons in the crew, but Red Coe got rid of them; he might have far from perfect equipment, but knew he had excellent men. The captain was expecting orders in December but was aware that war might arrive before his orders did.

Larry Bernard, also counting the days, prayed that the conflagration would hold off until after January, which was his time to leave. His ulcers began acting up again. The skipper came down with a case of intestinal flu right after he wrote Rachel not to count on his being home for Christmas, and everybody noticed that his guts improved before his disposition did. Gugliotta had no hope at all of getting out before the explosion. He alternated between the comforting knowledge on the one hand that *39* was the best boat around and that his fitness report stated, "would particularly desire to have him on board under wartime conditions," and the dreary realization on the other that his bride could be an old lady before he saw her again. To kick the blues, he went to a Chinese restaurant for fried *lapu lapu,* which he liked; saw the movie *Kitty Foyle* with Ginger Rogers, which he didn't like; then pigged it on candy bars, which he had never liked. Monk Hendrix, as a bachelor recently arrived, was less impatient, although his fitness routine accelerated.

Even the weather, seldom good, was extra capricious. Typhoons rolled in one after another with such fury that *S-39* was often forced to stand regular sea watches when in port. At times they had to leave *Canopus* and anchor separately because the boats banged against each other so hard in the wind that they couldn't stay moored. But the most obvious display of tension lay in the increase of nitpicking arguments. No statement, no matter how unimportant, went unchallenged. One afternoon in the crew's mess Bixler was describing the route from Olongapo to Manila. He declared, "the bus turns right as soon as you leave the gate and heads past the rifle range. Then in the valley you go straight until—"

"Oh no you don't," Nave, who had just come in, interrupted. "You forget that the goddamn bus makes a complete circle before reaching Subic and—"

"Fujigit, that's the Manila bus when it's going to Olongapo. What the hell do you know?" Bixler and Nave were now nose to nose, spit-spray from shouting mouths fogging the atmosphere. Half a dozen other guys joined in until the din reached epic proportions, and Schoenrock, very testy lately, pounded the counter with a soup ladle, yelling, "Shut up, you bastards. I don't need that flack in the galley." It worked, they all calmed down.

The cook had been sour on the whole bunch for some time. First, there was the monkey somebody picked up in Tawitawi and brought on board for a pet. His antics amused everybody except Schoenrock. With the seventh sense an animal has when somebody dislikes him, the monkey loved to wrap his tail around the overhead pipes in the galley and dip his bony fingers into Rocky's most beautiful creations, or carefully put a tooth through each cigarette in a pack the cook left on the counter before pushing them neatly back into the package. Then, when the cook wanted to enjoy a smoke, he couldn't get one lit no matter how many he tried. When Rocky discovered what was causing it, he went right to Coe with an ultimatum: "Either the monkey goes or I go." The capain responded by handing the monkey over to the Filipino crew of the laundry *banca,* but a few hours later the critter returned to his home away from home. He had leaped over the side of the *banca* and swum back to the *39.* It took some doing to remove him permanently.

The antics of the little beast hadn't helped Schoenrock's sense of humor. One morning Allyn Christopher noticed Schab tucking one of the cook's huge, melt-in-your-mouth pancakes inside the front of his shirt. Christopher nudged his friend. "What goes, you saving pancakes for the long cold winter ahead?"

Schab chuckled. "When Rocky's napping after lunch, come to the galley."

Christopher wouldn't have missed it for the world. When Schab sneaked back to the cook's sacrosanct territory, along with Pennell, Matthews, and electrician's mate C.I. Peterson, Allyn followed them in.

"Hurry up," Schab whispered, "we gotta work fast. Sometimes he's only gone for ten minutes or so." Pennell hoisted a bucket full of lead weights onto the counter while Peterson climbed up on a chair and secured a strong wire to the overhead. Then Schab held up the stolen pancake, and Peterson carefully ran the wire through it, fastening the bucket of weights to the end. Everybody snickered. It looked as though a heavy-as-lead pancake were supporting the heavy-with-lead bucket.

Matthews, who wasn't big but had the appetite of a lion, thought of the future: "Rocky's not gonna like this." Zeke's motto was don't bite the hand that feeds you. The other clowns paid no attention. Tayco, bringing back a tray of dishes from the officer's mess, took one astounded look at the suspended flapjack and backed out of the galley, muttering, "I no want to be here when he see this."

Allyn went through the boat rousing up an audience; even the officers got wind of it, so that when Schoenrock walked into the silent galley, rubbing sleep out of his eyes and smoothing his tousled hair, there were many witnesses to his shame. Hs eyes circled the crowd, then caught the abomination hanging in his galley. Everybody guffawed. Rocky's mouth trembled, then spewed, "You're a bunch of goddamn ungrateful bastards. After all I've done for you." People would swear later that he had tears in his eyes as big as crabapples.

And, as if that wasn't enough, there was the boxing match. Mike Kutscherowski, the *39*'s peace-loving pugilist who became a killer only in the ring, had made it all the way to the finals for the middleweight championship, the culmination of the Army-Navy, all-Asiatic boxing meets. It was to be refereed by the former Naval Academy heavyweight champ, Moon Chapple. Betting was heavy, and the excitement had a tonic effect on tempers badly needing diversion. In the crew's mess, many men were promising Kutscherowski all kinds of treats if he won the title, to all of whom the good-natured fisticuffs expert made the same reply, "I'll do the best I can."

Schoenrock, a long-time devotee of the manly art, came up with what he considered the ultimate inducement. "Ski," he proclaimed, "I promise to cook you a deluxe dinner of your own selection if you win. You—can—have—any—thing—you—want." He paused between words to hammer into the boxer's scarred head the full implications of his offer. "Filet mignon, chicken poached in wine, salmon with hollandaise." Kutscherowski's eyes bulged with the strain of trying to figure out what the fancy names meant. "I'll do my best," he said again earnestly.

The match took place on *Canopus* at an affair called a smoker. It lived up to its name because everybody smoked like crazy: cigars, cigarettes, pipes, most of which had been handed out free for advertising purposes. A blue pall hung over the ring accentuating the heat and humidity. Kutscherowski won. The *39* people went mad, shouting and screaming, pounding each other on the back, collecting money, and making plans to come through on all promises made to their champion. Schoenrock waited for the tumult to subside; then, with his customary dignity, told the sweating boxer, "Ski, when you're ready for that victory dinner, let me know what you want and when you want it."

The champ's voice was still hoarse from his efforts. "Gee whiz, Rocky, you know what I like best in the world?"

"No matter, I'll make it for you," Rocky assured him.

"I dunno why I like 'em. It just makes me feel good. I never ate nothing like it back in the States. I think it builds up my muscles." Ski's handler was untying the gloves now. "I'd really appreciate a whole box fulla papayas all to myself, but cold, see. I like 'em chilled."

The cook blanched. It was the final insult. How could anyone prefer a plain product of Mother Nature to a consummately contrived dish conceived by a master chef? Pennell tried to soften the blow. Knowing how much Rocky hated defrosting the ship's refrigerator, a job that came around all too often because of the rapid build-up of ice from tropic heat and humidity, Pennell volunteered to do it for him. (The machinist's mate had devised a quick method; pumping hot gas through the evaporator coils caused the big accumulations of ice to fall off in minutes. It may have been the forerunner of automatic defrost.) But even Pennell's offer couldn't get a smile out of the disconsolate cook.

Rocky and Stowaway Johnson decided to go out anyways, and hang one on in celebration of the victory. During the course of the raucous evening, the cook offered to pay for any tattoo that Johnson wanted to add to his already pictur-esque collection—that is, if he could find space somewhere on his hide. Johnson located an empty upper arm and promptly had it embellished with three horse's heads whose nostrils flared realistically when he flexed his biceps. Not to be outdone and drunk enough not to care, the usually more conservative Rocky had a coolie and ricksha tattooed on his thigh. Both men ordered tricolored jobs. Tops in flashy flesh.

A bright spot in the marking-time period was Fabricante's good luck. One morning he came aboard and said to Gugliotta, the duty officer, "Sair, I need to leave early. If you will say so today."

Gugliotta looked down at the tiny mess steward who seemed as pleasant, neatly dressed, and unruffled as usual. "I think that can be arranged. Any particular problem?"

"No, sair, no problem. I need only to put 5,000 peso check in bank."

The ensign's mouth fell open. "Good grief, Fabricante, did you discover a gold mine?"

"No, sair," the little man was smiling now, "I won fourth place lottery."

Gugliotta did some rapid calculation. Five thousand pesos translated into $2,500 American, a sum worth having in anybody's language. "Congratulations, Fabricante, what are you going to do with all that money?"

"Well, sair, first I like for you to have this," Fabricante held out a 20-peso note, "half for you, other half for Mr. Hendrix."

Gugliotta stalled as he sought a way to refuse without hurting the generous mess steward's feelings. "Tell you what, Fabricante, you hang on to that money for now, and sometime soon Mr. Hendrix and I would be real glad to have you buy us a drink."

Fabricante agreed. When he deposited his check, the Philippine government only took 90 pesos in taxes. Presumably the Japanese government got the rest.

As tension mounted during the month of November 1941, the men of the *39* boat listened constantly to Manila radio station KZRF, which broadcast news in many languages. It did not have much to report that was encouraging, especially with the sinking by U-boat, in October, of the U.S. destroyer *Reuben James,* further straining relations with Germany. They also read the Manila *Daily Bulletin* with great care. One of the columnists got a lot of horse laughs when he said it would be ridiculous to expect a German invasion of Russia. But what really pissed them off was such statements from U.S. Congressmen as, "Our navy will clean out the Japanese fleet in two weeks and burn up the island of Japan in one night," when they knew how their engineers sometimes had to work round the clock because the *39*'s engines had not been overhauled for a year and a half. There were leaks in the main ballast tanks and she often limped back to port on one engine. Her deepest dive, about 160 feet, always provoked leaks at various hull fittings. To keep everybody on his toes and the boat in readiness, Coe had called weekly inspections since the month of July. But if you can't make a silk purse out of a sow's ear, he certainly couldn't make a mechanically reliable vessel out of the patchwork pigboat.

At times the skipper became personally involved in the dirty work necessary to keep the prima donna functioning. One day during a torpedo firing run off Corregidor, Pennell, checking the motor room bilge, saw water coming in fast between the main motors, and *39* surfaced immediately for safety's sake. Before a hull inspection could be made to locate and assess the extent of the leak, equipment removal was necessary to dry out the narrow space. When everything was ready, Coe waved away other candidates and took on the job himself.

The captain kicked off his moulting straw sandals, hitched up his shorts, and motioned to Pennell to remove the metal floor plates. The welded grillwork beneath scarcely allowed a body the size of Coe's to insert itself into the motor-room bilge. In addition, the area was scummy-crummy with ancient grease and stagnant water that smelled like a dismal swamp. Down on hands and knees now, he asked Pennell to hang onto his ankles. The low pressure pump was at work cleaning the bilges, but noses wrinkled in sympathy as the redhead disappeared through the grillwork to probe for the leak below. Nobody could claim they had a skipper who balked at a dirty job.

On the brighter side, Pennell, who generally got along with machinery better than with people, had so far been successfully nursing the important compressors. There were two in the motor room to jam air into the bank of flasks. This air was used to start the main engines and to blow out the main ballast tanks when surfacing. It was also necessary as a general source of power to operate certain equipment and to move water between the auxiliary ballast tanks. And in an emergency requiring prolonged submergence, such as wartime conditions or mechanical difficulties, it would be needed to replenish air for breathing.

The main engines were used to charge the batteries. During this operation the air compressors were run by clutching them onto the propellor shafts. When Pennell first arrived, he noticed that the process dragged on much too long; common sense and basic arithmetic told him the compressors were running at about 30 percent efficiency. He decided to do some overhauling on his own and found the Corliss intake valves way out of tune. His work brought the air compressors up to approximately 75 percent, a most important improvement considering the essential services performed by them. Blessings like these were carefully counted because the possibility of a complete overhaul for *39* matched the prognosis for peace in the Far East.

For many months Admiral Thomas Hart had been viewing with alarm the tendency of certain important. U.S. politicians to make well-publicized, threatening speeches against the Japanese. He is on record as having written, "Nothing is ever gained by threatening the Japanese, their psychology being such that threats are likely to wholly prevent their exercise of correct judgment. Furthermore, such threats . . . tended to put the Japanese too much on guard against the preparations for war which were then being made in the Far East."

Hart did as much as possible with the limited material at hand to anticipate surprise attack. Foreseeing the probable loss of Manila Bay, the Admiral ordered the tenders to load all the spare ammunition, torpedoes, parts, and provisions they could carry. More torpedoes were stored in the tunnel allotted to the navy on Corregidor. Subic Bay and Manila Bay were mined, and by the end of November the tenders *Otus* and *Holland* had arrived, as well as a number of large fleet-type submarines from Pearl Harbor, bringing the total to 29 in the Asiatic Fleet; only the original six S-boats were vintage variety.

By 26 November the Admiral had received a Navy Department dispatch indicating very serious developments in American-Japanese relationships. On the 27th an all-night practice blackout was ordered in the city of Manila. On the 29th there was a definite war warning from the Navy Department. This was the day of the Army-Navy game, traditionally a slack-off period for the services both at home and in far-flung places like the China Station. Celebrations had been known to go on and on, and there were some who thought the Japanese might choose this time to launch their offensive. They didn't.

By Monday, 1 December, *S-39* was underway for operations off the southern tip of Luzon near Masbate Island. Three or four men were arguing the merits of various night spots in Manila, Nave's foghorn voice claiming to have eaten frog legs bigger than chicken legs at the Arcade Cafe. In the officer's wardroom, Gugliotta and Bernard were involved in a hot game of cribbage. Between rounds, Gugliotta was describing a Saturday night dance in one of the more remote towns on Luzon. When he and some others got back to Aparri from a hike, they were lured by the squeaky sounds of a four-piece band coming out of a shed. Peering in, they were immediately welcomed and led onto the dance floor by local Filipinas.

"The band never stopped playing," Guy explained, "but the end of a dance was signaled by an old gent ringing a bell. He also chalked up the number of dances each of us had, then charged us ten centavos a dance. But the big event of the evening was eating *baluts,* unborn chicks in the shell. A soft boiled egg was cracked so that part of the shell could be removed, exposing the ugly and smelly chick. The woman I watched very delicately bit off a black glob, which turned out to be the head, then pulled off a tiny wing covered with feathers and ate it bones and all. She disposed of the remainder in one bite. Meanwhile, naked kids were standing around with big, hopeful eyes, and the woman finally gave one of them the empty half-shell. The kid slurped down the juice, then dug a gob of yellowy green stuff out of the bottom . . ."

"That's enough," Larry Bernard yelled. "You'll make my ulcers act up again."

Coe who had come into the wardroom at the finale, said with a straight face, "Next time we go to Aparri, I'll challenge all of you to a *balut*-eating context."

When the *39* anchored in Masbate Harbor, the quixotic Philippine weather had decided to be kind in the midst of the rainy season, but a shimmer of stars flung across the sky blinked and often went out as rain clouds scudded by. The topside of the old submarine was covered with canvas cots on which reclining bodies were flaked out. Most were clad only in skivvies to take advantage of cooling breezes on the prickly heat that never cleared completely.

In the wardroom, duty officer Hendrix dreamed of the day he would find the report of his selection for lieutenant junior grade in the official mail or maybe by dispatch. Gugliotta had received his commission just before leaving Manila, so Monk was now the only ensign. Drawing a pad of paper toward him, he decided to write a long overdue letter to his father. "I'm learning a lot of good submarine and am used to it now when the boat flops" (Monk's term for a dive). He had just finished explaining that the mail clippers had to navigate a latitude right through the center of the typhoon area, and wouldn't run unless sure of clear weather all the way, when he dozed off. He was awakened by a loud, "Sir, sir, Mr. Hendrix, sir."

It was 0330, 8 December. Pennell's urgent tone of voice snapped Monk's head up. As he read the words of the message, he jumped to his feet, as wide awake as though he were about to hit a home run. "Take this to the captain immediately," he said.

Pennell had been on watch in the machinery spaces and had just made one tour through the boat when Radioman Bill Harris handed him the message that now sent him scrambling up the hatch with all speed, Hendrix at his heels. Picking his way among the bodies on deck, he spied the red hair of his skipper as the clouds parted; it was the last time for a long time that any man on *39* would welcome a bright night. As soon as Coe read the historic words, "Japan has started hostilities, govern yourselves accordingly," he told Hendrix, "Make all preparations to get underway." Pennell was ordered to rouse the sleepers at once and to strip the lifelines, benches, stanchions—items that fell into the unnecessary or personal-convenience class. Their elimination would reduce noise while the boat was submerged, increase speed, and dispose of white elephants that could be blasted loose by depth-charging, float to the surface, and disclose the boat's position.

By the time the second message came from CINCAF (Commander-in-Chief Asiatic Fleet), about 15 minutes later, "Submarines and aircraft will wage unrestricted warfare," all personnel and cots were stowed away below. In 11 minutes more, *39* was underway for her patrol area; by 0445 they had rigged ship for dive, which took place at 0700 much to everybody's relief. Although nobody spelled it out, a submerged submarine in broad daylight was much more reassuring than one on the surface, especially when you were new at the war game and didn't know when the enemy might pop up. Larry Bernard kept telling himself, it can't be true, it can't be true, even though he and all the others had been expecting it for over a year. A feeling of unreality was strong among officers and men.

Their designated patrol area was San Bernardino Strait, about 40 miles from Masbate Harbor. As soon as the ship submerged, the radioman became the sound man. The equipment used was near-obsolete hydrophone (underwater sound) listening equipment. Harris was listening hard as they made their way when he caught the su-woosh, su-woosh of propellers and reported, "Ship noises, possible screws on the port quarter."

Gugliotta, OOW (officer of the watch), ordered "Up periscope" and soon sighted the masts of a small ship about three miles away. He called the captain, and Coe, after taking a look, ordered, "40 feet"; at shallower depth he hoped to make out her type and size.

"It's a small cargo ship," he said, "but she's flying no flag. Take stations for Battle Surface but don't fire the deck gun right away. I want the signalman to bring up the searchlight and ask the vessel's identity."

Battle Surface was made, and as the dripping wet participants catapulted out, it was easy to see by their eager-cautious-fearful expressions that *39* did not have a blasé, hardened crew. The captain gave nothing away except by frequent tugs at his cap, even though the sun was not in his eyes. The signalman blinked "Who are you?" at the merchantman in international code but received no answer. The little vessel went right on going.

Coe ordered, "Fire a shot across her bow."

This brought the desired result. The ship stopped immediately, hoisted her flag, and identified herself by searchlight as the SS *Montanez* of Philippine registry. Gun and gun crew were secured, and *39* submerged. Were they disappointed? Yes and no. At 1740 they surfaced and started battery charge. That was the first day.

The Japanese saw to it that the *39* quickly got used to being at war. On 11 December the boat picked up enemy masts 12 miles to eastward just prior to darkness. They had been hearing the distant boom of depth charges all day, but now an advance screen of enemy destroyers began heavy, random depth-charging while Japanese cargo and troop ships made their way westward toward Albay Gulf. The explosions came closer and closer, and though *39* was pretty sure she was not being specifically tracked, she knew that a depth charge that found its target accidentally was just as lethal as one that found it on purpose. Pennell, whose Battle Station was in the motor room by himself, had noticed on the chart that the water depth in the area was 666 feet. Not given to flights of fancy, he had a sudden vision of one of the shattering crashes finding its mark and could feel the pigboat dropping, dropping, dropping to the depths, crushed like an eggshell with all hands aboard. When the session ended, those men who

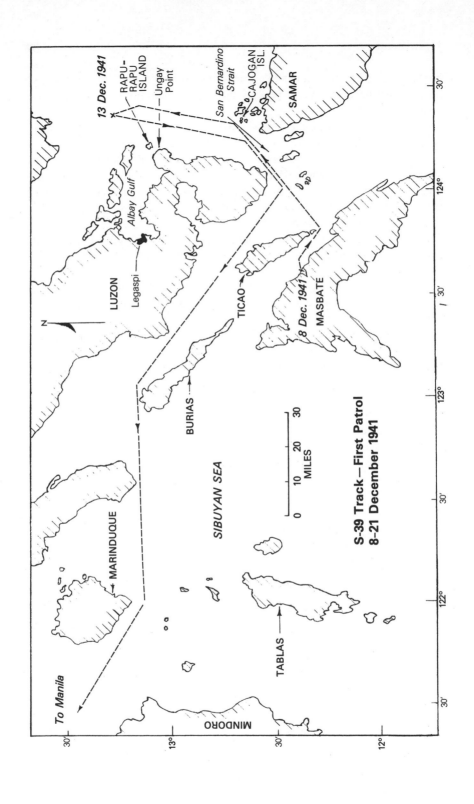

13 Dec. 1941

RAPU- RAPU ISLAND

Ungay Point

San Bernardino Strait

CAJOGAN ISL.

SAMAR

LUZON

Albay Gulf

Legaspi

N

124°

TICAO

8 Dec. 1941

MASBATE

BURIAS

30'

123°

SIBUYAN SEA

30

20

10

MILES

0

S-39 Track—First Patrol
8-21 December 1941

30'

122°

TABLAS

MARINDUQUE

To Manila

MINDORO

30'

13°

30'

12°

had been having trouble believing that a real war was in progress had become convinced.

With no fix since noon, meaning no chance to locate position by taking sights of celestial bodies or bearings of land or other charted objects, they did not know within a few miles where they were when they surfaced that night. The weather didn't help. Hendrix, OOD, was looking through his binoculars when he said to Quartermaster Rollins, "Take a look over there to the east."

"I see what you mean, sir, it looks like a submarine," the quartermaster said tersely, then turning to the lookouts asked, "what do you guys think?"

The two lookouts, training their binoculars on the same spot, said simultaneously, "I agree with that," becoming twins in the stress of the moment.

"Okay," Hendrix said, "call the captain."

Coe was topside lickety-split, binoculars focused on the same location while rain beat down heavily. He didn't hesitate long. "Make ready number one and two torpedo tubes," he said.

The two fish were fired, and everybody waited for the detonation. There was none. In the dark, and without navigational aids, they might have fired upon an object far beyond the limited range of the torpedoes, or a much larger mass whose distant outlines made it resemble a submarine close by. Charging batteries and running on the surface, Coe went close enough to discover, with the help of charts, that he had wasted two torpedoes by firing at Cajogan Island off the north coast of Samar. The novitiate had not yet ended.

By this time Japanese merchantmen as well as a considerable naval force were coming into Albay Gulf. Enemy transports and cargo vessels had no naval escorts until they were some ten miles northeast of Ungay Point, where destroyers out of Albay rendezvoused with them at dawn. The war was only five days old, but the men of the *39* felt as though they'd been seeing enemy masts for months without being able to do anything about them. At 0413, 13 December, *S-39* was surfaced when she sighted an enemy submarine close aboard. This time it was real. The *39* dove immediately, but dark and rain resulted in zero visibility; she was unable to attack. Frustration was still the order of the day. And then came a little game of hide-and-seek as the Japanese sub began tracking by active sonar, which S-boats did not have. Sound waves sent by oscillator pinged against the old pigboat and echoed back; by calculating the amount of time it took to send and receive the signal, the enemy sonar could ascertain the range.

Then suddenly, at 0550, Hendrix, on the periscope in the control room, said excitedly to the messenger, "Call the captain. I've got a target out here on the port bow," and to Quartermaster Rollins, "Mark the bearing, range about 12,000 yards; down periscope."

Rollins responded, "Bearing 345 relative. I'm starting a plot."

Hendrix said, "Left full rudder, steady on course 005." At this point Coe walked in wearing only skivvy pants and the disintegrating sandals. He had been trying to grab a few minutes rest. His blue eyes blinked away sleep rapidly as he said, "what's up?" Hendrix briefed him fast and told him he was heading for the target. Coe's face, bristling with blond stubble, lost its tired look. Larry Bernard had come in to take control of the dive.

"Pass the word Battle Stations Submerged," Coe said, then to Larry, "Come up a little bit more."

Quartermaster Rollins, scratching hard at the prickly heat on his rump that always flared up in moments of tension, passed the word on the public address system, while the telephone talker, Yeoman Smith, relayed orders to those concerned. Chief of the Boat Nave reported to the skipper, "All stations report manned at Battle Stations."

Coe, thoroughly awake now, asked Larry, "How's your trim?"

"Good, but I'd like to pump a couple of minutes." Coe nodded, and Larry said to Pennell on the trim manifold, "Pump 600 pounds from auxiliary to forward trim."

Pennell repeated the order, and when the action was complete Larry reported to the captain, "I have a good trim." Coe replied, "Stand by for a setup."

This would be Coe's first look at the ship he hoped to hit. As the only one seeing the target, he had to give as much information as he could to the approach party in the control room so they could determine the range, course, and speed. Accuracy was necessary to put the submarine in the best position for firing. The scene was reminiscent of the craze for seeing how many people could fit into a phone booth. The control room, 16½ feet fore and aft and 20 feet port to starboard, bristled with machinery, and a good chunk of it was taken up by the radio room. Battle Stations Submerged required that the approach officer, diving officer, assistant approach officer, plotting officer, chief of the boat, bow planesman, stern planesman, helmsman, quartermaster, trim manifold man, blow manifold man, telephone talker, messenger, and controllerman be present—14 in all, one-third of those aboard. Any quick movement dug elbows into nearby flesh. The claustrophobic could not survive long.

The skipper said, "Mark; angle on the bow 50 port; range three-quarter division high power; use 100-foot masthead height.

Rollins said, "Bearing 000 relative."

Assistant Approach Officer Gugliotta said, "Range 12,000. Can you make him out at all?"

Coe said, "Looks like a small freighter, 100 feet, and speed up, Larry. Give me the normal approach course."

During this period, until actual firing of torpedoes, observations were taken every few minutes with the speed kept as slow as possible to prevent a feather. This was the result of water running up the periscope, then down. Slow speed caused a dribble, fast speed caused a noticeable feather in the water, detectible by the enemy. But between looks, it was necessary to go fast to get close enough to fire. Less and less periscope was exposed above the surface as the range to the target decreased, and each observation was shorter, by now no more than five or six seconds. The mark 10 torpedoes used by S-boats had a maximum range of about 3,600 yards, but the ideal range for greatest accuracy was 1,000 yards. This was what Coe was hoping to achieve.

As Larry Bernard said to electrician Hiland, "Shift to series, 1,000 aside," and Gugliotta said to helmsman Norton, "Left full rudder, steady on course 275", both officers tied skivvy shirts around their necks to conserve their own sweat for cooling purposes, as well as to keep it from dripping onto the deck, where it turned slippery underfoot.

Hendrix, plotting officer, said, "I get him on course 240, we're about 8,500 yards off the track."

"Stand by for a look, 40 feet," Coe said.

Nave, for once as quiet as everyone else, started the scope moving upwards by means of a hand-held switch, stopping now and then at Coe's signal. As the scope rose, the skipper rose, coming off the deck until he reached standing position. The telephone talker, with his trailing wires, kept them out of the way with the skill of royalty manipulating a train.

Bernard said to controller Hiland, "Shift to parallel, half-switch," and a minute later, "Forty feet."

"Stand by, mark, angle on the bow 55 port; down periscope, speed up, Larry," Coe said. "Range, a bit more than three-quarter division high power." Gugliotta put the information on the Iswas, a circular slide rule used to set the submarine course and also to set relative bearing and angle on the bow which gave target course. He converted the periscope range scale to yards with a slide calculator.

The quartermaster said, "Bearing 074 relative," and Gugliotta came back with, "Range 11,000." Bernard added, "Shift to series, 1,000 aside," while preparations began for another observation.

Coe, eye glued to the rubber eyepiece again, his usually rosy complexion fiery from rising temperatures and anticipation, said, "Mark, he zigged towards; angle on the bow 30 port; down periscope, 100 feet and speed up again, Larry. Range just short of one division high power."

"Bearing 093 relative," Rollins said. Gugliotta contributed, "Range 9,000," followed by Hendrix, "I get him on course 210 degrees (T) making eleven knots."

After consulting his Iswas, Gugliotta said, "Recommend course about 20 degrees to the right," to which Coe murmured, "Okay," and Gugliotta told the helmsman, "Right full rudder, steady on course 295 degrees."

The skipper asked, "Sound, do you hear anything? Target is near the starboard beam." But sound operator Schab, in the torpedo room, replied, "Nothing yet, Captain."

The approach party began discussing the probability that the target was heading for the entrance to Albay Gulf, which would put him on a base course of approximately 230 degrees (T) (true course by compass) to pass just north of Rapu-Rapu Island. The captain asked the quartermaster to break out the U.S. Navy publication on Japanese Merchant Silhouettes and, thumbing through, decided that #61, a cargo ship, most closely resembled the target. While this was going on, the tight-packed group took the opportunity to shift restlessly, dig a finger in an ear or up a nostril, pop a fresh stick of gum into a nervously working mouth, or hitch up the blue dungaree shorts that no matter how faded always looked black from grime. But they all settled down quickly when the old man called for another observation and reported,"Mark, angle on the bow 30 port, range one."

Quartermaster Rollins said, "Bearing 092 relative," and Gugliotta, "Range 8,000." Hendrix reported, "No change, I get him on course 210 degrees speed 12, looking pretty good."

Larry Bernard knew what to expect, and he got it from Coe. "Speed up, Larry, we've got to get closer to his track, and I'm sure he's going to a more westerly course to head for the gulf entrance before long."

Sound operator Schab cut in: "I hear something, could be screw noises on the starboard beam but can't be sure."

"That's the target—stay on him and give us a screw count as soon as you can." Coe's voice stayed at the same pitch but his words came out faster than usual.

The next familiar "Stand by for a look" from the skipper was followed by, "Mark, he zigged towards; angle on bow zero; down periscope; stay at this slow speed, Larry. Let's head for him." The quartermaster replied, "Bearing 066 relative," and Gugliotta gave the range: "6,000 and right full rudder, steady on course 003." But it was slow work for impatient men. Three minutes later the bearing was 000 relative and the range 4,500.

At this point Schab reported, "I hear screws now, dead ahead, about 130 RPM."

"Good, stay on him and report any changes," Coe said. In a few minutes Schab came back with, "Target bearing is changing to the left. He may have zigged. I also hear more noise, screws at higher speed."

This brought "Up periscope" from Coe and, after finding the target, "He sure did zig. Mark, angle on the bow 60 port, 100 feet, and pour on the speed, Larry. Torpedo room make ready number one and two torpedo tubes, and tell Sound that the high speed screws are a couple of destroyer-type escorts."

The range was 3,600 yards, bearing 350 degrees. Gugliotta said to Coe,

"Recommend course 330 to give us a 105-degree track," got an "okay" from his captain, and said to helmsman, "Come left to 330 degrees." Hendrix, plotting, said, "Twelve knots is still good and checks with sound; target on course 250 degrees."

COB Nave relayed, "Torpedo room reports tubes one and two ready, zero gyro, ten feet depth set."

Coe said, "Okay, we won't get much closer, stand by for final setup and shoot. What's my firing bearing? Slow down, Larry."

Gugliotta fed him the information, 013: "I'll put you on it when you're ready."

"Up periscope. Mark, no change, angle on bow about 100 port. Down periscope." Coe said.

And for the last time this time, Gugliotta said, "Range 3,000" and the quartermaster replied, "Bearing 020."

The excitement in the control room was palpable. There wasn't a sound from those present as the skipper said, "Put me on the firing bearing"; Gugliotta turned the periscope to bearing; Monk said, "Setup checks, course 250, speed 12"; Coe said, "Up periscope, he's coming on, stand by."

A few seconds later the captain said, "Fire one." Nave, who as chief of the boat rated the honor, pressed the electric firing switch, and again when Coe said, "Fire two."

Torpedoman Bixler reported, "Both torpedoes fired electrically," and sound man Schab, "Both torpedoes running straight."

Now came the longest part of the 21 minutes since the approach had begun, the two- or three-minute interval between firing the torpedoes and knowing whether they'd found their mark. Coe kept wiping his palms on his skivvy pants but didn't bother to push back the strands of red hair that had come unstuck when he pulled away from the periscope. Nave kept opening his mouth as though he were about to say something, but nothing came. Larry Bernard folded his arms over his midsection and pressed down hard. He'd forgotten his belly, but now it was giving him trouble. Hendrix rubbed his eyes and blinked, rubbed his eyes and blinked. Some had clenched jaws; some were slack-mouthed. One man kept rolling his thumbs over and over each other. Each showed tension differently, but they were all listening, all breathing hard, all scared. Then two explosions were heard by all hands.

Coe, having a look through the periscope, said softly, "He's hit, going down by the stern and listing to port." Sickness stirred in the gut of every man present, but the memory of the baptismal depth-charging 39 had experienced put a brake on regret. The captain's next words stopped it completely. "Here come his escorts and one fired at our periscope; I just saw a splash nearby; 150 feet, Larry. Pass the word, rig for depth-charge attack." It was like a blast of cold air in the

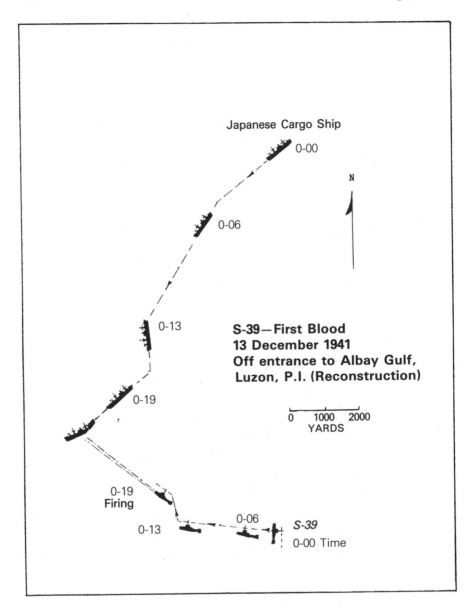

Japanese Cargo Ship

0-00

N

0-06

0-13

S-39—First Blood
13 December 1941
Off entrance to Albay Gulf,
Luzon, P.I. (Reconstruction)

0-19

0   1000   2000
YARDS

0-19
Firing

0-06

0-13   S-39
0-00 Time

100-degree control room. Schab's excited follow-up, "Two sets of high-speed screws approaching from vicinity of the target," caused further chilling.

They were in for it. There were four enemy destroyers, but instead of depth-charging they started echo-ranging and tracking. Coe and company figured that the Japanese submarine they'd encountered earlier might still be in the vicinity. The enemy couldn't be sure that the submersible they'd located wasn't their own. The Japanese sub couldn't be sure that the destroyers weren't U.S., so she was afraid to divulge her identity.

Coe ordered, "Rig for silent running." All electric motors not vitally needed were stopped. The gyro compass was kept running. The all-important but noisy battery ventilation motors were slowed as much as possible, as were the greatest noisemakers of all, the propellers. They had to be kept turning, though, in case it was necessary to make a knuckle. This consisted of a sharp turn and a burst of speed for just a few seconds, enough disturbance to create a mass of bubbles that would confuse the echo-ranging and enable the submarine to make a try at getting away. The sound waves that pinged against a target and echoed back were indiscriminate; a large fish, a mass of bubbles, or mud would sometimes do.

They were still at Battle Stations Submerged, which kept the best and most experienced people on watch. Silent running automatically meant that personnel movements were to be held to a minimum, especially in the engine room, where loose metal floor plates clanked when walked on. Sandals came off because calloused soles were quieter than leather. A broken belt buckle on Tom Parks's sweat-soaked shorts was snipped because it scraped against equipment. The smoking lamp (a term, stemming from early days when an actual little lamp was used to light pipes and cigars) had been out for some time.

The hourly cigarette break usually permitted when submerged was verboten. Air quality was a prime consideration in the relentless heat. Most of the men sat down on the deck right where they were to use as little energy and make as little noise as possible. The only people working hard were the helmsman and the planesmen, who had to operate the rudder and the bow and stern planes by hand now that power was secured.

In the torpedo room Ed Schab, still on watch, had shifted from the normal, powered JK listening gear to the SC, a long-range stethoscope mounted topside near the JK. As it was for everybody else, this was his first wartime experience with silent running. Wearing earphones, he was taking bearings when he began hearing something new, something other than the screws and the now familiar pings of the enemy's destroyers. He listened harder, moved around, took another bearing, turning the thick handle of the SC gear. Same thing. It didn't resemble the unmistakeable explosion of depth charges; it was a very regular bang-bang, unchanging in tone and quality. Schab didn't like it. It was creepy the way it followed him, never varying no matter how he turned to lose it

Coe was well aware that as long as they had four enemy destroyers pinging on them they were hardly out of danger, so he kept close check on the torpedo room. He had been sweating out the mystery sound with Schab for about ten minutes when his impatience became obvious. "Haven't you any idea yet what it might be?" He whispered.

Schab, who'd been having some unpleasant thoughts about the creepy noise, shook his head "no" just as Harris, radioman first class, came in. Ed handed over the equipment and Harris got down to the job. There was a touch of "We'll find out now that the expert is here," in Harris's manner as he set about covering the same territory Ed had. Schab sat back, praying that the leading radioman would come up fast with the solution. Waiting out the enemy still hovering above them was the worst part of the last five days. Everybody was exhausted, stubbly faces sagging from fatigue, the stinking air beginning to make eyes ache and temples throb from oxygen starvation. Expectations of living out the war were slim, but everyone had hoped to make it a little longer than this. To add the damned bang-bang and the fear of a secret weapon to the already existing misery seemed hitting below the belt.

"Well," the captain said impatiently to Harris, "do you still hear it?"

Harris gave the handle a big swing, a furrow of concentration between his heavy brows, beads of perspiration rolling down his jowls, listening, listening. "There it is again," he said. "I don't know what it is."

Schab, concentrating on every move the radioman made, suddenly caught sight of the metal tube leads that came through the hull; when Harris made a big, rapid swing, they twisted and banged together. Could it be? Ed wanted to shout as he watched it happen again when Harris trained around fast going from 15 to 90 degrees. Controlling himself, Ed tapped his skipper on the arm and pointed upward. Harris caught the action too. The mystery was solved.

For a few seconds it was almost reassuring to hear only pinging, but another hour went by and aching eyes had become red-rimmed and filmy. They were back to square one. Christopher, who kept having visions of a giant-sized, ice cold beer, thought to himself, how long, O Lord, how long? But nobody could answer that question. Increasing headaches were acting as a barometer of decreasing air quality inside the pigboat. Men who had been florid from heat were paling out from lack of oxygen. Nobody complained because there was no point in it. An S-boat was a great leveling agent; all suffered equally. Besides, why waste breath. It was too precious.

Depth-charging could blast you instantaneously out of existence, but pinging could wear you down until the lack of breathable air gave you the choice of surfacing or smothering to death. If you surfaced, you could shoot it out, hoping to do some damage and get away—not likely with four modern Jap destroyers on you. Or you could surrender and be taken prisoner, which was unthinkable. For *39* the point of surfacing and confrontation was getting near. Coe motioned Gugliotta to follow him into the wardroom. Guy silently picked his way across outstretched legs on the slimy deck; the only noisemakers were the enormous, dinosaur-vintage cockroaches plopping onto metal machinery.

"Guy, I want you to get all the confidential publications together," the captain whispered into his communicator's ear, "and if we have to surface, be ready to deep-six them."

Following instructions, Gugliotta went to the ship's safe, packed the confidential material into a canvas bag, and weighted it down with wrenches. Then he added his silent prayer to the rest of the silent prayers that he'd be taking them out and stuffing them back in the safe soon.

In the torpedo room Radioman Rice, who had relieved Schab, wanted to believe his ears but also wanted to be sure before he got everybody's hopes up that the pinging was getting farther away. Coming in quietly as a mouse, Coe took one look at the radioman's face and said, "There's a change. Have they given up on us?"

"It looks like it, captain," Rice said cautiously. "The sound is getting further and further away. I haven't heard anything at all for the last couple of minutes."

The word got around fast. Faces brightened as *39* began surfacing, and by the time Quartermaster Rollins started cranking the dogs of the hatch cover, there were a few cautious smiles. If only they could get rid of the foul air, things might be okay. All eyes in the conning tower were on the hatch cover, still held shut by the latch and water pressure. Then the hatch was out of the water, and Diving Officer Bernard relayed the depth to Officer of the Deck Hendrix, who told the quartermaster, "Open the hatch."

Rollins pulled hard on the lanyard that tripped the latch. With an angry blast the foul air blew out and fresh replaced it as the main engines were started. Officers and men had never known anything so good. For the first time they realized that air tasted. They opened their mouths and gulped it. They rolled it around their tongues. They smacked their lips over it.

The relief didn't last long. They immediately made ready for a battery charge and found a considerable amount of water in the large main induction piping through which ventilating air was drawn into the boat when on the surface. The source of the leak was a distorted gasket on the main induction valve located in the bridge structure aft of the open bridge area; the shocks from depth charges on 11 December had unseated the gasket. It had become badly crushed from opening and shutting since then, and no spare was carried on board. It was decided to force the distorted gasket into place, shut the valve, and keep it shut for the rest of the patrol. The hardest part would be to do the noisy job quietly and quickly in a patrol area crawling with enemy ships.

Bernard sent for Chief Machinist's Mate Paul Spencer and Jim Pennell to assess the task.

"Somebody will have to crank the valve shut from below because if it's operated by power it could cut off fingers," Spencer said. "It'll take three of us to force it into place and hold it there."

"I'll go get somebody," Pennell offered.

Coe had witnessed the rush of water when the valve was opened, and his concern brought him through the hatch to join the others on the bridge. It was a dark and hazy night, but the outlines of enemy vessels were discernible in the distance. In a few seconds Pennell was back with Earl Nave in tow. Though not a machinist's mate, Nave understood the problem from past experience on another submarine and had volunteered to help. He won a lot of respect for the action because a chief of the boat didn't have to do nasty little jobs like this, And most of them didn't. Some of the admiration given Nave was grudging, but all of it was genuine.

The three men got to work at once, unable to go as fast as they would have liked for fear of the noise. It was a hammer and screwdriver job. While the men worked, the skipper's eyes followed the progress of a clipper-bow Japanese "tin can" (destroyer) that loomed closer and closer. The machinist's mates were finding Nave's experience invaluable as they tried to get the hard rubber disc back where it belonged and the word was quickly passed below that the honker was not only working quiet but keeping quiet. "A miracle, a miracle," somebody muttered. It was a night for miracles. Although the Japanese destroyer could be seen throughout the repair session, she never saw *39*.

Frustration set in again next day. Albay Gulf was crawling with Japanese minelayers, transports, destroyers, and even a light cruiser. Visibility was poor because of rain and fog. The *39* sighted more cargo ships coming down from the north, but as they approached the entrance to the gulf, the enemy vessels were met by Japanese destroyer escorts to take them in. It was a very high-risk setup for a U.S. submersible, even if she could get close enough for a try. Excitement ran high when *39* sighted a transport on her stern, but it zigged away. The submarine could not close below 4,000 yards, which was beyond her torpedo range.

Then Coe got a wonderful idea. At least he thought it was and so did everyone else but Gugliotta. Except when his back was to the wall, Coe's philosophy was to be neither stupidly reckless nor overly conservative but to evaluate the situation and decide whether he had a chance of making a successful hit and staying alive to report it. Going in during daylight was out right now; surface approach at night was a problem for S-boats because their sonar couldn't be used unless submerged; going in submerged at night wouldn't do, either, because the periscope was inadequate after dark, especially in stormy weather. What to do?

"Guy, it'll be a natural for you," Coe said, "since you're torpedo and gunnery officer. We'll go in submerged after dark but with the radio mast up; you can sit on it with binoculars and con the boat into firing position. You'll be much more accurate than the periscope, and you'll be in contact with me by telephone. This way we should get a good firing setup."

Gugliotta was a Naval Academy graduate who'd been trained to obey his commanding officer. The brown eyes met the blue ones, and Gugliotta said, "Yes, sir," but the plan didn't appeal to him. It wasn't so much the idea of being a human periscope, riding the radio mast all alone like the lookout on an old-time sailing ship while everybody else was safely below; it was the schools of viperish iridescent sea snakes he had so often seen in the warm waters of the Philippines. Did they sleep at night, or were they out to attack any legs that might be trailing through the water after dark? Gugliotta had a fix on snakes. He just didn't like them.

"Gee, that sounds great," Hendrix said, his big enthusiastic grin turned on his shipmate, who mumbled "yeah" and wished the skipper had asked for volunteers and Monk had been it.

But before the plan could be implemented, the order came to return to Manila. On the way back, Schab caught a Tokyo Rose broadcast. The velvet-voiced lady announced the sinking of the *S-39* in her perfect, unaccented English, and there was pathos in her tone when she said, "The rest of you brave submariners want to be able to see your wives and sweethearts again, don't you? Why don't you surrender?" The quiver in the dulcet voice was heartbreaking as she added, "And now I'm going to spin a record for you that will really make you think." The song was "You'd Be So Nice to Come Home To," which provoked many a sigh from the crew. The women-hungry men thoroughly enjoyed the sexy voice without taking her proposals seriously; they figured she didn't either. What really upset them was to hear that the Japanese had taken over Shanghai's International Settlement on 8 December and that Blood Alley, a sailor's paradise, was no more.

That chaotic Sunday, to be known in history as Pearl Harbor Day, would forever remain in the memory of Bobette Gugliotta. At home with her mother and stepfather in Malba, Long Island, she had nothing special planned. There would be the usual stroll down country roads lined with peach trees in this small community between College Point and the Whitestone Bridge. There would be the *New York Times Book Review,* roast beef, and snow flurries wafting across smudgy storm windows. After dinner there would be radio programs—such as Eddie Cantor's show with his famous sign-off, "I love to spend each Sunday with you"—followed by writing to Guy, and winding up with the usual long session of reading in bed. Bobette was currently immersed in Upton Sinclair's Lanny Budd novels and was about to finish *World's End.* It was a curiously prophetic title. The world that the 22-year-old had known was ending, and a new era was about to begin.

Word of the catastrophe came by telephone from a friend. The next few days were hectic, with normal people reacting abnormally. Charles Dixon, Bobette's 45-year-old stepfather and an ex-merchant mariner tried to enlist in the U.S. Navy on 8 December. His age, plus an X-ray that revealed an old tubercular scar, kept him out. Bobette's mother, Aline, opened a can of Japanese crabmeat and upon finding glasslike slivers in it called the FBI; the bureau made an analysis and found the slivers harmless preservative. Bobette, who had done nothing throughout the past year but write letters to Guy, send him books, visit his family in New Jersey, and lose weight from lovesickness, pulled herself together and joined the American Women's Voluntary Service. The most important job performed by the uniformed women was selling war savings bonds that helped finance badly needed equipment. Bobette worked out of a booth at the Jamaica, Long Island racetrack and sold a good number of bonds to successful horse players who were put to shame by AWVS women beseeching them, in loud voices, to share their winnings with GI Joe so he could win, too. She was also good at collecting reading material, not so good at knitting socks, and no good at all at helping provide an honor guard for the dead. Unable to bear the sight of a flag-draped coffin with a naval officer's cap atop it belonging to a young aviator killed in training, son of an AWVS volunteer, Bobette left in the middle of the services. Sitting in the dressing room, she wept quietly, blaming herself for being a coward.

Caroline Bernard and her son were living with Larry's family in Deadwood, South Dakota. Although the town was well known for western characters such as Wild Bill Hickok, Calamity Jane, and Deadwood Dick, its current 3,288 citizens were true blue but not worldly wise. When the news of Pearl Harbor was broadcast, Caroline received many a commiserating call because Larry was in that awful place where all those battleships were sunk. The Philippines and Hawaii were lumped together in the minds of many townfolk, as they were in the minds of people in larger, more sophisticated centers. The U.S. was about to have a geography lesson. But Deadwood, highly patriotic, was eager to cooperate with the war effort, and when government rationing books were issued later, ranchers were doubly on the alert for cattle rustlers eager to make bucks in the black market.

Caroline didn't hear anything from Larry for some time, and knowing nothing of the routine employed to convey notice of death, she thought it would surely be by telephone, and quaked everytime the instrument rang. Late one evening the harsh jangle of the wall phone struck terror into her heart, but it brought good news, a cable from Larry.

Corenne Ward was chatting and listening to the radio with friends in San Diego, including the English aircorpsman John Bellamy, still awaiting delivery of a plane. Suddenly the swing music of Artie Shaw stopped and a breathless voice kept repeating over and over, "Ladies and gentlemen, the Japanese have bombed Pearl Harbor."

"Let's drive down to the harbor and take a look around," someone suggested. Nobody knew what they expected to see, but the idea of movement was a relief in itself.

It was a mild, sunny day, the kind that made San Diego boast that it possessed the finest climate in the world. The group swung past the Civic Center and onto the Embarcadero, where tons of lumber were stacked up to build new housing for the swarm of defense workers who had recently invaded the area and were living in tent cities. Sighting the headquarters of the 11th Naval District, Corenne thought of Tom Parks—as she had the moment the awesome announcement of war came on the air. She had heard from Tom not long before and was pretty sure he was around Manila, but no announcements had been made concerning the Asiatic Fleet. She would call his mother later. If Mrs. Parks hadn't heard from Tom, she might have heard from his brother Jim on the carrier *Langley*. With a little shiver that had nothing to do with the weather, Corenne realized how hard it must be for Mr. and Mrs. Parks, whose only children were both in a theatre of war so far away. Corenne came back to the moment with a start as the car ground to a halt. "You've been dreaming," John Bellamy said, helping her out.

Corenne smiled. "I guess you're right. I didn't realize we'd driven all the way to La Jolla."

They stood on the wind-eroded cliffs, feeling mist upon their faces from waves that crashed against the strangely shaped rocks and sent watery fingers probing into caves underneath. Looking out over the endless blue of a Pacific dancing with sun-sparkle, it was hard to believe that death and destruction lay beyond the horizon. It was their last opportunity to move about freely. Within a few hours the harbor was fenced off and the cliffs were declared out of bounds.

Corenne had no chance to become interested in a change of job, since she found out next day that the one she was in had been declared vital to the defense of the United States. By the time she arrived at the telephone building, there were guards at all doors. No calls to Mexico or anywhere out of the U.S. could be connected without a monitor to warn customers not to talk of weather conditions or troop movements. Callers were also warned not to speak Japanese, an order the employees considered little more than a bluff, since 90 percent of the operators wouldn't have known Japanese from Tagalog or Hindi. Blackouts went into effect throughout the city, and the major buildings were sandbagged. All military personnel were recalled to their bases, and people in the streets glanced over their shoulders first and spoke in whispers if they had anything to say about the war.

Corenne's friend Bellamy was a great help in those first frightening weeks;

he had gone through much more in Britain, where London was taking the terrible bombing that fortunate San Diego would never experience. Nevertheless, it took a while for the initial fear to subside and for things to return to near-normal—with the exception of rationing. The common folk obeyed the law and took only their share of scarce canned goods, red meat, tires, and gasoline. Of course, the ever-present hoods and crooks immediately set up a black market in ration stamps that spread from coast to coast faster than maple syrup on hotcakes.

And then John Bellamy's plane was ready and it was time for him to go. It was a difficult parting. Bellamy, to make sure Corenne's letters would reach him, asked her to write in care of his home address in Sheffield, England so that his mother could forward the letters to his proper wartime address. He was to be reassigned after he reached home and had no way of knowing where he would end up. Corenne was very fond of him, she wrote faithfully. But as the months went by, she realized that John Bellamy's dowager mother was not forwarding mail to her son from the American girl. Corenne's letters from John (and there were many before he became totally discouraged) asked again and again why she never wrote. Since John's letters bore no return address, after a while Corenne had to concede victory to Mrs. Bellamy.

Two stalwart crew members who had missed the S-39's first patrol were Schoenrock and Tom Parks. Parks had become the complete, dyed-in-the-wool, 100-percent devoted pigboat sailor by the time he got his dolphins. He had totally eliminated from his consciousness his old desire to be in aviation. After a night on the town, he met up with an aviation machinist's mate from a patrol bomber squadron. The encounter took place in the head at the barracks in Subic Bay. When the superiority of wings over dolphins came under discussion, Tom unfortunately did not have his pacifist friend Kutscherowski with him to keep him out of trouble. As the argument heated up, the aviation machinist's mate became abusive to the point of impugning the honor and respectability of Tom's mother, so the submarine sailor clopped his opponent in the jaw and was immediately decked by a punch to the solar plexus that left him gasping. By the time he caught his breath, the machinist's mate had shoved off. Tom realized that his hand hurt like hell, and it soon swelled up like one of Ski's boxing gloves.

Prewar tension had already resulted in a stab in the leg for Schoenrock during a fight on the beach. Coe had been able to finagle temporary duty aboard the *Pigeon* for the cook while his leg healed, but Tom's right hand was more serious. Parks went to the hospital, and the *39* went to sea. When he was released, 6 December, the hospital personnel office sent Parks to the USS *Holland,* one of the newly arrived submarine tenders, where he knew no one at all. Tom managed to persuade the personnel officer to endorse orders to Division 201 instead, familiar territory.

As he started across the bay, he caught sight of the old carrier *Langley* coming in and realized that he hadn't seen his brother Jim in over a month. And when he went aboard *Canopus* and found that the *39* was out to sea, he made a split-second decision that he never regretted: he went AWOL and spent the weekend aboard the *Langley* with his brother. Sunday night, as soon as he set foot on the *Canopus,* a heavy hand was placed on his shoulder by the master-at-arms. He was under arrest, spent the rest of the night in the brig, and after quarters in the morning was led out on deck for a captain's mast.

The informality and homey touches of an S-boat were lacking here—no sloppy shorts, bare chests, and sandals. The drizzly, gray light of the rainy season showed a grim-faced Commander Earl Sackett, his leading petty officer, a division officer, and the master-at-arms who had put Tom in the brig. With all speed Tom was set for a summary court martial. He began to realize that his impulsive act could have serious results. He hoped and prayed that what he'd heard was true, that the Navy took into consideration your previous record. His was clean, and there were extenuating circumstances, in this case a desire to see his only brother. What he didn't realize yet was that a war had started. Within hours the Navy was too busy for minor things like court martials, and besides, it needed all the hands it could muster.

By the time the *Canopus* had sailed back across the bay and tied up at the President Lines pier, Tom had heard the news. Although not even Admiral Hart knew the extent of the damage at Pearl Harbor. Parks, like the higher-ups, thought the Philippines the main target. The area was alerted for air raids, and shortly after, sirens began their high-pitched, ear-splitting whine. It was 10 December, the hour was 1210. Fifteen minutes later 54 Japanese bombers, accompanied by fighter planes, were sighted. Tom, mouth open and eyes wide as though in a trance, watched the faraway specks grow larger and break into two groups of 27 with the precision of an air show, before winging off into smaller units of nine with insolent ease. The flyers from Nippon knew they had nothing to fear by way of retaliation.

While Parks was wondering where the American fighter planes were, the first bombs bagan to fall, coming down at 1305 on Machina Wharf at Cavite, hitting minesweeper *Bittern* and submarine *Sealion.* That was only the beginning. The navy yard was bombed again and again, smashing ships and knocking out the power station so that no water pressure was available for firefighting.

Parks was assigned to a boat gang ordered to take a fire-and-rescue party of 30 men to the navy yard. The trancelike feeling continued as they crossed the bay, and Tom stared in disbelief at red flames skyscrapering up through enormous black billows of smoke. But when he landed at Cavite, it was not the spectacle burning all around him that made war real but the sight of what shrapnel could do to a human body.

The Filipinos suffered most in the Cavite disaster; over 1,000 dockworkers and shopkeepers were killed outright, and 400 more would die later in the hospital. As Tom stared at the bloody remains of what had been live people a few minutes before, he grew sick to his stomach and felt the cold grip of fear for his own life. The barracks had taken a direct hit; the torpedo and machine shops were in ruins; the *Sealion* had gone down; and he could see the superstructure of the *Seadragon* pocked with holes. But none of that mattered like the helpless dead.

When the battered fire and rescue party went back across the bay to Manila the next day, Tom cried unabashedly from anger, frustration, and fright as he watched Japanese bombers overhead and saw the futile antiaircraft fire popping so far below the planes that it would have been funny if it had been happening to somebody else. He consoled himself by thinking, we'll even the score in a few days, we'll get back at them. He was still expecting a battle fleet from Pearl Harbor to steam in and save the Philippines. Nobody had yet told him how impossible that was.

Fleet submarines *Sealion* and *Seadragon,* when caught in the devastating attack, had both been undergoing overhaul. Lieutenant Commander Richard Voge, captain of *Sealion,* had issued orders the day the war started that all hands were to come aboard fast if an air raid alarm sounded, because there were no shelters in the navy yard and the submarine was the safest place to be. The Philippine workmen had been trying their best to complete the overhaul and by working like demons were ahead of schedule, but *Sealion's* engines were still dismantled. Frank Gierhart, radioman second class from Cincinnati, Ohio, had been in the yard on business connected with *Sealion* when he heard the siren's wail. Running when he could and walking when he had to plow through the crowds of workmen and civilians frantically seeking shelter in a place which had none, Frank headed for home. He had put *Sealion* into commission and had been mighty glad to be on a new, up-to-date fleet boat after a two-year stint on the old *S-43* in Panama.

Frank scrambled across *Seadragon,* his heart beating louder than the wailing siren. He was scared. On the bridge Captain Voge urged Gierhart and others coming along behind him to get a move on. It was hardly necessary. By the time the bombers were sighted, the only men topside on *Sealion* were her skipper, the exec, and three gunners manning the machine gun. It was almost instantly clear that a single bantam-weight gun was impotent against 54 heavy-weight bombers.

As Frank dropped into the control room where most of the men were assembled, he heard the puerile ack-ack of Cavite's antiaircraft batteries, but not for long. The nine three-inch guns, with a range of 15,000 feet, might as well have been firing tennis balls into the air for all the impression they could make on high-altitude bombers. But it wasn't long before the holocaust taking place in Cavite stilled the sound of antiaircraft guns forever.

When the first bombs slanted down a few yards astern, Voge ordered all hands below, and minutes later two bombs hit *Sealion,* one completely destroying the machine gun mount just vacated. Fortunately, the first bomb exploded outside the hull, a few feet away from the crowded control room. If it had penetrated, most of the crew would have been killed. The impact shook the boat with the force of a giant hand, and three men in the control room were injured by bomb fragments piercing the pressure hull. But there was no time for tears because, almost simultaneously, a second bomb passed through the main ballast tank and exploded in the after engine room. The four electrician's mates working there were killed instantly. The room flooded immediately and the submarine settled in the mud, its sudden tilting slamming the men every which way as water started seeping through the bomb-fragment holes. All hatches were still above water, and the stunned and silent crew shot up them, escaping with all the speed of Battle Surface Drill, except the wounded assisted by their comrades.

It was worse outside than in. When Frank Gierhart emerged into the chaos of a thousand fires blazing like spin-offs from the fiery tropic sun and the explosions of zigzagging bombs wiping out people and landmarks before his eyes, he knew what terror was. The screams of the injured and dying were periodically obliterated by detonations, and the nauseating odor of cooked flesh was replaced by an oil stench when an errant breeze blew smoke from burning tanks through the hell that was Cavite. Gierhart was homeless now.

The day Cavite was bombed, another member of *Sealion's* crew, Fireman First Class Leslie Dean, had been sent to Manila to buy or scrounge whatever supplies he could find. It was every ship for itself, and each one wanted to have as many spares and as much food as it could carry. Dean was a good man for the job. His farmer-minister-carpenter father had never made much money at any of his trades and during the Depression earned even less. This had made a realist out of his son, who joined the navy in 1935 primarily to eat regularly and, by the way, to see the world. He'd never before been outside Mt. Vernon, Illinois. As soon as he could, he volunteered for submarines—extra pay the incentive. For the same reason he didn't mind being a messcook; the hat was always passed on pay day for services rendered and the extra bucks were worth a little sweat.

Like Gierhart, Les Dean had also put the *Sealion* into commission. Older than Frank, Les appreciated even more the pleasant life on a fleet boat; he had come up in the world and he wanted to stay there. Let newcomers to submarines live on the stinking pigboats; his four long years on *S-25* and *S-28* had made him a grateful graduate. Dean didn't get along with boatswain's mates but otherwise considered himself peaceable enough, not a personality to rub people the wrong way, somewhat forgettable in fact. He considered himself lucky as hell to have been in Manila when Cavite was bombed, but when he heard about *Sealion,* he took it hard. He was homeless, too.

Also in the Cavite Navy Yard when the war started was J.T. Lebow (no first name, just initials), another guy without a bunk to call his own. Lebow had six years of Navy experience; he had served on S-boats in Panama and then on the fleet boat *Cuttlefish* in Pearl Harbor. But when there was a shortage of radiomen in the Asiatic Fleet in early 1941, J.T. volunteered for the duty. He had bounced around on three different boats during the move to Manila, taking over temporarily for nonfunctioning radiomen. In the Philippines he had gone to the sub tender *Holland* as a spare. Filling in wherever needed, J.T. was as sought after as a substitute teacher and had served on *Sculpin, Sailfish, Spearfish,* and *Swordfish.* The conflict came as no surprise to him; back in Panama in 1940 he had predicted that war in Asia would involve the U.S. within a year. He was often right and not modest about it, which made him somewhat of a loner, except when it came to women.

In looks Lebow was not the traditional tall Texan but possessed the cockiness attributed to natives of the Lone Star State. In his spare time in prewar Manila, he had shot craps; guzzled scotch, beer, juleps; had some women and some fights. As the old saying goes, he was full of piss and vinegar, and behaved like many another sailor trying to do it all while he was still young and strong enough to enjoy it. He had a girl back home, Minnie Jeanne Nozero, but nothing definite had been settled between them. J.T. was too fond of the fair sex to ignore them in the warm and welcoming climate of the Philippines, or any other climate, for that matter. But like many another sailor who'd been blasted out of a nice setup, by the war, Lebow would have to be on the move soon or take to the hills and learn to exist on bananas.

The crew of the *Sealion* and other displaced personnel found temporary refuge in the new Enlisted Men's Club on the dock in Manila. They were immediately set to work digging a trench around the club, wide enough and deep enough for a man to take shelter in. This was to be used only if they were unable to make the mile run to the wall surrounding the old city, which was considered a much safer place to be. After a few days a bombing pattern became obvious. With clocklike precision the Japanese came in twice daily, at 1300 and 0100. Gierhart, Dean, and others began grabbing a blanket to tote along for wee-hours session. The ground was hard, wet, and chilly at that time of the morning. They were supposed to go right back to the Enlisted Club as soon as the all-clear sounded, but many of them, worn out from recent events, fell asleep and stayed the night. Gierhart's and Dean's main preoccupation was thinking about what would become of them if the Philippines fell, which looked more and more likely. The rumor factory went 24 hours a day, ranging all the way from a Japanese bombing of D.C. that had killed President Roosevelt to the sinking of the fleet in Pearl Harbor. They believed the first more possible than the last, because all those big battleships and fancy cruisers and new destroyers in Pearl were supposed to come and rescue them.

And then came news that wasn't a rumor. Until two days before the event, General MacArthur "forgot" to inform Admiral Hart that Manila would be declared on open city on Christmas Day. In a hastily summoned conference with his flag officers, Hart told them of the imminent need to evacuate personnel, equipment, and the *Canopus,* the only submarine tender left in the Philippines. Though he tried to control it, his bitterness at the cavalier behavior of his peer showed; the lives of men were at stake, men of the fleet who deserved every chance to escape so that they might live to fight more effectively another day.

Tom Parks hadn't had much time to think about whether *39* would take him back when she came in but the thought loomed more and more important. There were a lot of homeless Navy men and Marines, an estimated 4,000 of them, and only small vessels to put them on. Rear Admiral William A. Glassford, Jr., had already departed for Balikpapan with a cruiser, two oilers, and the *Langley.* When push came to shove, which would be soon according to scuttlebutt, space available for displaced men to catch a ride would be the submarines and inshore patrol vessels that were left. Whoever made it aboard would be lucky; the rest, the bulk, could soon be in the talons of an enemy swooping in like falcons sure of their prey.

Ships from many countries had sought refuge in Manila Bay, among them a modern French merchantman, *Marechal Joffre,* flying the Vichy French flag. The top brass decided to take *Marechal Joffre* into protective custody and put 100 U.S. Navy personnel aboard to sail her to an eastern Australian port, where she could be used by the Allies. But first a boarding party had to be formed for the purpose, and Parks was a member of the group chosen for the takeover. He didn't know much about Frenchmen, Vichy or otherwise, and was leery of the reception the "pirates" would receive. As they climbed into motor launches, he swallowed hard, recalling Errol Flynn movies where the boarding party always encountered gunfire and hand-to-hand fighting. The only thing missing would be sabers—maybe the French still used them.

When they neared the ship, the Americans could see officers and sailors hanging over the rails watching their approach. They couldn't read the expressions on the faces. But as the first member of the boarding party set foot on the *Joffre,* the skipper said, "Allo," with a big smile. Then the French sailors waved to the Americans, and Tom knew the takeover was going to be okay. He had one more hurdle to jump, and that was to find out if his billet was still available on the *39.*

6. The Vagabonds

When the *S-39* limped into Manila from her first patrol on 20 December 1941, the men found the city damaged, but were appalled at what they could see of Cavite from the bay. Obviously, the navy yard wouldn't be able to solve the boat's problems. Coe's first concern was getting the old pigboat patched up, especially if the next patrol meant going any distance. Leaks in the main engine circulating water system permitted full sea pressure in a system designed for much less. The boat also needed to replace six leaky torpedoes and to have periscope and binoculars dried out. But it immediately became evident that they'd have to spend most of the daylight hours on the bottom of Manila Bay, working on repairs as best they could and being serviced by *Canopus* at night. The main engine circulating water leaks would never be fixed and this would cause endless problems later on.

The hopes of the men for rest and recreation were smashed, but they got a lift when Chaplain McManus came aboard and asked everyone to write a message home that he would cable for them if possible. McManus refused to take any money because he wasn't sure he could send the messages out. He did, but the *39* boat people wouldn't know it for a long time.

Stepped-up air raids made working conditions even more erratic. In the city of Manila, Japanese bombers seemed remarkably accurate, since choice buildings such as the Manila Hotel and the Army-Navy Club were scarcely damaged. It was rumored that the Japanese High Command wanted these luxury quarters intact for their own use.

Out of a population of 16,000,000, only 29,000 Japanese lived in the Philippines, compared with 117,500 Chinese. In the 1930s young Filipinos had gone to Japan to study agriculture, fishing, and aviation, and a group of these became radicals. Some remained in Japan, some returned to the Philippines. When the war started, the Japan-based group, in contact with their radical affiliates at home, were responsible for directing much sabotage.

Officers and crew of *39*, when they could be spared, were scrambling around fast trying to hustle food and stores. Jim Pennell loved the old Miles, Bemment, Pond lathe on *39* and became concerned about having enough stock to turn on it. He solved the problem by snitching some from the *Canopus*, including a piece that was a good grade of brass over two feet long. This he wrapped in burlap and hid between the main motors for use in extremity, which wouldn't be long in coming.

Hendrix, rounding up supplies, was caught in a daylight raid in Manila and headed for the closest shelter, the trench surrounding the Enlisted Men's Club. After his first fear subsided, curiosity made him raise his head and look around. This was his first experience with a land attack. He saw reflectors being used by fifth columnists so the Japanese would have a good position to shoot at and knew that at night saboteurs boldly flashed lights at strategic locations as targets for enemy bombers. Hendrix also saw American soldiers shooting down the fifth columnists they caught sending signals.

When *39* pulled alongside faithful Mama San *Canopus* to be fueled, her personnel heard the air raid alarm sound off. Afraid they wouldn't have time to submerge before bombs started dropping, they chopped their lines with an axe to expedite clearing and managed to back away from the tender. They didn't have time to get very far before the first bombs came down, so they submerged inside the Manila breakwater. The harbor was so full of merchantmen and combat ships, constantly on the move to avoid becoming sitting ducks for Japanese airmen, that the pigboat was afraid she'd have her bridge mangled. Knowing her conning tower shears were showing in the shallow water, she raised both periscopes in silent warning that she was there and didn't want to be run over. Then she prayed for the best until the raid ended and she went back to the tender to complete the job of refueling.

But the crew had learned their lesson and tied up with only two lines, so when the bombers returned within a short period, *39* was able to clear fast and head for deeper waters. USS *Sturgeon*, making emergency speed of about 18 knots by the time she passed the breakwater, was some 300 yards ahead, and Coe and Hendrix on the bridge saw enemy planes circling over her. Knowing that Japanese pilots stood a chance of being decorated for blasting two American submarines out of existence at the same time, *39* submerged with all speed in the 60-foot water as a splash of bombs surrounded *Sturgeon*.

Coe and Hendrix looked at each other wordlessly; they never expected to see the fleet boat again. But two hours later, when they surfaced, *Sturgeon* came up alongside. It was a badly shaken crew, but the fleet boat hadn't suffered any real damage. Some stories had a happy ending. The postscript to this one was that U.S. newspapers carried headlines reading, "Japs Claim Two U.S. Subs Trapped in Manila Bay."

The four days from 20 to 24 December were the same hectic pattern for *S-39*, never knowing when a raid would start, constantly on the run from bombs or, to keep things really humming, dodging rockets aimed at them from shore by fifth columnists. The enemy was eager to have Manila all to himself. Every man on the boat, from the skipper down, learned by experience, but the learning had to be encapsulated into a very short space of time. Within the first few hours back in Manila Bay, air raids taught them to keep only single lines out; to keep the boat sealed except for the conning tower hatch; to maintain full water tanks; and to station men on the maneuvering watch ready to answer "bells on the battery." Because the engines were not reversible in S-boats, if they needed to back down they had to shift power to the batteries and motors. A full watch was kept aboard at all times.

Coe managed to let the men have some recreation; he had two sections stay aboard and gave the third section liberty, but only until dusk. When it came Schab's turn, he went ashore with Lipham, the striker who assisted Schoenrock in the galley. They found that, despite the war, certain things in Manila were going along as merrily as before. The Yacht Club and Wack Wack Golf Club were still serving meals to upper-class Filipinos, the men garbed in the *barong tagalog* (the embroidered shirt used on formal occasions), their wives wearing traditional *mestiza* dress, the *terno*, with its long skirt, puffed sleeves, and stand-up collar. The euphoria would not last long.

The two young sailors wanted to see what damage had been done to the city, and their curiosity took them a fair distance. When an unexpected air raid alarm sounded about four o'clock, they were far from the docks, and by the time the all-clear sounded and they had made their way back, the submarine had moved. Soon it would be dark, and there was no possibility of locating the boat under blackout conditions.

"Hey, Lipham," Schab said, "maybe we better check in at the club and see if they got any suggestions for us." The Submarine Command Post had been temporarily housed in the Enlisted Men's Club.

"Okay," Lipham said tonelessly, a worried look on his face.

Schab didn't like feeling lost. He knew the *39* had taken on a fireman, Les Dean from the *Sealion*, and that there were plenty more homeless men of all ratings anxiously looking for a submarine to latch on to. He and Lipham were expendable. As they walked across what had been lush green turf, now so chewed up by bombing that it looked like a dancehall for dinosaurs, Schab's usually optimistic spirits sank. He wondered if he'd be alive next week. There was that girl he'd met at the skating rink in San Francisco. He really wanted to see her again.

But when Ed asked the duty officer what they could expect if they couldn't find their submarine in the morning, his answer was, "You've got two choices. You can take as many guns and as much ammunition as you want and hide in the mountains near Baguio, or you can go to Corregidor." Then Schab and Lipham really felt low. Besides, the officer was cleaning out his desk and stuffing papers in his briefcase as if he expected for sure to see a son of the rising sun sitting in his swivel chair.

"What'll we do, hole up here for the night?" Lipham asked.

Ed did some quick thinking. This could be their last night ever of freedom. They had seen plenty of bars still operating in Manila; they both had money in their wallets after being at sea; and this might be the last chance they'd have to spend it. "What the hell," Schab said. "Let's go."

What started out glum became jolly, then riotous as the night progressed and whiskey replaced beer. There were sympathetic females, too, willing to lend an ear and share a drink. Around midnight, when everybody became a buddy and a soulmate—and witty—they ran into a couple of radiomen from one of the big boats and decided that these two were especially brilliant, since they were fellow submariners. But by two in the morning, when the guys from the fleet boat began telling what a rough time they'd had when their air conditioning went out for two days, Schab and Lipham exchanged looks of disgust and slid their drinks down the bar to a new location. Schab muttered, "Coupla candy asses, that's what they are." It was the pigboat sailor's scornful name for fleet-boat sailors and their life of luxury.

By dawn's early light, Schab and Lipham weren't sure if it was raining or if their eyes were just bleary. "Yours look like pee holes in the snow," Lipham commented to Schab. "Yeah," was all the retort Schab had left in him. "Listen, we got to find *39*. There's lots of motorboats around here. Maybe we can talk some joker into taking us out to look for her. I got a few pesos left."

In a short time they were bouncing over the waves, still a little drunk, but the cool air was doing its work along with the sobering effects of not finding their submarine. They were almost back to battery when they noticed a commotion over by the seawall with people signaling to them. When they got within shouting distance and heard somebody yell, "Are you from *39*? You better get your butts over there fast, they're looking for you," things began to look brighter.

As they neared the *39*, Ed could see Captain Coe sitting astride the rail on the bridge in his frayed khaki shorts, watching the approach of the motorboat. Schab could also see that the lines were all singled up and ready to go. They'd made it by the skin of their teeth—that is, if the captain still wanted them. The two missing links exchanged sheepish glances and began worrying about their future. As they came aboard, the blue eyes under the officer's cap seemed to be reading their minds, but after a long, shriveling scrutiny, Coe just said, "Party's over, boys. Shake a leg." The culprits started breathing normally again.

Now that he was safe, Schab suddenly had a complete change of mind. He figured Captain Coe had known that *39* would be in bad shape if she lacked a vital communication man and a back-up cook, and that they'd never been in danger of being left behind in Manila. On second thought Schab decided the submarine might have gotten along okay without Lipham but couldn't have functioned without a crackerjack radioman like himself.

Frank Gierhart, *Sealion* refugee, still didn't have a boat by Christmas Eve when word came that Manila would be officially declared an open city the next day. This meant that no combat personnel of any kind could be found within her borders if the city and its inhabitants were to be spared further bombing. Those who were temporarily housed at the overcrowded Enlisted Men's Club had to be removed at once. They immediately set to work stripping the place of everything but toilets and washbasins; They figured that not only would usable loot be welcome to retreating Americans but, if the structure wasn't bombed out of existence, little would be left to aid and comfort the enemy. Since food and clothing had already become scarce, any kind of edible or wearable was squirreled into pockets, jumpers, or jackets, or tossed into sheets that were tied around necks so hands could grip communication equipment and furniture. The strangeness of the silent procession making its way in the dark to two open barges, which would serve as rooms at the inn for Christmas Eve, was surpassed only by the scene when the barges were loaded. Gierhart and others found themselves seated on chairs, leaning against tables and desks, or straddling radio equipment while a couple of old tugs pulled them out into the middle of Manila Bay and left them there to spend the night.

The frightened men did plenty of drifting but very little dreaming; nightmares were more like it when anybody dropped off to sleep, which seldom happened and never lasted long. At any moment they expected mines to explode below them and bombs to drop from above. If they'd stopped to think, they would have remembered that the bay itself wasn't mined, only the entrance, but you couldn't expect logic under the circumstances. They couldn't smoke to relieve tension because cigarettes and matches glowed in the dark. Fortunately, they didn't know how real the threat from the sky was; the Japanese would continue bombing for a number of days in spite of the agreement that the attacks would cease at midnight on 24 December.

Daylight, when the tugs were supposed to come back and tow them into Mariveles, did not bring improvement. Dawn came, grizzly gray—nothing happened. Eight o'clock and still no tugs. This was even worse than sitting it out at night; anything in the harbor was fair game, and the two big barges filled with men were super targets. The men kept watching the sky, looking for the first specks that might become planes. By nine o'clock nobody could even crack a joke. Finally, at ten, the tugs came back and towed the barges to Mariveles, where the men were housed in the Quarantine Station barracks. There they waited for submarines to come in, praying there'd be space available when it came their turn to hitch a ride. Gierhart was lucky; Moon Chapple took him on as a passenger along with four or five others. Admiral Hart didn't want submarines that were going on patrol to carry so many people that they might be hampered if they got a crack at the enemy, but the *38*, on her first patrol, had taken a terrific depth-charging after sinking a Japanese transport and sustained a battery explosion that had badly wounded three men. Some of the crew thought Chapple took chances that went beyond fifty-fifty, but Gierhart figured he'd rather exit this way than have the enemy stalking him in the mountains of Baguio.

Tom Parks was reinstated on the *39* boat. The same stroke of fate that brought bad luck to the *Canopus* wiped out his AWOL offense for all time. Despite camouflage, the doughty tender took a bomb through her after deck-house that penetrated below and exploded in the shaft alley. The boat crew's quarters were smashed, along with all of Tom's gear. He had only the clothes on his back. But the personnel and ship's offices were also hit, so Tom's records, including reports on the captain's mast and summary court martial, were completely destroyed.

Tom wasn't the only one with a clothing problem. The crew generally was in the same situation, having lost their belongings on *Canopus*, and the officers had left theirs at the University Apartments. It was a ragtag group, but that was the least of their worries

Unbelievably, Schoenrock managed to come up with turkey, cranberry sauce, mashed potatoes, gravy, and pumpkin pie for Christmas dinner. At the bottom of Manila Bay, with bombing still in progress, Rocky served it with his usual aplomb, and everybody chowed down like trenchermen. Things weren't so bad. Sure, they were submerged and it was hot as hell, but the air wasn't foul yet, and at the moment no enemy was pinging on them. It was almost possible to pretend there wasn't a war on.

In Wilmington, Delaware, Rachel Coe was doing exactly that, trying to pretend that December 25, 1941, was a routine Christmas Day. But daughter Jean was old enough to ask childish but embarrassing questions, like, "If Daddy sinks the bad people, can he swim home?" Rachel tried to turn such queries aside with a laugh, not to divert herself but to divert her elderly and ailing Quaker parents. The Gowthrops were still, in their hearts, far from approving of war in any form or for any reason.

That evening after the children were in bed, Rachel thought back over the last months. By the time she had arrived in Wilmington, after a 15,000 mile journey by sea and by land, the memory of having an *amah* to take care of her two children was just that, a wonderful experience that seemed to have happened to someone else back in a dim, remote past. So it had been with a great sense of relief that she saw her parents waiting for her on the platform of the train station. There were helping hands at last.

In the cab on the way home, Mr. Gowthrop held his granddaughter on his knee and tilted her solemn little face upward. After a long scrutiny he said, "She's skinny as a straw, but we'll take care of that directly we get home. We have a surprise waiting for you, Rachel. You never know what you'll pick up in those heathen countries. The baby needs looking after, too." These cryptic statements were soon explained.

As the cab driver put on the brakes, the front door of the house opened, and Rachel saw a familiar face peer out—the family doctor. For a moment she thought they were stopping at his house first to say hello, but when her mother got out, carrying baby Henry, and her father followed with Jean by the hand, she realized she was home. As soon as greetings had been exchanged, the doctor picked up his little black bag and asked Rachel to remove Henry's clothes.

With the directness of a testy old Quaker accustomed to speaking his mind and going right to the point, Mr. Gowthrop said, "I asked the doctor to be here when you arrived so he could check the children immediately and get stool specimens, or do whatever's necessary to turn them into healthy American young ones. Jean is skin and bones."

"But I've always been thin," Rachel said in self-defense. "Jean just takes after me."

"There's a difference between slender and skinny. Thee art slender," Mr. Gowthrop said with finality. Rachel knew that when he lapsed into Quaker talk there was no arguing with him.

While they waited for nature to take its course, the physician clipped a small bit of flesh under the baby's tongue which he said would have prevented Henry from speaking clearly and was the cause of an old ailment called being tonguetied. Mr. Gowthrop nodded with a smile of satisfaction. And when the laboratory report revealed that both children had worms, Mr. Gowthrop refrained from saying, "I told you so," but his triumphant expression proclaimed that he'd been right all along about the Philippines being "an uncivilized jungle full of monkeys running up and down trees." But both Grandma and Grandpa Gowthrop were taken aback by three-year-old Jean's Pidgin English: "Okay, okay, missy Jean go chop chop and see why baby Henry cry."

Despite household help, the constant presence of active young children was a strain for Rachel's parents, and she would have preferred living in the house she and Jim had built in Annapolis when he was teaching at the Naval Academy. Unfortunately, the Coe house was rented, and it would be some time before Rachel could get into it. By then, she kept telling herself, she wouldn't need it anyway; Jim would be home and they'd have duty elsewhere. His letters were cheerful, but it wasn't hard to read between the lines that he had been hoping and praying his orders would come before war did.

It wasn't hard to keep busy. First and foremost, the children were a full day's work. For diversion she played bridge and regaled her friends with tales of the China Station, including everybody's favorite. In Hongkong, when Rachel had asked the famous Jellybelly the Tailor, to make an exact copy of a suit she had, it came back complete with a mended cigarette hole in the skirt.

Her friends also enjoyed hearing about the nylon stockings sent to her in Manila in 1939. They were from the first batch ever made. Mr. Gowthrop was given some because he did a great deal of business with the Du Pont Company in Wilmington, where the product had been developed. With her interest in textiles, Rachel's fascination with the new synthetic had induced her to put on the girdle necessary to hold up the stockings and wear them downtown in the Manila heat. In one of the city's department stores, she created a sensation when a saleswoman exclaimed, "You're wearing stockings, but they're not silk." In moments, a group of store personnel gathered to feel Rachel's legs and exclaim over the miraculous new fabric. When she told them the hose were made of nylon, which was made from coal and air, they looked at her as if she was crazy. But the fiber soon went to war, becoming parachutes, glider towropes, and other essential items.

All of this was stopgap for Rachel as she marked time and wondered if the waiting period would ever end. She got her answer on December 7. Inheriting a bit of Quaker directness of her own when people talked nonsense, she got tired of answering the phone and repeating the same words endlessly: "No, I haven't heard anything from Jim. No, I don't know what happened at Pearl Harbor and have no way of finding out." She tried to be patient with her civilian friends, reminding herself that they knew little of military life and assumed that the wife of the captain of a submarine would have inside information. But even Rachel, who well remembered the pigboat stench that followed Jim home and the cramped torture chamber of an officer's mess, where she'd struggled through the diesel oil and turkey dinner during her pregnancy, was unable to imagine the impending voyage of the *39* as part of what the crew had started calling the R.A.F.—the Retreating Asiatic Fleet.

There was fierce competition for food throughout Manila and environs. Fearing the worst, the Army had sent officers from Corregidor into the city to buy up everything they could find and stockpile it on the docks until transportation arrived. Money talks even louder than usual in wartime, especially when it's gold, and the army had plenty of that. For all practical purposes, civilian firemen and police were almost nonfunctioning. Air raids had shattered street lights, so looting had begun, illuminated mostly by oil tanks burning on the

Pasig River. Flames splattered salmon pink against dark rain clouds, fitfully lighting thoroughfares empty of moving vehicles but filled with fleeing people toting baggage and heading for the docks. Even fishing bancas could demand and get 500 pesos per person for a ride out of Manila.

Nursing her wounds, *Canopus* was able to move to Mariveles, where she continued to service her young as best she could. Her crew had become so adroit at camouflage that they even set small fires burning on her decks so the enemy would think her too badly damaged to waste more bombs on. The cooperation of *Canopus* personnel and what remained of the Cavite Navy Yard work force enabled *39* to be patched enough to meet her schedule. By 29 December the boat had picked up spare parts and taken on fresh water, fuel, and provisions, the last consisting mostly of canned and dry goods. Fruit and vegetables had stopped coming into the markets of Manila as the enemy converged on the city. Coe was worried because the ship's supply of produce was scant. It was not regulation then for crews to carry vitamin C tablets, so scurvy was a genuine threat. The engines were still in bad shape but there was no help for that.

The last thing remaining to be done was a trip to Corregidor, where some torpedoes had been stored in underground tunnels allotted to the Navy. (Most replacement parts and torpedoes had to be left in warehouses on the docks of Manila because of the short evacuation notice given the Navy.) Monk Hendrix, in charge of procuring the "fish," took a party along with him that included Ed Schab. There was a badly bombed ship tied up at the Corregidor docks near the *39*, and on the way back from the tunnels, Hendrix decided to board the abandoned vessel just to have a look. Among the bits and pieces scattered about her decks were a few usable handguns. Schab remembered the officer who had advised him to take a gun and go hide in the hills, and he had a sudden impulse to possess a firearm. His reasoning was that if he had to abandon ship, he'd have some means of defense.

"Mr. Hendrix, is it okay if I take one of these guns?" Schab heard himself ask.

"There's nobody here to object," Hendrix said. "Go ahead."

When Schab got back to the *39* and had a few free minutes, he carefully cleaned the gun and wrapped it round and round with greasy rags to preserve it. Hendrix, catching sight of the operation said, "Schab, if we get captured you can be sure the Japs won't let you tote that gun along with you."

But that didn't deter Schab. He put it in his locker, which, like those of the rest of the naked crew, held little of anything else. Ed's had only a picture of Dorothy Reynolds and her last letter, ten months old, to which he added the weapon. Now and then, during the next few months, he'd take it out, examine it for rust, and put it back. It gave him a feeling of security.

Many of the crew had Filipina girlfriends who were more than casual acquaintances. During the crowded, hectic, dangerous ten days between patrols, these men made attempts to visit the scarred city, find their girls, and say goodbye. Allyn Christopher tried and failed. At 0200 on 30 December, the *39* passed through the U.S. minefield outside Manila Bay and started on patrol to Tablas Strait, about 150 miles away. There were men aboard the old sub who had a tight feeling in the chest and a dampness around the eyes. Quiet Zeke Matthews muttered, "Sure will miss that place, best place I ever knew," but cut it short when he saw Tayco and Fabricante. They were leaving not only friends but family and children behind. It was a subdued group that had gathered in the after battery compartment when COB Nave blustered in and called out, "What's for chow, Rocky? Make mine filet mignon and strawberry parfait smothered in whipped cream, like what I had last time I was in L.A. and went to the Coconut Grove."

Schoenrock pursed his lips in disgust, not even deigning to throw a glance Nave's way. It was painful enough for a cook to be short of foods that were merely life-sustaining, let alone be reminded of unattainable delicacies.

"Did I ever tell you about the time . . ." the honker continued.

"Stop shouting," Bixler interrupted, "the Japs can hear you. You wanna get us depth-charged?"

"Piss on the friggin' Japs," Nave said scornfully. Then, in an exaggerated whisper that cut across all other conversation, he added, "Betcha none of you guys ever took out one of them Wampus Baby Stars like I did. What a build." With curved hands he outlined 16-inch breasts jutting straight out from his chest. "Like watermelons, they were. That's who I took to the Coconut Grove." His triumphant expression said, match that if you can.

"Did the Wampum Baby Star take you for all your wampum?" Bixler jeered. It wasn't much of a joke, but everybody needed a gloom-buster, so it got more of a laugh than it deserved. Besides, it was at Nave's expense. Even the new guy off the *Sealion* laughed, Les Dean, who didn't like anybody much on *39* so far. But the loud-mouthed chief of the boat had served a purpose, and to do him credit he wasn't totally unaware of it. Everybody brightened. Schoenrock dared to face the question he'd been avoiding all afternoon: would navy beans taste okay if you seasoned them with chili powder and cumin, which he had on hand, instead of salt pork and molasses and onions, which he did not have? He'd try it and find out. It would have to be served as a meat substitute over rice. Not that he didn't have a little meat tucked away, but he was saving that to make something good when the going got rough.

Schoenrock wasn't the only one concerned with food. As they headed for Tablas Strait, the skipper was evolving a plan for picking up some of the fresh stuff they needed so badly. Coe, whose specialty was navigation, broke out one of the many charts he had indiscriminately scrounged from *Canopus*. He'd probably never use most of them, but the seas they would be sailing later they had never sailed before, and he'd need all the help he could get. Like Schab's gun, it gave him a good feeling to know he had them. Distance did not lend enchantment with main engine clutch problems developing, and after experiencing superefficient enemy air raids, Coe no longer had illusions that retreat would be simple.

After Christmas dinner, when 39 was sitting on the bottom of Manila Bay, Coe had started a letter to Rachel. He hoped to finish it later and mail it somewhere, sometime. It was only a hope, but he didn't tell her that. Instead, he scribbled, "By now you must know, my darling, that censorship is in full swing. There's not much I can say, but I think of you and the children often. Things are quiet, I'm in excellent health and don't worry. . . ." He was sure that Bernard, Hendrix, Gugliotta, and the crew all had half-finished, dumb-sounding, fake-cheery letters stashed away in their lockers, too, hoping they'd be mailed someday but finding it hard to believe.

Smoothing out the chart on the wardroom table, Coe picked out the tiny barrio of San Agustín at the entrance to Tablas Strait. The 39 had neither pesos nor gold nor yen, and the American dollar would be worthless. But this close to Luzon, the villagers of San Agustín were probably not Moros or headhunters; they might even be cooperative. If not, Coe wasn't above stealing whatever he could get, because he knew that a seaside town of few inhabitants had an ever-present supply of fish, rice, and fresh fruit. The venture might not appear in his patrol report, but he had already decided that some things were his own business.

He sent for Bernard and Schoenrock. When they arrived Coe swung right into his plan. "We'll be close to the town of San Agustín within the hour. They're bound to have supplies we can use. There may not be much choice of fruits and vegetables, but what do you need the most, Schoenrock? I'm going to send Mr. Bernard in the wherry with Tayco or Fabricante as interpreter. Don't forget how small the wherry is and it will already have two people in it. If we should be lucky enough to find a lot of food, what items would take priority?"

Schoenrock turned the question over in his mind while the skipper and exec waited for the oracle to speak. "Onions, pineapples, limes. They keep good and go a long way. Bananas, mangos, and papayas spoil fast, especially in the heat we got submerged. Taro and breadfruit store good but the guys don't like them. But look," Schoenrock's expression turned from calculating to earnest, "don't turn anything down. If there's nothing but bananas bring bananas, a whole boatload. Anything but coconuts."

"Got that straight?" Coe asked Bernard.

"Yes, sir. I think I'll take Fabricante. He's smaller than Tayco—there'll be more space for food in the wherry."

Sound reported hearing nothing suspicious in the area, and the night was as black as a night could be. After surfacing, Bernard did some more intensive listening before he climbed into the wherry and signaled Fabricante to follow.

The dip-dip of oars was the only noise except for the rustle of coconut palms when they neared the beach. As Larry dragged the wherry up on the sand, Fabricante whispered, "Sair, if we see Tagalo peoples, I talk." Fabricante almost seemed to be enjoying himself, and Larry figured maybe the expedition gave him a slight edge over Tayco, a bit more importance.

It was eerie walking through the dark town, past nipa huts built on stilt legs below which even darker shadows lurked. Ladders had been drawn up, which meant that family members were tucked away for the night. A snort from a pigpen beneath the privy in the rear of one of the shacks made Larry jump. The town was only one block long, and the dirt road, muddy from recent rains, was slippery going. If they didn't meet up with somebody or something soon, they might have to climb trees and pick coconuts, which Schoenrock considered undesirable. They couldn't take forever, either; the skipper had asked them to be as quick as possible. General interest in the project had been roused on the boat and Larry did not look forward to going back empty-handed. They had almost reached the last structure at the end of town when Fabricante clutched Larry's arm and said, "Store, store."

Larry peered through the murk. Sure enough, the town's general store loomed before them, if anything so small could be said to loom. They had just started unlatching the woven bamboo shutters when Larry heard a rustle that didn't come from a palm tree. Looking back, he saw Fabricante face to face with a compatriot who had his hand on the vicious and efficient bolo knife thrust in his waistband. Non-English words were exchanged, and the stranger's tone did not sound entirely friendly. As the discussion went on and on, Larry grew impatient; time was being wasted. "Tell him we're Americans," he said to Fabricante. "Tell him the truth about our needing food and having to get away and all that."

Larry heard Fabricante invoking the name of San Juan, El Labrador, the patron saint of the Philippine farmer, to whom all gave thanks to ensure bountiful crops. Maybe Fabricante was threatening to ask San Juan to curse the fields if the native didn't share his food with the submariners. Whatever was said, it seemed to work; the townsman ushered them into the store, lighted a kerosene lamp, and helped carry the basketloads of food down to the wherry. They couldn't come up with onions, but pineapples, limes and other local produce would stave off scurvy for a while. Larry completed the mission by leaving an IOU with the storekeeper, which he promised to pay when the U.S. fleet returned to the Philippines. The native scratched his head over it, turning it this way and that, but it made Larry feel better, and he hoped he could keep the promise.

Tayco's turn to act as interpreter came next. For the first few days in the patrol area, Tablas Strait was as quiet as a church. Captain Coe was impatient. He was learning that a large percentage of war was waiting, but there wasn't much point in hanging around where nothing was going on or likely to be. He decided to send Hendrix to the town of Looc on Tablas Island, with Tayco as interpreter, to find out whether the locals had seen the enemy or any strange ships, especially those flying a flag with a rising sun. The nocturnal visit did not take long. Hendrix reported that they got the same negative answer from several townsmen: nothing unusual had been seen. Tayco added, "Captain, they say the truth. They know Japanese are here and we leave. Much they do not like this because they were almost free. Japanese will not let them free like Americans."

That same night Coe decided to post lookouts on peaks on the southeast coast of Tablas Island. One man would cover the strait from Tablas to Semirara Island; the other would keep watch from Looc Harbor to Mindoro Island. Bernard asked Nave to select two men to be rowed ashore before dawn and picked up after dark. Nave chose Christopher and Parks for the first day. Each one carried a firearm, a flashlight, and a simple code; their job was to give the *39* advance notice of any vessels approaching Looc Harbor. If the weather was clear during the day, they could see a distance of some 25 miles. After sunset, and before rendezvousing with the wherry, they could flash signals so that the submarine would be alerted to possible targets. The watch went on for six days, with changes of personnel. Comparing notes, Parks and Christopher agreed that it was lonely and scary on their separate mountain peaks, even in daylight. Any noise in the bush might be a Tagalo so surprised at seeing a stranger that he'd let loose with his bolo knife. But the descent down the mountainside in the dark was worse. You didn't know if that sudden rustling was your shipmate who'd been on the other peak, the enemy, headhunters, or a boa constrictor. Nothing was sighted.

On the last day of the mountain watch, while the boat was on her way to pick up the lookouts, she went aground near Looc Bay. Fortunately, she was going at slow speed and on the motors, allowing Hendrix to back the propellers so that the old pigboat barely hit bottom. But it was enough to bring the captain on the run, and sure enough, the sub was stuck in the muck to the point where it could not simply back off. Although the sound of aircraft was rare in the Tablas area, at that moment a plane was heard in the distance. The sound was hardly reassuring with the submarine on the surface and aground besides.

"Get all hands topside, we'll have to sally ship," Coe ordered.

Asleep in his bunk, Bill Hiland had been dreaming about his hometown in Ohio, but nobody had to wake him up. The impact of skull banging against bulkhead as the boat went aground put him right on his feet. Since the batteries were his babies, he immediately assumed that something had gone wrong with them, but as the crew poured through the hatch, he heard the captain say, "All hands go aft and on my signal run forward. When you reach the bow, run aft. Keep doing this until I tell you to stop."

The men obeyed with alacrity, the approaching aircraft acting as an extra

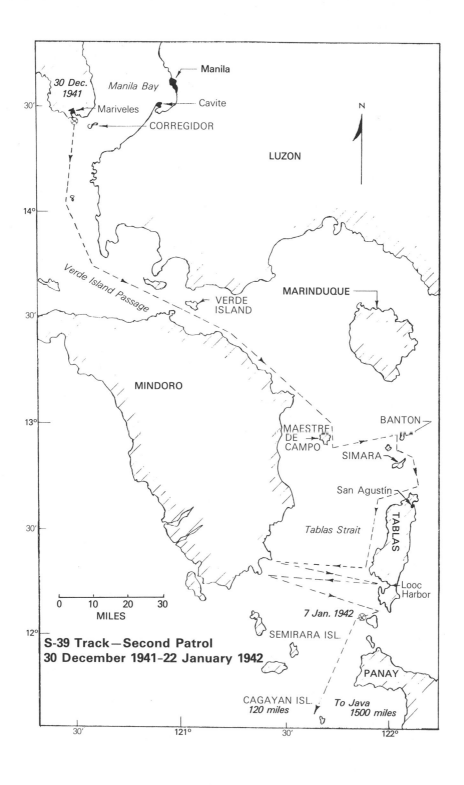

Manila

Manila Bay

30 Dec.
1941

Cavite

Mariveles

CORREGIDOR

LUZON

N

Verde Island Passage

VERDE
ISLAND

MARINDUQUE

MINDORO

BANTON

MAESTRE
DE
CAMPO

SIMARA

San Agustín

TABLAS

Tablas Strait

Looc
Harbor

0   10   20   30
MILES

7 Jan. 1942

SEMIRARA ISL.

S-39 Track—Second Patrol
30 December 1941–22 January 1942

PANAY

CAGAYAN ISL.
120 miles

To Java
1500 miles

30'

14°

30'

13°

30'

12°

30'   121°   30'   122°

incentive. The running back and forth gave the desired pitching motion, and Coe had just ordered the propellers full speed astern when someone exclaimed, "Holy Moses, it's an American plane, and it's gonna make a run on us." The P-40, no doubt sure that she had located an enemy sub, zoomed in. It was a heart-stopping moment, but the barechested skipper in his tattered shorts charged into the conning tower, grabbed the American flag, and got back out in time to wave it frantically at what may have been one of the last U.S. planes operating in the Philippines. The P-40 backed off without bombing or strafing, avoiding the kind of incident that would not be unknown as the war progressed. Noisy "whews" were heard as Coe ordered sallying resumed and went back to scratching the prickly heat around his ankles.

The rocking went on for almost an hour, the men making as little noise as possible to avoid alerting possible foes. Suddenly there was a small yelp and a stifled "Jesus Christ." Other half-smothered bleats followed; arms and legs were flailing about. Nave's sibilant stage whisper, "What the hell's the matter with you guys?" brought the answer, "I never seen a bee who went to sea before." It was the ultimate insult. A swarm of bees, changing residences, had somehow chosen the hapless 39 boat crew as honeycomb material. What with harassment from above by their own aircraft and from below by a swarm of bees, the men stepped even livelier. At last the boat broke free and was able to pick up Parks and Christopher, who had almost resigned themselves to the miserable thought that they had been marooned for sure.

Discussing the adventure later, Christopher asked Parks, "Suppose something had gone haywire and the boat never did come back to get us? Did you think of that?"

"I thought of it," Tom said.

"Can you picture me, a fair-skinned, blue-eyed Norwegian kid running around in a tattered G-string day after day, covered with blisters and sluffing off skin like a snake? I'd always stay pink and shining. No matter how many *baluts* I'd munch to prove I was just a friendly albino native, I'd end up with a bolo in the back. You're dark, you tan good, and you're not too tall. You'd be okay."

"Until I opened my mouth," Parks said laconically. "My Tagalog's pretty limited." The only bright spot had been the sandwich they took with them and the meal, such as it was, waiting when they got back at night. Schoenrock could no longer serve de luxe.

On the seventh day, the starboard engine clutch started slipping. All remaining adjustment was taken up, but next day the port clutch followed suit. Then both clutches slipped on battery charge. The machinist's mates toiled side by side with Chief Engineer Larry Bernard on repairs, which included turning out homemade eccentric bushings on the lathe and inserting S-springs. The bushings, made from Pennell's stolen hunk of brass, enabled them to gain a 1/16-inch additional adjustment to the port clutch—enough to hold, for a while. But clutch repair was a major job. It required the constant labor of turning, lifting, jacking up, and otherwise manhandling the heavy flywheel, clutch assembly, and more. All this performed in midget quarters, foul air, and a degree of heat that matched hellfire. Chief Machinist's Mate Paul Spencer and Jim Pennell worked 23 hours straight. Pennell resented the fact that nary a word of thanks was passed along to him from the skipper and that Spencer got all the credit. Pennell, intense at all times, was showing a testiness not unique during the discomforts of S-boat patrols.

The immediate problem had been temporarily corrected, but inspection revealed four cracked clutch shoes. Even Scalia, who had supreme confidence in his own ability, had to admit, "They gotta really be overhauled at a pro navy yard."

Coe decided to start working south toward Java as instructed. By this time the port clutch was the only one in operation, and although they were lucky to have it hold at two-thirds speed, it meant making six nautical miles per hour at the most. The 1,500-mile journey was going to be a long, slow take, and while it was going on, the Japanese would be consolidating their hold on the Philippines. But Coe, pondering *39*'s problems, had no time to brood over the enemy's progress. The boat was now carrying 46 men, four more than usual. There had to be utmost conservation of scarce food and water. There weren't enough bunks or stowage space. The leaks in the engine circulating water system continued, and the captain knew that if the boat was forced deep, as in depth-charge, the pressure would make the rupture of lines or failure of gaskets highly probable. Overhauling gate valves in the system was also beyond the ability of the ship's force. Two temporary patches on the skin of the old pigboat were potential casualties that could go at any time. The first was an 18-inch steel plate covering a 1-inch hole in the bottom of a fuel oil tank; the second was an 8½-inch plate welded over a ½-inch hole on top of the main drain, motor room aft. Increased water in the motor room bilge during all-day submergence indicated that this patch had already started leaking. Then there was the problem of ancient wiring combined with high humidity, causing frequent grounds in electrical gear. Repair around the clock was a constant drain on the electrician's mates.

So, in the kind of shape that would have required major surgery in peacetime, *S-39* began her long safari. There wasn't a man aboard who wasn't aware that if the Japanese had taken the Dutch East Indies by the time the old submarine got there, the future wasn't worth thinking about. They didn't complain, but Les Dean found himself disliking the setup more every minute and praying he'd be transferred to a fleet boat in Java. At first he didn't rate a bunk, so he slept on the deck in the torpedo room. Hot as it was, it wasn't as torrid as the bunk he was finally assigned, which turned out to be against the bulkhead and away from the passageway, where there was at least some slight circulation of the viscid stuff that pigboat sailors breathed submerged.

Finally, Danny Tella, one of the four Italian descent engineers (known aboard as the Black Watch), took pity on Dean and let him "hot bunk. Since Tella's bunk was on the passageway, this enabled Dean to get some sleep, but it didn't make him like the crew any better. And, as though they sensed it, they began making him the butt of some of their jokes. Dean knew he was letting it show that he felt the comedown from a brand-new fleet boat, and knew it was a mistake, but couldn't seem to stop. Tedium alternating with terror in malnourished bodies close to exhaustion created a breeding ground for fall guys. Dean became one.

7. Dutch Treat

On 8 January 1942, seven miles south of Cagayen Island, *39* sighted an unknown periscope broad on port bow, estimated range 6,000 yards. It had to be Japanese because no friendly subs, Dutch or British, were in the area. Coe and company hustled around until they got what they thought was a fair solution of the target course and speed. Coe called for Battle Stations Submerged and commenced the approach from about 6,000 yards. The enemy submarine's course was estimated to be about 135 degrees, speed 4 knots. After 28 minutes of tracking, they fired one torpedo set at 40 feet at an estimated 1,500 yards, then immediately went deep and made a radical course change because of indications that the Japanese sub had turned toward them preparatory to firing. Sound reported the fish was running straight, but no hit was heard. After 15 minutes of trying, sound was unable to pick up the enemy submarine, so Coe ordered periscope depth and searched for the target. He couldn't find him. An hour later *39* surfaced but still could not locate the other sub. She continued on her way, hoping for better chances at the enemy.

There were plenty of worries, but the prime concerns as the days went by were the ailing innards of the patchwork pig—requiring more and more labor with less and less success—and the shortage of potable water for drinking and cooking. What they had left began tasting of diesel gas and salt. Nothing disguised the flavor; it triumphed over coffee, and permeated rice or anything else cooked in it. It was hardly thirst-slaking but helped curb appetites—which was just as well, since there wasn't much to eat. Temperaments suffered. Bodies showed the lack of rest, sunshine, and vitamin C. Many men developed ulcerations on their legs behind the knees; later they were told that this was an early symptom of scurvy.

People worked off tension in different ways. Pennell had been hurting since late November after receiving word that his brother had died. He had always been interested in boxing and manipulated the gloves pretty well. Impressed by Kutscherowski's prowess and his having been a sparring partner for Billy Conn (a light heavyweight who had gone twelve rounds with Joe Louis), Pennell persuaded the big teddy bear, as he called Ski, to punch around with him. They did it with such zest that they frequently emptied the after battery room in less than a minute. But as the second patrol wended its weary way, and Pennell lost track of days and dates from working around the clock on disintegrating machinery, he began to show strain. His one consolation had been that the small amount of time spent in bunk, when he could cut loose from the torrid motor room, compensated for everything because he shared an electric fan with a lanky gunner's mate striker, Arky Sturtevant. Suddenly Sturtevant decided he wanted full use of the fan. After reasoning, begging, threatening, and explaining the concept of sharing, Pennell tried punching. Sturtevant returned it hot and heavy. It didn't last long, though, because a third party quickly inserted himself between the gladiators, and Pennell found himself trading glares with the old man. A reprimand from J.W. Coe cooled the atmosphere fast, fan or no fan.

Larry Bernard's sense of humor, which generally favored the whimsical, became more satirical. Although the nightly surfacing for battery charge brought relief from the heat, war conditions and the S-boat's lack of radar did not permit a general exodus of the crew topside to gulp fresh air and cool off frazzled nerves. Only the watch was allowed on the bridge, consisting of the officer of the deck, a couple of lookouts, and the quartermaster. This small group enabled the officer of the deck to count noses fast (which he literally had to do aloud) if a quick dive became necessary. For the same reason, only the bridge hatch was kept open. Even the captain had to announce his intention before setting foot on the bridge. However, the O.D. might allow one or two others to "come up for air" if he thought it safe and knew they'd been working hard without a break.

After having been below for a number of days, Jim Pennell requested permission to come on deck, and Bernard granted it. Soon after pushing through the hatch and enjoying the luxury of a few draughts of clean air, the machinist's mate asked the engineering officer where they'd be headed in the morning. Larry struggled with temptation, lost, and couldn't resist saying in a quaking voice accompanied by dramatic gestures, "We're going out to meet the enemy." The startled Pennell was not quite sure how to take it.

Monk Hendrix set an example for everybody by doing an incredible number and variety of setting-up exercises in the torpedo room or after battery whenever possible. He made it look effortless as he smiled his way through as long a session as patrol conditions would permit. Restricted space prevented him from holding mass calisthenics, but he talked up fitness to each and every man, and seemed to have the same amount of energy no matter how sparse the food became.

Earl Nave profaned the sacred more frequently than ever before. A heavy smoker, he'd had a small cough that now began erupting into hacking bouts that left him unable to talk for a minute. His detractors, taking unfair advantage, claimed that fear could make a man lose his voice and that the chief of the boat could be cracking up. His supporters noticed that Nave seemed to be dropping flesh even faster than the average weight loss of 15 pounds per man per patrol. The gaunt look was universal.

Little irritations loomed larger. Men who played poker, cribbage, or acey-deucey were more likely to flare up when losing or gloat harder when winning. People who smelled, which meant everybody, sometimes complained about other people who smelled. The only clean-off available was a little torpedo alcohol applied to the rankest spots. Water was much too precious to waste on washing bodies or clothes. The lashing tropical rains they'd all bitched about in peacetime were prayed for now so that during the nightly battery charge a tarpaulin could be rigged on deck abaft the bridge to catch the badly needed downpour. It was manna from heaven, this clean-tasting wet stuff, especially with the engines pooping out and the voyage getting slower and slower. Water could keep men alive long after food had ceased to matter. It could keep batteries alive, too, but there was only a limited amount left of the required distilled type. If *39* ran out of it, they'd be forced to use potable even though it harmed the batteries.

Reading, an ever popular diversion, was limited by lack of new material. In the haste of the exodus from the Philippines, food and spare parts had taken precedence for space available. What had been aboard to read at the time of departure had been aboard through the first patrol and before, and was still aboard unaugmented. Drooping old copies of *Reader's Digest* were thumbed again and again, and the *Saturday Evening Post*, especially issues containing Alec Hudson's submarine stories, began falling apart in the excessively hot and humid conditions. There were too few "Pocketbooks," such as Zane Grey westerns and Earl Derr Biggers's and Charlie Chan detective stories, and not nearly enough long-lasting blockbuster novels. Margaret Mitchell's *Gone With The Wind*, Kenneth Roberts's *Oliver Wiswell*, Hervey Allen's *Anthony Adverse*, and Rachel Field's *All This and Heaven Too* were read and reread; competition was fierce to see who would get them next. Even a dozen old 1938 copies of Submarine Squadron Five's weekly newspaper, the *ISWAS*, experienced a revival until the tattered pages fell apart. Nor was there much possibility of finding anything new if and when they ever reached Java; with so many ships headed that way, there wouldn't be enough available in English to go around.

In peacetime, Ed Schab had enjoyed looking through the glass portholes in the conning tower for diversion. He never saw much but bubbles and seaweed, but he played a little game: he'd pretend he was intrepid explorer of the deep William Beebe in his bathysphere, gathering material for his book *A Half Mile Down*. Schab hadn't read it, but he liked the title. Now, even this harmless pastime was no longer possible. Steel plates had been welded over the portholes to prevent their shattering during a depth charge. The men of *39* were learning that war is hell in little ways as well as big ones.

Each man had his own style of thinking about the life he was living. Tom Parks, who kept working through his frowzy copies of Kipling et al., again and again, declared to Scalia, "Patrol runs are days and days of boredom interspersed with moments of sheer terror." Scalia, vociferous but not poetic, responded, "You said it, kid." Zeke Matthews, never much of a yakker, just nodded his head in assent.

Les Dean brooded even more about the nasty cracks made at his expense. He thought that the crew in general, and the engine-room people in particular, did too much sneering and jeering. If he made a slip, it was particularly galling to be ridiculed in front of the commanding officer and exec. One time, oil can in hand, he was about to check an oil cup under the deck plates. Hitting a finger hole first to pull up the plate, he heard a guffaw behind him and a loud, "Looka him will you. Izzat what they do on them fleet boats, Dean, oil the finger holes first? What craphouse elegance." And another voice joined the chorus: "*Sealion* sailors was specially chosen because they're so smart. They hadda pass a oiling-the-finger-hole test." Convulsive laughter followed.

Dean had learned not to talk back because his words were bent out of shape every time. He seethed in silence, and thought, Watch my smoke, you bastards, when we get to Java. I'll get off this tub fast and back to the big time with decent people. The only guy he could talk to, the only crew member who didn't twist his words, was Bob Norton in the torpedo room. Otherwise nobody loved Les Dean, and Les Dean loved nobody.

Everybody began looking like unbaked bread to Schoenrock. Even Tayco and Fabricante seemed pallid from living all daylight hours submerged. Rocky was only making two meals a day now, and those were not the best. Because there could be little work done submerged, Coe decided to try reversing schedule. Dinner was served in the morning when everybody could hole up afterward and divert energy to digesting the big meal. Breakfast was served at night when activity took place in the cooled-off, oxygen-renewed atmosphere. But as dinner got smaller and duller, it didn't seem to matter much. Rocky had long since used up the fresh fruits and vegetables from San Agustín. The only meat left was corned and canned, plus a small amount of dried chipped beef; the latter, creamed and served on toast, the crew called "snot and foreskins," which appellation infuriated the sensitive cook. He informed the men haughtily that he'd run out of the canned milk needed to make the dish and they'd be thinking

Submarine Tender USS *Canopus* with Submarine Division 201; *S-39* on the far right. *National Archives*

Above and opposite (top), *S-39* in the Far East on the eve of the war. *Courtesy of U.S. Naval Institute*. Opposite (bottom), a ship's party at Tsingtao, 1939.

Above, S-boat cleanup day. Below, *S-39*.

Personnel of the *S-39*, 1940.

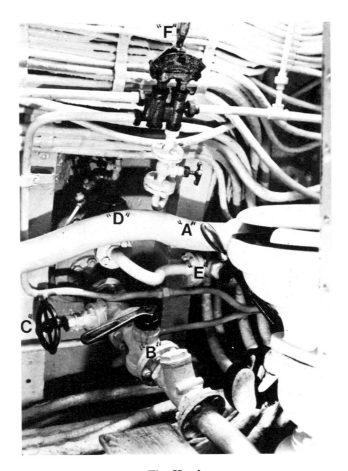

The Head
Directions for operating

A. Before using
See that:

1. Bowl flapper valve "A" is closed.
2. Valve "C" in discharge line is open.
3. Valve "D" and sea valve in water supply line are open.
4. Then open valve "E" next to bowl to admit necessary water.
5. Close valve "E".

B. After using

6. Pull lever "A" up.
7. Release lever "A" and *hold down*.
8. Rock air valve "F" lever to charge.
9. Position to charge measuring tank 10 lbs above sea pressure.
10. Open plug cock "B" in discharge pipe line.
11. Rock air valve lever to blow.
12. Position to blow overboard.
13. Close plug cock "B"

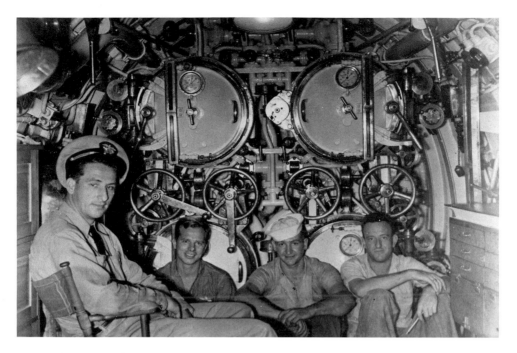

Above, torpedo room of the *S-39,* looking forward at torpedo tubes. From left, Klinker, Bixler, Sappington, Nave. Below, captain's inspection (Coe).

Right, James W. (Red) Coe. Below, Coe with infant son in Manila. At bottom, Rachel Coe in Shanghai.

Above, left, Larry Bernard; right, Caroline
Bernard. Below, right, Dottie Lautrup.

Below, Les Dean. At right, Frank Gierhart. Bottom, U.S. Navy Enlisted Men's Club, Tsingtao

Top left, Guy Gugliotta; right, Anne Gugliotta, WAVE ensign. Below, Bobette Gugliotta at the New York headquarters of American Women's Voluntary Service.

Above, Edward (Zeke)
Matthews (left) and Allyn
Christopher. At right, Jim
Pennell.

At left, Richard Ellis. Below, left,
Tom Parks; right, Corenne Ward
Parks.

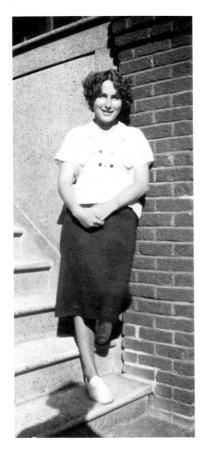

Above, left, Dorothy Reynolds Schab; right, Ed Schab. Below, Slick's Bar and Grill, Tsingtao.

Above, a softball game between *S-38* and *S-39*. Below, left, Wreford G. (Moon) Chapple; right, Mike Kutscherowski

Allyn Christopher (left) and Ed Schab. Below, Ed Schab with Browning automatic machinegun.

Top left, Pop Bridges; right, Bill Hiland. Below, Keeven M. (Gunner) Hurtt.

Left, Bill Harris. Above, Paul Bryan with depth charge launcher. Below, Earl Nave (left) and Bob Bixler loading torpedoes.

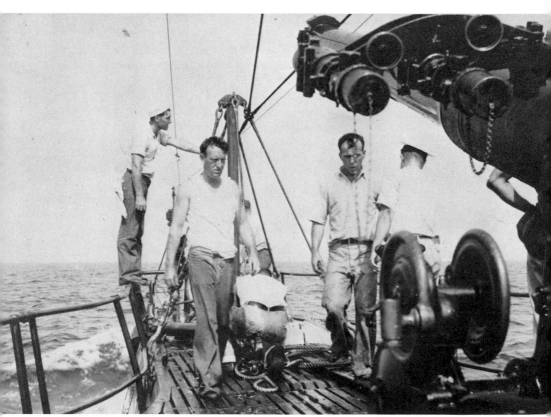

Above, left, Pop Bridges and Dutch
Mandekic; right, Stanley (Dutch) Mandekic.
Below, Earl Nave.

Above, J.T. Lebow. Right, Minnie
Jeanne Nozero Lebow.

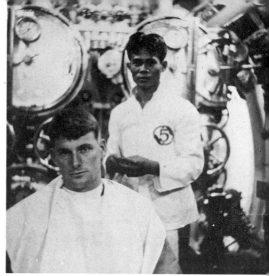

Right, Lyman C.
(Swede) Bloom. Above,
left, Amador Tayco;
right, Cecilio Fabricante,
doubling as barber.

Left, Charles (Monk) Hendrix. Above, Francis E. Brown. *U.S. Naval Academy.* Below, Walter L. (Rocky) Schoenrock

Above, rescue boats approaching *Katoomba*. Below, left, *S-39* survivors aboard *Katoomba*; right, Dan Dryer, Australian radioman who heard *S-39's* call

Above, *S-39* crew on board *Katoomba*. Below, *S-39* abandoned on the reef

of it with longing before they reached Java. But what everybody was really thinking of was beer—great, foaming schooners of it that left the lips white and sticky and the belly bloated.

The *39* had been ordered to delay en route to Java and patrol for a while off Balikpapan, Borneo, but the order was canceled because the clutch problems were getting worse all the time. Instead, *39* was told to head directly for Soerabaja and the navy yard there. But with the starboard engine clutch completely inoperative and the port engine, running at two-thirds speed, being used for both propulsion and battery charging, could they make the Dutch East Indies? Larry Bernard and his engineers alternately cursed and prayed over that port clutch because it had reached the limit of adjustment. By the time *39* limped in to meet her escort in Madura Strait, hacksaw blades, chisel points, and other odd pieces of metal had been used as contrivances to keep her engine and shaft clutched together. The last three days en route to Soerabaja were made with sandpaper inserted at the clutch shoe faces to keep the surfaces from slipping.

As *39* came in, her bleached-out crew came on deck to feast their eyes on the island of Java and its sparkling white houses with red roofs set off by emerald greenery. Flagpoles in almost every yard flew the Netherlands ensign; its red, white, and blue gave a homey touch. After weeks of traveling submerged, it didn't take long for the men's pale skin to burn from the tropical sun reflecting on the water. But it hurt good; nobody wanted to go below no matter how badly he blistered. They could hardly wait to go ashore. Christopher said, "Ice cream." Gugliotta said, "Oranges." Hendrix said, "Showers." And Schoenrock, speaking for everyone, said, "Beer." It was 22 January. Unfortunately, in little more than a month, the East Indies would fall to the Japanese.

The first person on board as they tied up was their assistant paymaster, whom they had last seen on *Canopus* in Manila and had hardly dared hope they'd see again. Considering the beating the tender had taken, Lieutenant Charles Osborne was just as glad he was alive as they were. Everyone's eyes switched to the bulging, mail-carrier-sized bag Osborne had slung over one shoulder. He conferred with Coe, then said, "Please line up alphabetically while I set up shop here on the main deck. If I can persuade a couple of men to procure a couple of benches, or whatever else they can find, to make a seat and desk for me, I'll see that you all get paid." There were so many volunteers they were trampling on one another's feet.

Osborne was soon in business and didn't seem to mind the smelly, un-civilized-looking creatures who extended sweaty palms black with grease and grime to receive the most beautiful greenery of all, U.S. dollars. He had no pay records but simply asked, "What did you get last time?" Then he calculated by two-week periods, with a table he had ready as a multiplier, what each individual was owed since his last payday. When somebody called out, "What would the Bureau of Supplies and Accounts think of this, sir?" Osborne replied with a grin, "I'd be court-martialed. Don't anybody let on, huh?" The secret was safe. In gratitude nobody even uttered the traditional term for payday, The Eagle Shits.

True to his dream, the first thing Gugliotta did was to buy a slew of oranges, which he wolfed as he walked down the streets of the navy yard. He was not alone. The citrus-starved officers and crew couldn't get enough of the wonderful stuff. About half a mile away from the docks, where open, grassy, tree-bordered acres looked more like the grounds of a private estate than a service installation, the Dutch navy had quarters. These were modern, well-built barracks for enlisted personnel and large, comfortable rooms and apartments for officers, which the Dutch were generously sharing with their U.S. counterparts. Lieutenants Bernard and Gugliotta immediately headed for the showers and scrubbed to their heart's content. (They were startled by the toilets, which contained a rack of liter-sized bottles of water instead of the usual rolls of tissue. Once the routine became evident, they decided to carry their own paper.) By borrowing here and there, they managed to scrape together enough clean clothes to make a presentable uniform, and with that they took off for town.

At that time, Soerabaja's population numbered some 300,000; it was a cosmopolitan city of theatres, museums, restaurants, and sidewalk cafes. After a bit of sightseeing, Larry and Guy dropped into the nearest cafe and ordered a native curry that was so hot it almost blew their heads off but furnished a wonderful excuse for downing quantities of the inimitable Dutch beer. It was still possible to forget, for a few hours, that there was a war on. They were so glad to be alive, clean, and comfortable that they didn't even comment on the strangeness of a society that was conducting business as usual with the Japanese breathing down their necks. The Dutch masters of Java seemed such slaves to the easy routines and established traditions of colonial rule that they also seemed blind to how quickly it would all be swept away.

That night, for the first time, Bernard and Gugliotta experienced the joys of a "Dutch wife." Soerabaja, 6 degrees south of the equator, was so torrid that it made Manila cool by contrast. With no air-conditioning, the Dutch had invented an oblong bolster, about three feet long, that could be clutched between the thighs or clasped to the chest to absorb heat during sleep—a welcome device.

The next day, Gugliotta and Bernard found they were slated for a spell at a rest camp and also discovered that it was still possible to make phone calls home. They took off for the cable office and lined up with scores of other Americans waiting their turn. The lines were clear, the voices distinct; many women wept with joy that day and could scarcely utter a word, so happy were they to find sons, husbands, or sweethearts alive, even though censorship forbade the men from disclosing their location. But Caroline Bernard had plenty to talk about when the call came from Java. The baby was on his feet and running. She had sent pictures, but of course Larry hadn't received them. She would send more, but where? Oh, in care of the Fleet Post Office, San Francisco. Okay. Larry's whole family was gathered in the kitchen listening to the conversation, so there wasn't much privacy, or time either, but that didn't matter. The next day Caroline went to church, as she had every day since the start of the war and would until it ended. There she prayed and lit a candle for her husband's safe return.

Bobette Gugliotta was totally unprepared for the telephone call from Soerabaja. To begin with, she had never talked at such a long distance in her life and hadn't even realized it was possible under wartime conditions. When she heard Guy's voice saying, "I'm okay, I'm fine, how are you?" she could scarcely clear her throat in time to utter the banality, "I'm fine, too." Nor could she think of another thing to add, because small talk just didn't seem to fit the occasion. But the call ended soon enough.

One of the nicest parts of the experience was sharing it with Guy's family. When she telephoned her sister-in-law Anne in New Jersey, it was amazing how much more Bobette remembered of what she'd said to Guy than she actually did say. It was what she would have liked to say, if only she'd kept her wits about her and not been choked up. Harmless poetic exagerration.

Dorothy Reynolds didn't dislike her secretarial job at Owens, Illinois Glass in Oakland, although she'd been restless and wanting to do something different and exciting for a long time. But everybody had been saying that war was likely to break out at any moment, and it did. Dorothy still had plenty of dates and loved dancing to big-band music at the Bal Tabarin ballroom in San Francisco, but there had to be more to life than this. She was almost 21 now, still living at home, and although several men had mentioned wedding bells, she had made a silent pledge not to marry until she'd had a chance to see Ed Schab again, the fellow she'd met at the roller rink when she was only 16. That is, if she ever got the chance.

What really made her dissatisfied was having her brother announce one night at supper that he'd joined the Marines and, as soon as he finished boot camp, expected orders overseas. Young enough to forget the dangers, Dorothy envied him. For years she had longed for a tornado to whirl her away, like her namesake in *The Wizard of Oz*, to Spain, France, or Hawaii, and whenever she was in San Francisco and saw the big ocean liners tied up at the docks, she imagined sauntering up the gangplank to go someplace, anyplace, amidst a flurry of farewells and friends yelling, "Don't forget to write." Then she came back to reality with a thump, especially when she passed recruiting posters with slogans like "Join the Navy and See the World" and realized that the military was for men only, and that a girl from a family that didn't have money to throw around might just as well forget going anywhere more exotic than Lily Coit tower.

And then one day when Dorothy was on her lunch hour, somebody left a *Time* magazine on the counter of Walgreen's Drugstore where, for 20 cents, she was polishing off a giant hot dog laced with sauerkraut plus a large cherry Coke. Glancing down at the open pages while she slathered mustard on the roll, she read that a woman named Oveta Culp Hobby had been asked by Chief-of-Staff George Marshall to map out plans for a Women's Army Auxiliary Corps. This would be a real departure because, aside from nurses, the Army had never accepted women, although in World War I the navy had yeomanettes and the marines had marinettes, but for clerical duty only.

A great resolve was forming in Dorothy's mind. She would keep tabs on this Oveta Culp Hobby and watch the papers for further news. The minute the "go" sign came, Dorothy would heist herself down to the nearest recruiting office. Most important would be the travel, especially if you could go overseas. As she paid her bill and bought an O. Henry bar for an afternoon snack, she wondered what the uniforms would look like, whether you could wear makeup, and how short you'd have to cut your hair. But when the world marched to war, the bill to create the WAAC had not yet been passed.

Dorothy kept hoping she'd hear that the servicemen she'd known were okay. She hadn't heard from Ed Schab for several months, nor had she writtten him for a long time, but she wasn't particularly worried about him. A boat to her was a great big imposing vessel that floated on the water, carrying the rich and famous to gay Paree or Rio by the Seeo. A pigboat, which was what Ed had called his submarine in his last letter, was so remote from her youthful experience that its perils were unimaginable.

Half the *39*'s crew and all the officers except Hendrix were sent to a rest camp in Malang, in the mountains behind Soerabaja, where cool breezes blew through the lush countryside and only an occasional Japanese plane was heard. Then, on 3 February, the war hit Soerabaja with a bang. Bombings increased in intensity daily.

Hendrix, left in charge of repairs, was impressed by the Javanese workmen. With Stone Age equipment and man's most ancient tool, bare hands, they did an accurate and thorough job. The Dutch Navy Yard had covered piers, nicely spaced, enabling the submarine to come alongside the dock with ease and go about her refit without being delayed, or drowned, by tropical rain showers. The neatness, tidiness, cleanliness of the whole setup was a tonic to Monk after the catch-as-catch-can, lucky-to-be-alive journey. Although the repair facilities were overloaded by American, British, and Dutch vessels, extra delays to the *S-39* were caused by the Javanese workmen's terror of submerging alongside the dock. The minute the air raid siren went off, the workmen would come pouring out of the hatches, leap across the deck as fast as their short legs could go, and head for the air raid shelters. Some bypassed the sturdy, beehive-shaped steel and concrete shelters and ran to crouch down in open fields, seeming to derive comfort from proximity to Mother Earth.

Monk worked out a solution by putting one chief petty officer on the engine room hatch, another on the forward torpedo room hatch, and himself on the bridge. The instant the alarm sounded, the two chiefs and Ensign Hendrix scooted down the hatches, secured them, and flooded down the boat. But the workmen never accepted the idea that they were much safer inside a submarine with water closing over their heads. Pennell was delegated to reassure them, and coax them into continuing to work on clutches and other machinery while submerged. Much of this was in pantomime because of language barriers.

Hendrix became friendly with a young English-speaking Javanese foreman who had great curiosity about the American way of life. He had completed high school and several years of special training. Monk was impressed with how much he knew about engineering and how much more he wanted to learn, including trigonometry and calculus.

The conversations progressed to life in the Indies, and the foreman, very bitter, said that the Dutch ruled his people with an iron hand and treated them like dogs most of the time. Natives were not allowed to speak Dutch, among themselves or with their masters, but could only converse in the indigenous language. The officers and crew of the *39* had immediately been told, "Don't spoil the natives. Stop giving them food, money, and souvenirs." Although people of color in the U.S. Navy at the start of World War II did not have equality, since they were permitted only the rating of mess steward, this kind of approach had not been usual in the Philippines. To be fair to the Dutch, those of mixed native and European blood were socially accepted. But looked at another way, it could be construed as the ultimate in racism to assume that the so-called taint of native blood was automatically erased by the addition of white. An Indonesian independence movement had begun to smolder early in the twentieth century but did not catch fire until 1940. The advent of the Japanese was only a brief interruption to the people who had waited centuries to rule their own land. In 1945 the Nationalists would proclaim the Republic of Indonesia.

Frank Gierhart, displaced *Sealion* sailor, had been lucky to hitch a ride on the *38* to Soerabaja, where Moon Chapple left her. Gierhart had hoped to stay aboard the *S-38* as a replacement for a radioman who wanted off, but in this instance his luck didn't hold. Another homeless *Sealion* sailor and former *38* boat man, Ray Barnham, got the nod. Gierhart was sent to the staff of ComSubs Asiatic but was constantly on the lookout for another boat. He didn't like staff duty or the idea of being left behind in Java any more than he'd liked the idea of being left behind in the Philippines.

ComSubs Asiatic was modestly headquartered in a house in the suburbs of Soerabaja, with radio receiver set up in a garage. Gierhart was constantly aware

of the relentless advance of Japanese forces. They had steamrollered the Philippines, Celebes, and Borneo; according to all indications they would soon do the
same to Sumatra and Java. The waiting period wasn't all bad for Gierhart,
though. He found not only the Dutch navy but local civilians friendly, and had
the good fortune to meet an attractive Dutch girl, Mary Moelenkamp. He was
welcomed by Mary's family, and the romance progressed to the point where
marriage was discussed. And then 39's radioman, Harris, was sent to the
hospital, and Frank Gierhart was given the choice of remaining on the staff or
replacing Harris. Despite the charms of Mary Moelenkamp, he accepted 39 boat
duty with alacrity. He and the young woman planned to take up where they'd left
off—sometime in the future, in some other place.

J.T. Lebow, radioman, also found himself helping set up communications
headquarters for subs fleeing the Philippines. Although his stay in Soerabaja
was short, he was there long enough to make some observations. He noticed that
Javanese prostitutes, though frequently no more than 11 or 12 years old, had body
development far in advance of early puberty, and that the going rate for their
services was one gilder, about 16 cents. He also found that he had to alter his
appearance. One of the few sailors sporting a beard in the itchy-steamy weather,
J.T. was forced to shave it off because every time he went into town, kids
followed him around pointing and tittering, probably thinking he was one of the
disciples they had seen pictures of in missionary Sunday Schools.

And then, the Japanese were so close that J.T. and others were called in not
to construct but to destruct, trying to render the Dutch naval base useless. They
smashed equipment that might aid and comfort the enemy, and blew up oil tanks
(unfortunately, most of the oil reserves were stored in the interior of the island,
and there was no time to reach them). Fate did not steer Lebow to the S-39 just
yet. For now, he was off and running, this time to Darwin, Australia, where an
attempt by the Americans to set up communications would be just as ill-fated as
it had been in Soerabaja. Lebow had really planned to drop a line to that nice
Minnie Jeanne Nozero back in California; he knew she'd worry about him. But
he couldn't spare the time—the heat was on.

The small, dark-haired girl rubbed sleep out of her eyes and climbed aboard
the bus that would take her to Chaffey Junior College in Ontario, California.
Minnie Jeanne was wearing a sweater and skirt but had discarded her high
school bobby socks and saddle shoes to don high heels and rayons. The wartime
rayon stockings had a tendency to bag no matter how tight you rolled them or
how high up you snapped them on your garter belt, but she was saving her few
pairs of nylons for the day when J.T. Lebow came home on leave. She wasn't in
love with him, she reminded herself, looking wistfully out the window at the flat
southern California landscape, mostly because she hadn't seen or heard from

him for such a long time. Funny how they'd met. Minnie and her mother had been on the train en route to her grandma's funeral when the fast-talking young sailor struck up a club car conversation. Minnie Jeanne had never met anybody like him and was spellbound. But Mrs. Nozero didn't think much of the non-Catholic, wild and ornery Texan, and neither did her conservative, Italian-born husband when he met him later on. When Pearl Harbor rocked the world, it barely twitched the little inland town of Etiwanda that the Nozero family called home. The even more remote Asiatic Station, from whence the notorious J.T. had mailed a handful of letters to their only child during the last couple of years, was so far away it wasn't on the mental map.

At Chaffey Junior College Minnie had acquired another boyfriend of sorts, who was about to join the Navy. She went to dances with him once in a while but sat out the jitterbug numbers. More romantic pieces like "Paper Doll" were her favorites, especially when played by Glenn Miller. The friend mentioned marriage. Minnie wasn't interested. First there was school and her determination to graduate and follow up with work as a legal secretary. And then there was J.T., although she had no idea where he was.

Minnie Jeanne's early indifference to the war had disappeared as her knowledge of the situation increased. Many of the fellows at Chaffey were enrolling in the V-12 naval air program, which would enable them to continue their schooling, since the junior college specialized in aeronautical engineering. Minnie was absorbing a lot of talk about the glamor of pilots and planes in the wild blue yonder. Submarines were grubby, anonymous plodders for the moment.

Tom Parks, along with other crew members, returned to the shipyard after a few days at rest camp in Malang. While enjoying cool breezes in the mountains, he had struck up a friendship with a Dutch sailor who spoke English, and the sailor gave him a note of introduction to his parents in Soerabaja. Parks and several shipmates visited them, but the Dutch couple made it obvious that they didn't approve of the Americans. After an uncomfortable half-hour, the young men departed. In contrast, Tom found the Dutch sailors warm and friendly, confirming his observation that special bonds exist between seafaring men of all nationalities, especially submariners.

Parks had been hoping since arrival in Soerabaja to have news of the *Langley* and brother Jim. The antiquated carrier, the Navy's first, known to her crew as the "covered wagon," was also the slowpoke of the seas. Parks comforted himself with the thought that *Langley* would eventually make it, she would just take a little longer getting there, same as the equally antiquated *39* boat had. He knew *Langley* was slated for Java along with the British carrier *Seawitch*. But when all hell broke loose on 4 February, and the Japanese dealt

Admiral Hart's allied ABDA (American, British, Dutch, Australian) Fleet a death blow that started by knocking out *Houston* and *Marblehead*, a chain reaction was set up. One after another went down like ninepins, smashed by the enemy.

Then Tom Parks went down, too, felled by severe food poisoning. He had to be transferred to the hospital shortly before *39* was due to leave. With his body acting the way it was, he knew he'd be left behind. As all these misfortunes piled up, it was just as well that Parks had no way of knowing that on 27 February the *Langley* would be so severely damaged that she would have to be scuttled. Most of her crew and aviation personnel were rescued, but Tom's brother, Jim Parks, was among the 16 lost.

As work on the *39* accelerated, the tempo and atmosphere began to resemble the last days of Manila. Air raids increased, and more and more submarines competed for scarce parts, experienced workmen, and enough food to see them through to the next port—assuming they were lucky enough to find one that wasn't controlled by the enemy. Many Americans were mystified by what they considered the Dutch "ostrich" attitude. As yet nobody worked on weekends, and none of the white colonials, military personnel included, would dream of getting himself a cup of tea or a beer or lighting his own cigarette if he could find a native to do it, even though bombs were dropping all around. The attitude seemed to be, if we ignore the war, maybe it will go away.

There were Dutch submarines in port, and Gugliotta got to know a few of their officers. One evening, one of his Dutch friends invited Guy to dinner. As Gugliotta went aboard, he was greeted by the topside gangway watch, who informed him that the lieutenant was ashore. Gugliotta had heard that Dutch submariners were a very relaxed bunch, and the living proof was that his friend the duty officer was drinking beer at Modderlust, the naval officers' club. The astonished American also noticed that there were only about eight men on board, no officers, and all this while they were putting in a battery charge. In a short while his friend showed up, and the two men dined aboard as planned, exchanging sea stories. But it was an eye-opener in casualness for Gugliotta.

Allyn Christopher had enjoyed the spectacular scenery as he traveled the narrow-gauge railroad up the mountains to Malang. Although he couldn't get as much ice cream as he would have liked, the Dutch chocolate bars made a good substitute. It was possible to rent a bike in Malang, and Christopher and friends pumped up hill and down dale in the picturesque country. Every day a black German reconnaissance plane (on loan to the Japanese) would zoom overhead, but the rest camp had no strategic importance, so the pilot would buzz off again.

Once back at the navy yard, Christopher found the planes too close for comfort. As members of a work party, he and Zeke Matthews were sent to the pier for supplies one afternoon. Suddenly bombers swooped in, and the men were caught flat-footed out in the open. Matthews, not given to exaggeration, swore later that the planes were so close you could see the pilot in the cockpit; Christopher claimed you could see his eyelashes.

Matthews, of the large appetite, found that the smart move when an air raid alarm sounded was to head for the chief's quarters, where he could drink beer and munch pretzels, storing up calories for whatever deprivations might lie ahead in an uncertain future. Normal procedure for the *39* as soon as a raid started was to flood down alongside the dock and sit on the bottom to wait it out. There was enough depth to cover the boat completely, and watch was kept by periscope. If they had to stay on the surface because the status of repairs prevented closing some of the hull's openings, they hustled their portable 50-caliber machine guns up from below, mounted them on the bridge, and opened fire on enemy aircraft that came within range. They never hit anything, but it made them feel better. Dutch submariners were doing the same, with the same results.

Jim Pennell managed to make it to the rest camp at Malang for one day before everybody was recalled because of stepped-up attacks by the Japanese. If Pennell thought he had worked hard before, he now found that it had been only dress rehearsal. Repairs had to be completed fast, and *39* had to get out before the foe got in. Coe and company had nightmares in which the enemy captured them right there at the docks, completed the refit, painted a Japanese "I-boat" number on *39*'s hull, replaced the crew with their own, and sent the old pig out to sink American ships.

Most of the work had been completed when Pennell discovered heavy leakage in the starboard main motor lubricating lines. The fault was in two union joints so old that they could not be replaced by standard unions; the men had to improvise again, and time was all-important. The engineers endured endless hours and killing heat until the job was done, and one of them paid a high price. When Pennell, drenched in sweat and bleary-eyed, came up across the brow and fresh air hit him, he collapsed like a wet rag. He regained consciousness in a narrow, white bed in the Koenlike Kojoon (Royal Sick Corner) near the Dutch barracks. When he recovered, his belongings were transferred to Allied Head-quarters and so was he. The *39* had lost another member of her crew. Scalia would also be left behind.

Because S-boats had no fathometer, no pitometer log to indicate depth, distance, and speed, no radar, and no bridge pelorus that could be read in the dark, one of their greatest hazards was grounding. It was a particular problem in the shallow waters off the Philippines, Borneo, and Java when many of them were trying to make it to Soerabaja without adequate charts. Ancient explorers in sailing vessels had an easier navigational job than an aging submersible groping her way through unknown waters, pursued by a modern enemy fleet and aircraft, trying to stay concealed, and praying she'd be able to avoid the snarling scrape and sudden shock that meant grounding.

S-36 on her second patrol, was not fortunate enough to escape disaster. In the general retreat she had traveled more than 100 miles without being able to get a fix, and suddenly the boat was on its side, beating in the surf and badly holed. She had run aground on Taka Bakang Reef in Macassar Strait and was irretrievable. Machinist's Mate Swede Bloom, who hailed from a dairy farm in Wisconsin, was one of those on board her. He had just made chief when the war started, but in the melee that followed he had been unable to get the proper gear. Swede particularly craved the cap, that most important article of clothing that separates the men from the boys. It was Bloom's first grounding. He didn't know that it wouldn't be his last. He was able to salvage little by way of personal possessions. The only consolation was that he hadn't been able to buy his chief's cap yet so he couldn't lose it.

The officers and crew of *36* were picked up by a Dutch merchantman and taken on to Soerabaja. Swede was given the temporary job of helping the division engineer sort through and mete out spares of all kinds that individual submarines in Manila had garnered indiscriminately from *Canopus*. Now they were trying to determine which sub needed what and to furnish it, if possible. When time permitted, Bloom scurried around trying to locate that chief's cap. He couldn't find one. Then the air raids heated up and Bloom doubled as a gunner on a Dutch anti-aircraft 40-milimeter gun, since most of the natives, not feeling great responsibility to defend their Dutch masters, took to the hills. He was first loader, while Sam Hernandez, who had been chief of the boat on the *36,* swung the gun and a Dutch warrant officer acted as gun captain.

Bloom made friends with the warrant and was invited to his home. It was a smashing good evening. To begin with, the Dutchman's wife had invited one of her girlfriends for Bloom, who hadn't had the pleasure of a date since Manila. While they were all sitting on the porch drinking beer, the Japanese began bombing the docks close by. With Dutch aplomb—or foolhardiness, depending upon the point of view—the warrant officer simply crouched down by the porch railing, pulling his dog alongside him, and motioned the others to do the same. The roar of planes and exploding bombs shattered the tropical night. As an air raid shelter the porch lacked security, but the jolly companions hardly cared at that point.

Although Swede knew he was supposed to return from leave before midnight, and fully intended to do so, time went fast. Suddenly it was two o'clock in the morning. He made hasty farewells and hotfooted it over to the barracks where the displaced crew of the *S-36* was quartered. The base was blacked out as usual, so when he entered in the dark he didn't notice anything out of order at first. Then, groping for a cot, the utter quiet struck him. The usual squeaks, snores, bleeps, and bloops of sleeping men were missing. As Swede felt his way along the row of cots and touched empty after empty, the awful truth sank in.

The gray light of dawn enabled Bloom to get the story. While he had dallied at the warrant's house, the crew of *S-36* had been ordered to board a train, which would take them to a tender, which, in turn, would take them to Australia. It was much nicer down under right now than in Java. The date was 14 February. Bloom didn't know it, but Admiral Hart was relieved of his command that day—a valentine he didn't deserve—and the *39* set out on her third patrol. As luck would have it—good luck as far as Bloom was concerned, the untrustworthy old prima donna no sooner got out than she had to come back in because of a fuel leak. Bloom was disconsolately walking along the docks, wondering what would become of him, when he bumped into a body, looked up, and recognized Red Coe. Their surprise was mutual, and the captain asked, "What the devil are you doing here?"

Bloom told his dreary little story, feeling more sorry for himself by the minute but making it short because he could see that Coe was in a hurry.

"Want to go to sea with me?" Coe asked.

"Yes, sir, but I haven't any records or gear or anything."

Coe just motioned Bloom along, and they hopped aboard. Bloom felt good. It sure beat staying in Java, with Japanese prison camp a possibility in the very near future. He would have been completely content except for one thing. He still didn't have his chief's cap. Maybe next place, wherever next place might be.

There were a couple of conspirators aboard *39* as she set out once more after a quick repair. Schab, with his usual zest, had really enjoyed Soerabaja in spite of the bombings, the grueling work, and more heat rash covering his fair hide than he'd ever seen before. The beer had made up for everything, and by departure time Schab had gotten hold of 26 quarts of Heineken, everybody's favorite. Unlike Dutch submarines, American subs were not allowed to carry alcoholic beverages except for "medicinal brandy," which, in peacetime, had been truly used only in case of illness. But Schab thought of the hot-as-a-furnace pigboat and the long days at sea. He thought of the simple truth that every minute could be his last. He had never had a reputation as a boozer or a rowdy; in fact he was quite a nice guy. Was there any reason why a nice sailor, who never did anybody any harm, shouldn't have a little cache of the cooling, nourishing beverage that was even recommended for pregnant women?

The next step was getting it aboard (not too difficult) and hiding it (very difficult) somewhere safe. Twenty-six quarts would take a lot of space on a tight little submarine where inches counted. There was one catch in the plan for Schab; he just couldn't drink beer unless it was chilled, or cool anyway. He just couldn't get it down. He needed a place where the bottles could be snaked out one by one as the days went by and put into the refrigerator. That is, if the cook could be persuaded to let Schab use the refrigerator.

Schoenrock's consent came first, otherwise there was no point in even trying to bring the beer aboard. "Of course," Rocky agreed, "providing you share each bottle with me."

"That's exactly what I had in mind," Schab lied, "but where can we stash it?"

"Easy. Come on, I'll show you."

Rocky led the way to the forward battery room, glanced around to make sure nobody was watching, then pointed overhead. There was an adequate space right above the officer's wardroom—somehow that made the beer taste even better.

The designated patrol area for the *39* boat was a 60-mile square in the South China Sea not far from Singapore. It took five days to get there. They were uneventful for *39* as she made her way through Karimata Strait, except for sighting a submarine 2,000 yards on port bow on opposite course. They assumed the submarine to be the Dutch *K-12*, slated to pass them during the night en route to Soerabaja, but they dove anyway.

Those same five days were not uneventful for the Allies in the Far East; the disaster pattern continued unabated. Singapore fell on 15 February. Darwin, Australia, was so severely bombed that the port city had to be abandoned as a naval base the following day.

The euphoria of clean quarters and fresh food and drink that the men of *S-39* had found in Java was dissipating. They were back on the pigboat again, and although they were on patrol, they were also on the run. Nobody expected to return to Soerabaja, and doubts had begun to set in as to whether Australia would be available. Distraction was indicated. Coe, very much aware of morale and grateful that it had been so high, knew that the men needed a lift to keep it that way. A successful encounter would be good medicine in the midst of all the bad news. To be completely realistic, he felt that things would be a lot worse for the Allies before they got better. There weren't enough planes, ships, fuel, spare parts, workmen, or friendly ports. But there was no use dwelling on the irremediable.

For seven days *39* patrolled her 60-mile square, hoping to make contact with the enemy. The captain was getting tired of writing "Nothing sighted this date" in his report night after night. Among the crew, boredom and frustration led to griping about anything and everything. Schoenrock discovered that his occasional attempts to serve a canned stew they'd taken on in quantity in Soerabaja brought a flat refusal to eat it. Shaking a fist at everybody in general, Rocky yelled, "Whatsa matter with you jerks? They didn't have nothing else. The Dutch navy, the Limey navy, and our navy all needed food, yeah. We gotta stretch out our fresh stuff. You wanta get scurvy again?" The stew consisted of a can full of mashed potatoes into which a big meat sausage, made from strong-smelling mutton, had been rammed. The concoction bore the curiously appropriate name of Klapstok, and the men hated it. They also hated the tea that had been the only substitute available for the coffee they loved and had almost run out of.

Rocky made cakes and flapjacks for his spoiled customers more often, although he knew if he used up the flour too fast, it wouldn't last out the patrol. But that was a calculated risk; flour could be spoiled by roaches, mildew, and other tropical hazards. Limited storage and refrigeration were bad enough, but having food ruined before it could be used was a cook's nightmare on lengthy patrols in old S-boats, where the constant sweating of men and machinery caused a humidity so high that decay was accelerated. Craving the praise to which he'd been accustomed, Rocky consoled himself by quaffing the daily dollop of secret beer with Schab.

On the brighter side, Chief of the Boat Nave, forced to double as pharmacist's mate, had finally been given something new by way of medication for the four cases of gonorrhea that had resulted from joy in Java. The new tablets had been introduced to *39* by a Dutch doctor at the sub base in Soerabaja. Nave reported to the captain that the drug, called sulfathiazole, was the best remedy he'd run into. Three men were completely cured and the fourth much improved.

The few new things to read that had been picked up in Java had soon made the rounds and began dropping leaves. Bickering blossomed. Dean, still nursing a grudge, was even less inclined to follow the example of Frank Gierhart, his shipmate from the *Sealion*, in forgetting about big, well-stocked, neat, air-conditioned submarines and making the best of this one for now. Sensing Dean's continued scorn for *39*, his tormentors turned their attention to him again for lack of other material.

And then, on 28 February, *S-39* received orders to diverge from her designated patrol area and go on a special mission to an island off Sumatra. The message read: "271525 Job for S-39 x CSAF forty seven x Party about 40 British including Rear Admiral Spooner and Air Vice Marshal from Singapore reported on Chebia [Tjibea] Island of Toadjoe group [Kepulauan Tudjuh] Dutch chart six one since Feb. twenty x Rescue if possible x On leaving head for Sunda Strait report result x Japs in force at Palembang and Bangka Strait x Watch for air and surface patrol x."

At last there was action. Coe, wanting to get at this mission of mercy as quickly as possible, covered the 90 miles in 23 hours, real speed for the old S-boat. He even used some early morning daylight hours to travel on the surface, since submerged travel was so much slower. But he dared not take too many chances of being spotted by the enemy. Arrival time was 0030, 1 March. The *39* was a quarter-mile off the southwest point of Chebia Island on a bright night with the moon approaching full. The plan was to cover the entire southwest side, signaling by blinker gun so that the British refugees on Chebia, wherever they were located, would have ample opportunity to see it and signal back. Of course, the submarine, whose greatest hazard was always exposure, was in plain view of foes as well as friends, but the skipper figured that a quick dive could be made if need be and that rescue was impossible without risk. Using the same reasoning, *39* traveled on the surface for several hours before reaching Chebia, so that if survivors had gone to nearby Katchangang Island to take advantage of its more sheltered beaches (within rowing distance from Chebia), they would be able to see the rescue vessel approaching in the bright moonlight.

Chebia was a small island, but the signals brought no response. Coe stopped near a palm-fringed beach that showed silvery white in the moonlight; he had done his duty, gone as far as his orders demanded, but without results. Everyone aboard wondered if that was it. The answer soon came when the old man said, "I need a volunteer from the rated men aboard to accompany Mr. Hendrix ashore to reconnoitre the situation and see what can be found. I want to make it clear that there are dangers involved. The Japs could be hiding there. They might have baited a trap for us, and they won't hesitate to shoot or take prisoners." The moment Coe mentioned the word "volunteer," hands started waving—so many that Coe told Hendrix, "Better put all the names in a hat and draw." Of 33 rated men, there were 23 volunteers.

C.I. Peterson, electrician's mate first class, was the lucky fellow who got the nod. He and Hendrix, armed with pistols, took off in the wherry for the beach. The tropical breeze was a caress, the gentle curve of the shoreline straight out of a B movie where bare-breasted beauties suddenly emerge from behind the scratchy trunks of coconut palms. Hendrix and Peterson were uncomfortably aware that they were almost as well delineated in the moonglow as they would have been in broad daylight. A foe, especially with a pair of binoculars, would be in no doubt that Americans were rowing their way in.

At the soft scrape of wherry on sand, the two men tumbled out and ran to the dark shadows beneath the palms. It seemed an endless stretch of white beach to cover in a half crouch. Neither would have been surprised to hear shots ring out. The island was only a dot, half a mile wide and a mile long, covered with lush undergrowth. The men moved as quietly as possible, and though neither had been trained in jungle warfare, the dexterity necessary to maneuver through a cramped S-boat, plus the recent experience of running silent during depth charge, stood them in good stead. Once they were away from the beach, the blackness of heavy foliage fell about them like a cloak.

Suddenly Hendrix thrust a detaining arm in front of Peterson, then pointed ahead. There was a clearing in front of them, sufficiently illuminated by moonlight to show that a settlement had been there. The supports upholding native shacks had been axed until the structures collapsed. Then such violent smashing had taken place that the simple dwellings had been reduced to scattered haystacks. The two men did some fancy footwoork around the clearing, stepping over pots and pans thrown helter-skelter, hanging plants tossed to the ground, and splintered tables and benches. Neither dared speak aloud yet, although there was nothing resembling life in evidence anywhere.

Noticing the broken hulls of very young coconuts, whose soft, custardy insides were savored by native babies and adults alike, Hendrix picked up several pieces and handed one to Peterson for inspection. Both men ran their fingers around the moist and pulpy meat; obviously the chunks had been recently broken with little time to dry out. The mystery deepened. Who had lived here and where were they now? No householder destroys his own dwelling unless forced by an enemy. But an enemy, deprived of his prey, might in anger destroy a deserted village. And where were the British? Had they been here and fled to another part of the island? Or had they been rescued?

Hendrix gestured that they'd better return. They picked their way back through the inky black tangle of underbrush as stealthily as they'd come, but when they got out on the beach this time, they traced several lines of shoeprints that led to the water but did not come back indicating that the wearers had left by sea. Neither Hendrix nor Peterson was a big man, but the prints were much smaller than theirs and showed a very square, military toe. The Japanese had been here.

During the 40 minutes the men were ashore, Coe continued to send various calls by blinker tube, directed to all parts of the island. He included proper ANDUSREC challenge recognition signal for the date, and messages such as, "British party, U.S. submarine calling British party," but with no success. When Hendrix and Peterson got back and told their story, the decision was to make a complete circuit of Chebia, sending messages continuously. Coe wanted to be completely satisfied that they had done everything within their power to locate the refugees.

Running about a half-mile offshore, officers and crew were grateful that the old man was a top-notch navigator. The shore was very steep, and a heavy surf pounded against jagged cliffs dropping 50 feet into the sea. No other beaches were sighted that would have made another landing by wherry possible. Coe, the OOD, and two lookouts all scanned the coastline with binoculars, at the same time keeping an eye out for the enemy at sea. The quartermaster continued to send signals by blinker light. The old submarine took a pounding she could ill afford, rocking like a washtub in the rough seas. Everyone aboard was disappointed at the negative results of the search so far, and concerned about the fate of the 40 British. From the skipper on down they were also disappointed because they wanted the satisfaction of bringing off the rescue, a matter of pride. They had no way of knowing that the Chebia story would be detailed in various volumes of naval history as one of the earliest special missions carried out by a U.S. submarine.

At 0518, with dawn imminent, *39* had to submerge, but Coe stayed close to the island, still searching by periscope for signs of the British party. No life was seen on either Chebia or Katchangang, but at 0740 life of another kind was sighted five miles to the east: a Japanese destroyer headed on a southwest course, range 12,000 yards. Had he seen them? There had been ample opportunity. It was probable that the enemy maintained a lookout with a field radio on an island in the group of which Chebia was a part and that the destroyer had been called out after *39* was spotted during the night. The can appeared to be varying speed from 0 to 25 knots, and changing course frequently. This kind of behavior indicated that he was pausing to listen for a submarine but zigzagging to avoid becoming a target himself.

That was exactly what *39* had in mind. She started in pursuit, but against the fast-moving destroyer the submarine could not close range below 6,000 yards, and the limit of her torpedo accuracy was approximately half that distance. Within the hour the destroyer disappeared between Chebia and Lalang Islands on a westerly course. Coe figured this would put the Japanese vessel in the area where *39* had waited during the night for the landing party, strengthening the probability that the destroyer was searching for the American submarine.

8. Retreat With Honor

Two days passed. The entries in the patrol report read, "Nothing sighted this date." Then, on 4 March, another bright, moonlit night, several dark shapes appeared on the horizon, 2 points on the port bow. They apeared to be crossing the submarine's bow to starboard. Nobody said, "This is it," but there was a noticeable heightening of tension as *39* submerged and commenced approach. Coe could not see the target through the periscope, so he changed course to 300 degrees to close with the enemy.

Then they picked up enemy vessels on the port quarter. The boat changed course to 180 degrees and attempted to close at 6 knots, the range now being approximately 7,000 yards to the closest ship, which was a destroyer. Again *39* changed course, to 130 degrees, continuing speed at 6 knots. With all the power (which was little enough) and all the seamanship (which was considerable) at their disposal, officers and crew worked mightily to get within firing range. But they could not close below 6,000 yards, and the enemy vessels were soon out of sight. It was heartbreaking to lose a chance at a large Japanese force of five destroyers, one cruiser, and one aircraft carrier. The *S-39* surfaced and headed southwest. She had received orders to make tracks for Perth, Australia.

Red Coe, rubbing his eyes and dragging his feet so that the shlush-shlush of the disintegrating straw sandals sounded louder than ever, headed for his bunk to catch a few hours of shut-eye. As he passed the galley, Schoenrock said, "Sir, could I speak to you for a minute?"

"Fire away, Schoenrock." Coe yawned and tried not to. "What's the problem?"

"It's a bad one, captain. The refrigerator's broke down."

Coe swallowed the yawn. It was not the kind of news that acted as a soporific. "Get an auxiliaryman to work on it and report to me later," he said. His eyes were closing again in spite of himself. A half-dozen hours sleep picked up here and there, but no more than a pair at any one time, didn't add up to a lot of rest in the last couple of days, and the worst part of losing it was that it hadn't done any good. But Coe was not one to worry about what couldn't be helped; that was part of his success as a skipper. As soon as his head hit the pillow, he was out.

Four hours later, at 0744, Larry Bernard, who had the watch, said to the messenger, "Call the captain, I think I see smoke on the horizon." Still on the periscope, Larry said to Quartermaster Rollins, "Mark the bearing, no range estimate; I can only see what looks a little different from haze on the horizon."

Rollins reported, "Bearing 202 degrees."

Coe appeared, his voice sleep-roughened. "Got something out there, Larry?"

Bernard, wary of jumping to conclusions, said neutrally, "I'm not sure, but I thought you ought to take a look."

Coe asked, "What's your depth?" and Bernard answered, "Forty-two feet."

"Up periscope," the captain ordered, then took a long, careful look around. "It's certainly slick up there, but I don't see anything. Come up a couple more feet." Everybody watched him and waited for further comment. "You're right, Larry. I see smoke and a small shape out there. Let's head for him and see how his bearing changes. Mark bearing."

It was difficult for Bernard not to show a little more interest now, although he tried hard to keep it under control. There was nothing to get excited about yet, he kept telling himself. When Hendrix and Gugliotta eased into the control room, ready to start an approach on the target, Bernard had assumed a poker face again.

"Forty feet, stand by for a setup," the captain said. "Up periscope, mark the bearing. It must be a ship; the bearing is drifting to the left. We'll do it again in about ten minutes." The old man headed for the wardroom and a cup of the ever-scarcer coffee that nobody wanted to give up for the all-too-abundant tea.

When Coe returned and got back on the periscope, he said, "Not much change. Mark the bearing," then told Larry, "The sea is like glass. Let's go down to 80 feet and speed up, lead his bearing by ten degrees. Take another look in ten minutes, Larry. It's going to be a long approach. I'm going to turn in." To flake out for fifteen or twenty minutes was the wise thing to do for reasons of accuracy and endurance later. If only, this time, they could get close enough. Coe took himself off. The talk in the control room after he left dealt only with the business at hand; nobody was ready to get happy yet. Even the ever-enthusiastic, ever-opimistic Hendrix kept his thoughts to himself.

Bernard had taken two more looks when Coe came back to the control room, refreshed by his catnap. "Can you make out anything yet, Larry?" he asked.

"I can make out a small bump now."

"Let's hold this speed a little longer and try to close the range for a good look," Coe said. "Come left to 150 degrees. We'll lead him a little more."

Another interval elapsed. The occupants of the control room now included Les Dean, acting as trim manifold man. He felt that it was better than lapping in (grinding) injection valve discs for the air compressors, which was the way he spent most of his off-watch time. Besides, nobody was heckling him for a change. All he wanted was to go unnoticed, be left in peace, and not be made a fool of in front of the captain and exec.

The next time Coe had a look through the scope, all hands present were still doomed to a state of suspension. They heard the skipper say, "I can barely make him out, mark bearing. Give him an angle on the bow 70 port; down periscope. Best guess at his range is 16,000 yards."

Nave asked, "Do you want to go to Battle Stations, captain?"

Coe replied, "Yes, but have all hands stand easy on station for now. It's going to be a long approach."

The next 20 minutes dragged and dragged and dragged. More than one man present had mentally kissed off the target as another might-have-been when Coe, at the periscope, said, "I can make him out better now. Mark bearing, angle on the bow, 60 port, Range a bit less than three-quarter division high power. Down periscope; 80 feet, and speed up."

Assistant Approach Officer Gugliotta said. "I get 13,000 yards using 100 feet masthead height."

Hendrix, plotting officer, allowed excitement to creep into his voice. "He's zigged toward us about 25 degrees."

"We might change course a little to the left to compensate, say 120 degrees," Gugliotta added.

But Coe decided to stay on course and close range faster. Ten minutes went by; although neither the captain's voice nor his expression showed heightened interest, he sent for a sweat towel to wrap around his neck. When he got back on the periscope, he said to Larry Bernard, "Forty feet and all stop. Can you hold it long enough for a look? The sea is as smooth as glass and I want to stay up as high as possible."

"Okay, I've got a good trim," Bernard answered, then, "40 feet."

"Up periscope and stand by; mark bearing," Coe said. "Angle on the bow 70 port. Range, a bit more than three-quarter division high power; down periscope; 80 feet," and to the controllerman, "1,000 aside." Then, for the first time, there was a change in his tone of voice. "She's a fat tanker, and I don't see any escorts."

Scratching his prickly heat at a great rate, Quartermaster Rollins said, "Bearing 185 degrees."

Gugliotta contributed, "Range 11,000 yards." There was still a long way to go.

Monk Hendrix said, "He's tracking on course about 070 degrees, going very slow. I get only about 4 knots."

Coe said, "My first ranges were probably off. He must be going faster than that unless he stopped or slowed for a while." Turning to the telephone talker, Matthews, the skipper said, "ask Sound if he can hear the target bearing 185 true."

A few minutes later Matthews relayed, "Sound says we're making too much noise. He can't hear anything else."

Coe replied, "Tell all stations we are making an approach on a large tanker that seems to be all by himself. He's a long way off, but I think we can catch him."

During the next 20 minutes of pursuit, the temperature in the control room climbed another five degrees. When Gugliotta said in his quiet way, "Range 9,000," it began to look as though there might be a possibility of closing in. And when Matthews, on the telephone, relayed, "Sound reports screws at 190 degrees true 110 RPM; he can stay on the target now at this speed," and Hendrix announced, "He's speeding up now, I get 7 knots," all heads nodded in approval.

The old man said to Quartermaster Rollins, "Let me see *Jap Merchant Ship Silhouettes*. I want to try and pin down who this baby might be. He's a big one." Everybody was trying to suppress excitement; you could have heard a pin drop when Rollins handed Coe the large paperback volume that opened like a secretary's notebook. Coe began flipping pages to the section on tankers. The small control room bulging with men and activity made possible quick looks over the old man's shoulder every time he stopped and read the vital statistics that went with a particular vessel. It seemed a long time before he said anything, but it was only impatience that made the few minutes stretch. Holding up the book so all could see the pictures, Coe said, "It looks like either *Tatekawa Maru* or *Itukisima Maru* could be our target, both ten thousand tons displacement."

Somebody muttered, "That's a lotta ship." Coe caught it and said, "It's a lot of ship and an important ship. When we first sighted this tanker, her position was only a few miles from the destroyers, carrier, and cruiser we saw earlier when we couldn't close. This tanker is on the same base course, steaming behind by about four hours and apparently trailing the task force for fuel replenishment at sea." The skipper didn't have to draw conclusions aloud; everybody knew that it would be somewhat more than inconvenient for the enemy if the fuel supply for the task force suddenly went to the bottom of the sea.

Coe said, "We'll fire four torpedoes, because a modern tanker like this, with large-capacity pump and unusually good watertight compartments, would be able to sustain severe damage without sinking."

After another observation, Gugliotta could report, "Range 4,500 yards," and Hendrix, "A good speed solution now at 9 knots." The approach had taken

70 minutes so far, but with the knowledge that *39* was reaching firing range, the tension in the crowded room became palpable. Coe ordered telephone talker Matthews, "Tell TR to make ready all torpedo tubes, set zero gyro, depth 6 feet on numbers 1 and 4 and 9 feet on numbers 2 and 3."

Matthew's reply, "Sound reports a change in the sound of the target screws; he may have zigged," brought sighs. Did this mean another disappointment? The captain said, "Let's have a look. Up periscope." There was a lot of breath-holding until he added, "He zigged toward," which kept hope alive. "Tell Sound that was good work picking up a zig, and tell him to keep the bearings coming."

There were other signs that things were picking up, such as Coe's next order to Gugliotta, "Tell me when Sound has us 5 degrees from the firing bearing."

Seven or eight minutes later, after completing calculations with the Mark VI angle solver, a hand-operated mechancial device to determine firing bearing, Gugliotta was able to report, "Five degrees from the firing bearing."

All ear-digging, rump-scratching, crotch-adjusting, nose-picking, and eye-twitching stopped. Coe, in a squat, said, "Up periscope. Put me on the firing bearing. Torpedo room stand by." He rode the scope up no higher than a half crouch; the sea was absolutely calm and clear and he wanted to expose a minimum of periscope, so he ordered, "Forty-five feet."

Then came the long-awaited words, "Coming on, stand by. Fire one—fire two—fire three—fire four." The orders were spaced a few seconds apart, and Chief of the Boat Nave, lips folded into a thin line, carried them out. Almost immediately came, "Down periscope."

Now all eyes turned to Matthews on the telephone. The eyes of the usually self-controlled Zeke danced with agitation as he sputtered, "Torpedo room reports all tubes fired electrically, and Sound reports all torpedoes running hot and straight." Nobody moved, nobody wanted to. Nobody breathed, nobody dared to. After approximately 40 seconds, there were three distinct explosions, followed by three distinct shocks that jarred the close-packed bodies in the control room.

The moment the explosions came Coe went back on the periscope. He knew that the torpedoes had been fired from an ideal position, about 1,000 yards range, 100-degree track, and zero gyro angle, but only seeing was believing, especially after the long run of hard luck. So when he reported, "The tanker is heeling way over and settling down by the stern" he didn't even try to keep excitement out of his voice any more.

A loud cheer went up in the control room, Matthews telephoned the happy news to all stations, and much hugging and back-pounding took place. And when Coe said, "I think every man should have a look," they lined up. Nave, following the officers, shouted, "She's firing at us with her deck guns forward and aft, trying to hit our periscope—it won't do you no good, you sonsabitchin'

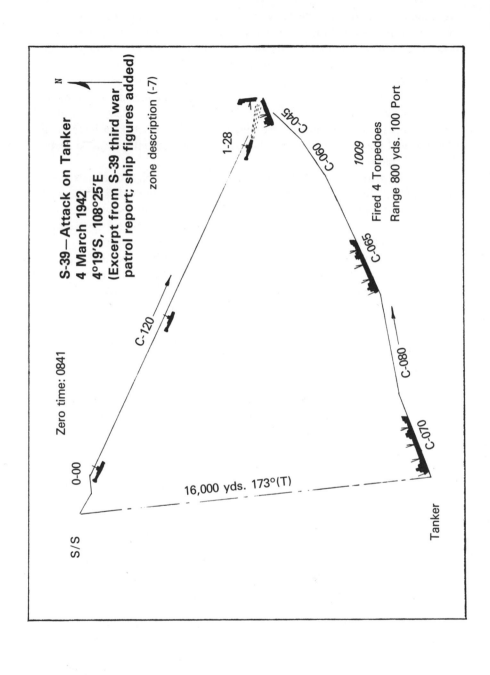

S-39—Attack on Tanker
4 March 1942
4°19'S, 108°25'E
(Excerpt from S-39 third war
patrol report; ship figures added)

zone description (-7)

N

I-28

C-045

C-060

1009

Fired 4 Torpedoes
Range 800 yds. 100 Port

C-065

C-120

C-080

Zero time: 0841

0-00

C-070

16,000 yds. 173°(T)

S/S

Tanker

bastards," then caught himself and glanced quickly at the skipper, because he tried his best to control his language around the old man. But Coe hadn't noticed a thing. He had dug his hands deep into the pockets of his tattered shorts, and the smile of satisfaction on his face belied heat and tension. There were no marks of rank on the bare chest with its sweat-clotted strawberry blond hair, but his dignity didn't need dress whites.

Somebody who spotted Tayco and Fabricante way in the back of the line called out, "Hey, you guys, let these guys go next. The Japs took over their country, not ours." The two Filipinos were passed along to the front and took their turns. Fabricante muttered his reactions in Tagalog, but the clenched fist he shook conveyed his feelings. Tayco, more at ease in English, commented, "Our captain do good work. Will not give fuel to enemy, that tanker again." Morale had needed a boost. This was it, and the order, "Secure from Battle Stations, set the regular watch," came as a welcome change.

The tanker took over an hour to sink. A single, mighty burst of flame, about 50 feet high, erupted from her and burned for several minutes forward of her stack, then quantities of light smoke or steam gushed forth aft. Many large streams of yellowish liquid were pumped over her side, but she continued to settle by the port quarter, going down completely at 1116. Meanwhile, 39 had reversed course and was moving away at slow speed.

At 1239, sound operator Frank Gierhart picked up three sets of fast-moving screws ahead and on the port bow. He also heard occasional pinging. Coe, who thought his well-earned sleep had come at last, had just punched his pillow into shape when he got the report. A minute later he was on his feet, giving the order, "Rig for silent running." Back on the scope, Coe reported one DD (destroyer) dead astern on the same course, range 5,000 yards. When Gierhart responded, "I hear two other sets of screws on each quarter growing stronger," the relaxation changed to apprehension.

At 1255 the order "Man Battle Stations Submerged" went out, and the weary men lucky enough to be off watch, rolled off their stinking, moldy mattresses and stumbled to their feet again to join their weary captain. Coe ordered a depth of 105 feet. Apparently the tanker had been able to radio for help before sinking, and 39 was reaping the harvest. The click-clack-wham of depth charges exploded six times in rapid succession, reverberating throughout the boat. The old craft quivered as though she had suddenly developed palsy. Fear painted every man's face before he could try to wipe it off. The glassy sea had been great for sinking a tanker. It would be equally great for locating and blasting a submarine out of existence.

Twelve minutes later, Sound reported he could no longer hear screws—a good sign, but it didn't last long. At 1335, the chilling wham-crash of an aerial bomb exploded close aboard. Japanese flyboys were helping their seagoing comrades, and the men of 39 had seen enough of their work in the Philippines to feel fear return full force. In the torpedo room Schab and Bixler solemnly shook hands. Swede Bloom, who had survived the grounding of *S-36* and almost being left behind on Java, thought his luck had run out. He wasn't so sure now how grateful he was to Captain Coe for taking him aboard. He tried to convince himself he wasn't scared, but his bladder thought otherwise. Fortunately, he was in the engine room, where he could relieve himself often. He could squeeze out only a few drops, but that didn't prevent him from having to go and go and go. He wasn't the only one.

Allyn Christopher's knees started shaking so hard that he wrapped his arms around them tight and diverted his thoughts by watching Tayco and Fabricante. The two Filipinos had knelt down, closed their eyes, and clasped their hands in prayer, doing openly what everybody else was doing covertly. Much fingering of St. Christopher medals and crosses took place, and those who didn't have them wished they had.

The Dutch chart indicated a depth of 130 feet in the area, so Coe ordered the ultimate of 120 feet; he knew that a submarine could be seen in clear tropical water at approximately 100 feet. Another aerial bomb exploded. Water slithered off tense, half-naked bodies as though trying to match the increased moisture oozing from the seams of the boat. The 39 seemed to be weeping at the thought of her own death. In the control room, Diving Officer Bernard said, "She won't go down, captain. I'll bet we're on the bottom."

Coe ordered Navigator Hendrix, "Check how much water we've got here."

Hendrix replied, "We should have 130 feet according to my DR position."

Muttering, "That damned chart must be off," Coe turned to Bernard. "Larry, put a bubble in number two until we break loose, and put on a little speed. The bottom must be awfully soft—there was no jar or scraping."

Breaking loose couldn't be done simply by using the screws, going ahead, or backing. The captain's order would lighten the boat by blowing some water out of the main ballast tank closest to the waist of the submarine. If they blew too much, they risked losing control and popping up to the surface, a sitting duck for the Japanese milling around up there.

The boat started to rise. Bernard said, "Ninety feet, vent number two main ballast tank." Nave carried out the order and everybody held his breath. With the motors turning over for 3 knots during the last few minutes, 39 had been sending up clouds of mud—which was, no doubt, the way Japanese bombers had spotted them in the crystal clear waters. If they couldn't steady at 90 feet and move off, the future looked dim.

It worked. The boat slurped free. Quietly as a jellyfish, 39 eased away, continuing to run silent, taking a southeast course. It was only 1343, there was plenty of daylight left, and they were aware that the Japanese didn't give up easily. Schoenrock made his way to the galley as though walking on sponges. Without clicking a knife, he put together a tray of sandwiches and a pot of coffee. Like everybody's mother, he thought food could dissipate worry, heal wounds, and make present and future look brighter. Edibles, water, and coffee were all scarce—but if you never surfaced, what difference could it make how much you had on hand? Besides, the reefer still wasn't working, and the auxiliarymen had said it never would until *39* reached a port that had the spare parts to repair the antique mechanism. Since Rocky knew that this possibility would be an impossibility for a long time, he figured he might as well use up the ham he'd been saving before it spoiled.

That the submarine was still not out of the woods was emphasized by the fact that the captain was still in the control room, keeping tabs. When Schoenrock glided in with his tray of food, Coe set an example by eating a sandwich and washing it down with coffee, but some people couldn't swallow a thing. The heat had grown unbearable, and the air was beginning to smell as if the body of a dead animal had burst from an accumulation of foul gases. Dirty clothes didn't help. The patrol was 19 days along now, and the few items each man owned stank from constant use. Soerabaja had not been able to begin replacing wearables for the many ships of the Retreating Asiatic Fleet.

Three hours passed. Things began to look a little brighter, but they had to assume that the enemy was still bent on avenging the death of the tanker. And then Schab, who had relieved Gierhart on Sound, picked up two sets of high-speed propellers aft. Though they moved up the port side and went out of range ahead, Coe figured they were the same destroyers who had depth-charged *39* earlier. There would be no respite from battle stations and silent running yet.

Heads began to ache from the combination of emotional acrobatics and high carbon dioxide level. Coe couldn't do anything about the former but he could about the latter. He ordered an inspection of the battery ventilation. Electrician's Mate Hiland reported a relatively high concentration of CO_2 throughout the boat. Not knowing how long they'd have to stay down, the captain said, "I'm not ready to bleed in fresh air or oxygen from the storage flasks yet. What would you think of spreading some CO_2 absorbent around?"

"Sounds like a good idea, sir," Hiland replied.

The dry white powder was carried in gallon cans. Hiland, Matthews, and Mattingly spread it on a couple of the bunks in the forward battery and a tabletop in the after battery. It helped—for a while.

At 2200 the can (main storage batteries) was almost flat and the air so bad that even the fact that no screws had been heard for almost seven hours seemed unimportant. Coe decided to lie to for a couple of hours so they could put both engines on the battery charge.

Word was passed that surfacing was imminent, and the motor machinist's mates made ready for the S-boat ritual that took place at the end of a long dive. The electrical main-motor breakers on these old craft were located in the forward end of the engine room, enclosed in large steel boxes open at the bottom. Because there was no air conditioning, the breakers became scummy with condensation at the end of an extended dive. Feeling a slight surge of energy at the thought of surfacing, Swede Bloom rigged an air hose with an educting connection that led into a five-gallon can of carbon tetrachloride, and proceeded to spray the breakers until the condensation was cleaned off. It was a nasty job, and the engine-room crowd took turns at it because the fumes left a sickening taste in the mouth that lasted until the following day. The men were lucky that this was the only problem they'd encountered so far as a result of such liberal use of the chemical. Later, illnesses and deaths would be attributed to its inhalation, and it would shortly be so strictly prohibited that not even a small bottle would be allowed on any submarine.

The exhausted officers and crew had never craved surfacing so much. They were familiar now with the tremendous eruption of foul air that would literally blow open the conning tower hatch as soon as the quartermaster knocked the latch clear with his mallet, and they could hardly wait for it to happen. When the order was given, heads were raised and mouths fell open to gulp the fresh stuff. A few seconds after the pigboat belched out her foul air, a bit of sea water and silt always washed in, but this time the men were surprised by the quantities of mud that slithered down and blobbed onto the deck as though a giant child up above was making sand castles. Then they remembered how they had churned up the bottom when the enemy was hunting them.

"I hope we don't see no Japs," somebody commented.

"You're just liable," Nave said between hacking coughs that shook his thin frame. "They're all over the place like horseshit at a rodeo."

Coe knew the area was under enemy control and that the Japanese were easily able to keep surveillance of all routes south to Australia. He hoped to be heading for Sunda Strait by 0100, 5 March, and to reach the entrance the following day. Early morning was the best time for transit because Sunda currents were notoriously strong and treacherous and there were many small islands to avoid as well. But before they could undertake that journey, whose completion would put _39_ into position to head for Australia and a friendly port, the badly discharged batteries had to be made ready or they wouldn't have enough juice to go anywhere.

Unlike an automobile battery, which is constantly being charged by the generator when the engine is running, a submarine battery is simply discharging when in use. When the boat is submerged it uses up its energy by driving the propellers through the main motors, as well as supplying all other energy needed for lights, pumps, blowers, and so on. Eventually it will discharge completely to its low voltage limit (LVL) and must be charged before that point is reached. Coe had been keeping close check through the long submergence, wanting to conserve the batteries as much as possible for days ahead that might be even rougher than this one. Now, a battery charge was imperative; he couldn't take the chance of reaching the LVL. A flat battery left no choice but to surface, unless you could sit on the bottom or do the impossible and keep a stop trim indefinitely. The skipper didn't lack imagination; the future could be full of counterattacking destroyers or other antisubmarine ships that could hold 39 down for a long time. That future could be tomorrow or a few hours from now.

There were many groups of little islands in the vicinity, and the old man decided to lie to on the lee side of one of them, in a nice little cove with a lot of tangled and intertwined tropic greenery as a backdrop. The night was lit by moon and stars, as it had been throughout most of the patrol. As soon as both engines were on the battery charge, the boat quickly freshened from the control room aft through the engine room, but since this didn't do much for the torpedo- and motor-room watches, these men were allowed to come up to the bridge, two at a time, for 15 minutes of fresh air.

Electrician's Mates Hiland and Peterson had lined up for a charge before surfacing. They had to water the batteries by getting under the decks, which gave them only about two feet of clearance. Hiland, normally inclined to be chubby, commented, "Jeez, losing weight on these luxury cruises has some advantages. I don't have to squeeze so hard to get my butt in here."

The two recorded the specific gravity of each pilot cell, along with the temperature and height of electrolyte. When the charge was started, they speeded up the battery ventilation to carry away the gases being generated and to keep the batteries cool; otherwise, they heated during the charge, and this particular heat was extremely dangerous because a good amount of highly inflammable and explosive hydrogen was being generated. The lower the battery, the longer the charge and the more hydrogen released. The gas could accumulate in pockets in the boat in spite of increased ventilation and all efforts to dissipate it. No smoking was allowed during the process, although some authorities considered it best to have a small flame burning in the overhead of the battery compartments to catch and burn escaping hydrogen before it could collect and form an explosive mixture with air. A battery explosion was the nightmare of every skipper and the bugaboo of every duty officer, who had to monitor the whole operation by periodic inspection to make sure nothing abnormal existed. But the duty officer was rarely an electrical and battery brain, so usually depended upon the wisdom and experience of his electrician's mates.

At sea, the procedure differed slightly. With everybody on board, the chief engineer was the monitor. So tonight Larry Bernard, whose deeply circled eyes seemed to be receding with each passing hour, reported "ready" to Hendrix, OOD, who gave permission to start the charge. The dark stubble on Monk's face created a caved-in look beneath his cheekbones, which matched the way he felt. But he didn't have time to think about it. Getting the charge completed was the thing.

Hendrix and lookouts Christopher and Tayco were on the bridge when

Machinist's Mates Dean and Tella came up for their 15 minutes of fresh air. Suddenly Tayco whispered excitedly, "Bright light, sair. Look like searchlight on port quarter."

Hendrix needed only a quick glance to agree. A searchlight was playing over the greenery of the island. If it continued on its course, it would be opposite *39* soon. "Answer bells on the battery; captain to the bridge," Hendrix ordered.

In nothing flat the redhead appeared, assessed the situation, and asked, "How's the charge?"

Hendrix replied, "It's well along sir. We just put it on one engine."

Coe muttered, "There's not enough water to dive in within miles," then said to the OOD, "Turn to head for the light and flood down so that we don't present a big silhouette. That's probably one of the cans we've been seeing around here for the last few days."

Hendrix's message to control was, "Open the Kingstons on number two main ballast tank." Coe added, "Pass the word to man the deck gun and stand by to pass up ammunition," and to the torpedo room, "Make ready all torpedo tubes; set depth six feet, zero gyro angle."

Gun Captain Schoenrock was on the ready in short order. With his crew training the gun in the direction of the searchlight, he reported, "Manned and ready, first round of ammunition is in the scuttle."

Suddenly Allyn Christopher was scared like he'd never been scared before, even when the aerial bombs exploded. His body turned to water, the stuff he was wishing he was submerged in. Relentlessly, methodically, the searchlight came on. They all watched as it easily picked out details of palm fronds and lianas coiling around tree trunks. Christopher could have sworn that he saw the beady eyes and twitching muzzle of a monkey peering through the leaves. Allyn screamed silently, they'll pick us out easy, we're on the surface, I could get killed, that deck gun's no good against a big Jap destroyer.

The light was within a few yards of them now. The men on the bridge were so completely frozen that they could have been figures in a wax museum. The inexorable beam flitted along treetops, then dropped down skittishly—as though playing a game—before zooming back up again. Now the searchlight was no more than a few feet above their cables. If the operator brought it down, he would surely make out the pale, open-mouthed faces on the bridge. This was just what he was looking for, and had been looking for, ever since the death of the tanker.

The men stared at the beam, their rolled-up eyes and the brilliant light overhead making them look strangely like portraits of haloed, medieval saints imploring heaven's aid. It was not in vain. For some reason the operator did not play his light downward until after he'd passed the submarine. No one spoke until the searchlight was well off in the distance, and then the only words were Coe's quiet order, "Stand easy at gun stations," and to Hendrix, "Get back on the battery charge and go ahead on one engine. I'll tell the quartermaster to give you a course."

Later, when Christopher was describing his reactions to Kutscherowski, he said, "It was worse than walking naked down Main Street in my hometown."

And Ski, who sometimes got his images a little mixed, nodded wisely as he shadowboxed with the edge of his bunk. "There's nothing like the good earth, huh?"

"You take the good earth," Allyn said. "I'll crouch in the cradle of the deep."

"We was scared down here, too. We dint know what was going on." Ski feinted and dodged, then cuffed himself lightly on the jaw. "I miss my sparring partner Pennell. Hope he made it out of Java okay."

"Tom Parks, too," Christopher added.

It was approximately 0010, 5 March, when *39* put one engine on propulsion and set a southwesterly course for Sunda Strait. So far she was on schedule. Most important would be the early morning start next day. Part of the time they would be going through the tricky strait at relatively slow, submerged speeds. These would not guarantee good control to keep them on their planned track against the ever-present adverse currents for which Sunda was famous. The only thing predictable so far about this third patrol was that difficult navigating and piloting lay ahead.

At 0409, while they were traveling on the surface and completing the battery charge, three dark shapes were sighted. They dove immediately. They were afraid they'd be sighted in perfect silhouette because they were between a full moon and the prospective targets. Then Coe tried to close in hopes of getting a crack at them, but he couldn't see anything by periscope nor could Sound pick them up. About an hour later the submarine sighted smoke over the horizon on port quarter. Obviously, *39* had not estimated the course correctly and the targets had gone around end out of reach. The rest of the day the boat had a breather, hitting a relatively strong, favorable current. At 1856 they surfaced about five miles north of a group of small islands near the northern entrance to Sunda Strait. All was serene. They were not aware of the terrible toll that had been extracted in the Battle of the Java Sea and how badly the Allies, had been hurt. Ed Schab, given permission to enjoy some fresh air on the bridge, sighted wreckage floating by and commented happily, "Looks like we finally gave 'em a dose of what they gave us at Cavite." He wouldn't know for some time that he was looking at the flotsam of his own ships.

Gugliotta, officer of the deck, had one engine on charge and one on propulsion when the old man joined him, carrying a cup of coffee, relaxed and wanting to smell the fresh air. As a navigation expert, Coe had no illusions about the ease of traveling through Sunda Strait; might as well make the most of these moments of peace.

"How you doing, Guy?" Coe perched on the railing. "I see we still have a beautiful, bright, moonlit night. Too bad it has to be wasted. Your wife never had a chance to get out here, did she?"

"No, sir, she would have enjoyed the Philippines." From force of habit, the officer's glance kept roving over the surrounding territory. There was a small island nearby.

"Some enjoyed it and some didn't," Coe said. "Some complained all the time about the heat, the bugs, the food, all that. I was lucky, Rachel enjoyed every minute. When I met her back in '33, she was working in Honolulu and saving her money for a round-the-world trip. Can you imagine—"

Suddenly Gugliotta cut into the captain's reminscence: "Clear the bridge, dive, dive." Then to Coe, "There's a submarine about 2,000 yards on the port bow."

The lookouts shot down into the control room, followed by Coe sliding down the ladder into the conning tower and on to control. Gugliotta dropped into the conning tower; he pulled the bridge hatch cover shut; and the quartermaster dogged it securely. They made the three split-second actions seem one fluid motion. Gugliotta and Quartermaster Rollins eased into control where Coe was ordering, "One hundred feet."

The bow and stern planesmen, who had been the lookouts, knew the urgency of getting down in a hurry. The OOD who, with submergence, became the diving officer didn't even need to give the order, "Full dive on the planes"; the men already had them there. The boat was at periscope depth in 39 seconds going down fast. The faster, the better, because not only the whoosh but the high-pitched throb of propellors could be heard, as one torpedo streaked over the engine room and another over the forward torpedo room, leaving no doubt that the Japanese submarine had seen its American counterpart silhouetted by moonlight and knew its exact location.

Sound was unable to pick up the enemy submarine's screws. The Japanese sub had been difficult enough to detect on the surface but after the excitement died down, Coe thought it worthwhile to take a look by periscope. Despite the brightly illuminated night, he saw nothing. About 2145, studying the chart, Coe said to Navigator Hendrix, "Are you pretty sure of our position?"

"I got a good cut before dark and I think my DR [dead reckoning] shouldn't be very far off since then," Monk replied.

"We're going to make our planned start of transit. What do you think we'll find by way of currents on the surface?"

Hendrix hesitated for a moment. "The best information I've been able to dig out of these Dutch sailing directions is that the currents are variable in direction and velocity in this area."

"We didn't need the Dutch to tell us that." The redhead let a trace of irritation creep into his voice. He would have preferred not to practice psychic navigation. "What do you think is our best course?"

Hendrix said, "I'm going to guess at a fairly strong easterly set and recommend course 240 degrees."

Since the encounter with the Japanese submarine had caused a delay that could put *39* on a later, less favorable schedule to start transit of Sunda Strait, Coe decided to surface, put on as much speed as they could on one engine, and resume battery charge on the other, to reach their destination as soon as possible. At 0500 they dove, and the helmsman immediately felt the stong currents pushing them off course. At 0533 two Japanese destroyers were sighted patrolling the Java shoreline about 5 miles distant. At that time *39* was making turns (motor speed) for 3 knots but was logging 6 and steering up to 50 degrees away from their course desired to be made good. No attempt could be made to start an approach on the destroyers because all of the old man's attention had to focus on keeping clear of the many small islands and trying to get safely through the insistent currents that kept shoving the boat sideways.

In the narrowest part of the strait, Frank Gierhart was heard to say, "Bet if we surfaced I could spit on either side and hit an island." Swede Bloom muttered, "Jeez, I could swear we're going through ass backwards." In the control room Coe ordered, "Up periscope," took a careful look around and said, "All clear, I see a group of small islands to the northwest. Do they check with your DR, Monk?"

"Yes, I think I'll recognize them," Monk replied. "Permission to take a round of bearings?"

"Go ahead when you're ready."

Navigator Hendrix was on the periscope now with Quartermaster Rollins standing by. Monk took a round of bearings on several islands he had identified on the chart. Coe asked, "How're we doing?" as he looked at Monk's calculated position.

Hendrix said, "I can hardly believe it. I'm sure my fix is good, the landmarks appear to be well charted, but since entering the strait we've been making good a course of 130 degrees while steering 180 degrees, and making good a speed of about 7 knots with turns for 3."

The helmsman reported, "I've got full right rudder on, but she won't come to course; we keep drifting to the left of 180 degrees."

Coe ordered more speed.

Larry Bernard was trying to get a few hours' sleep, but instead he kept wondering how long it would take to clear the strait. he kept reminding himself that once *39* got through, the worst would be over. After that, the chief engineer would just have a routine 24-hour day, and the all-too-familiar worries about the machinery, until they reached Australia. On this happy note he dozed off.

In the control room Monk plotted another round of bearings and reported, "We're doing better, but we're still being pushed to the east and getting too close to the coastline."

Studying the chart Coe, said, "I think we're okay but it looks good and clear for several miles to the west so let's change course in that direction."

When Monk advised course 240 degrees, Coe ordered, "100 feet, come to course 240 degrees." And to the diving officer, "Put on more speed, make turns for 6 knots."

That was the turning point; shortly after, the helmsman reported, "No trouble staying on course now. I need only 5 to 10 degrees rudder."

They had made it to the wide part of the strait where there was less struggle with currents because they were able to dive to 100 feet, and clear the most violent riptides and eddies. But suddenly Sound reported hearing depth charges in the distance. There was instant increase in urine, saliva, and sweat. The probability that the Japanese submarine had informed the tin cans of *39*'s presence flashed through every mind. Half an hour later, at 0930, Coe ordered slowing down and periscope depth, and the thin faces, bluish-gray with beard and fatigue, began to relax. But it wasn't over yet. Squeaking signals, similar to those on a previous patrol off Legaspi, were heard by Sound on the starboard bow and thought to be a submarine. Then they saw a single-pontoon naval observation biplane three miles astern, patrolling the narrow part of Sunda Strait they had recently cleared.

It was just as well they didn't realize how complete the enemy control of the area was. The waters were crawling with Japanese surface ships, submarines, and aircraft, triumphant from the Java Sea battle. Any one of them could have been *39*'s nemesis from the moment she disclosed her presence by sinking the tanker.

They surfaced at 1800 hours, gaunt with oxygen starvation, and felt the usual surge of spirits at washing out their lungs with breathable air. A few hours later the boat cleared the strait and set course for Fremantle, Australia. Indications that the crew felt the worst was behind them were remarks like, "Christ, I thought it would never end," and "Whew, what a relief." As they grew more confident that they were out of it, comments with a lighter, more typical touch emerged, such as, "Me scared? Hell no, I just kept wondering why that crappy Klapstok stew stuck in my craw and wouldn't go down," followed by, "Hey, you mean crappy Klapstok or clappy Krapstok?" Everything got a laugh.

And the old man called attention, as he had before, to Gugliotta's sure-footed way of whipping down the hatch face-forward like any ordinary flight of stairs. Guy explained, as he always did, that he had learned it on ladders when working for his father, a contractor. Everybody enjoyed the well-known dialogue, taking comfort in the familiar as people do when an ordeal is over.

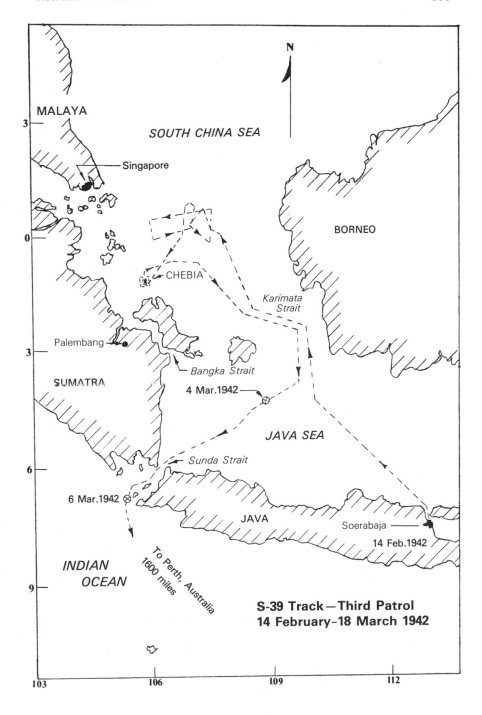

N

MALAYA

SOUTH CHINA SEA

Singapore

BORNEO

CHEBIA

*Karimata
Strait*

Palembang

Bangka Strait

SUMATRA

4 Mar.1942

JAVA SEA

Sunda Strait

6 Mar.1942

JAVA

Soerabaja

14 Feb.1942

*INDIAN
OCEAN*

To Perth, Australia
1600 miles

**S-39 Track—Third Patrol
14 February–18 March 1942**

Hiland got up an "anchor pool" and "date of arrival" pool. The chances went like Schoenrock's hotcakes, even though nobody would have any money until they got paid in Australia. Nave began wondering how Australian girls were built, and gave technicolor descriptions of the kind, size, and shape of dolly he expected to find the minute he set foot on Aussie soil.

The final indication that the crew felt the ordeal safely over was Kutscherowski's exchange with Captain Coe. Still within the margins of the superrelaxed atmosphere, the good-natured boxer said to his skipper, "Cap'n, I been wondering about something for a long time."

"What would that be?"

Ski glance down at the captain's unlovely footgear. "Them slippers, sir. The straw's all sticking up and out the bottoms and leaking out the sides. Don't it hurt to walk on that rough stuff?"

"Feels good. It scratches the prickly heat on the soles of my feet."

Kutscherowski glanced down at Coe's bare legs. It was true that the skipper's ankles showed signs of rash. But the soles of his feet? The control room wondered if Ski would have the nerve to ask the old man to prove it. You could almost hear the boxer pulling the question back and forth in his mind, but he decided on, "I guess it's kinda like them Indian fakers that walk on nails."

The captain had maintained a perfectly straight face throughout, but a lot of people thought he winked one red-rimmed blue eye as he said, "Exactly." The scuffs continued to disintegrate, and Coe continued to wear them.

The boat settled down to what passed for normal. Schoenrock fed everybody as much ham as he could, but the thrice-baked meat began to stink, and what little fresh stuff was left slimed over from lack of refrigeration; even the cockroaches wouldn't touch it. They threw everything but dry goods over the side. Rice, beans, and canned tomatoes took over until those supplies gave out. From then on it had to be Klapstok all the way. Although officers and men had always eaten the same food, once in a while Rocky had fixed some little extra for the wardroom, and Tayco and Fabricante had seen to it that whatever was left found its way to the crews' mess. But these days there were no treats, and Fabricante said sadly, "Captain eat too, all esame esmelly estuff." Tayco added longingly, "I wish I had big plate fried *lapu lapu*."

But in the wardroom one morning after coming off watch, Gugliotta thought, hell's fire, I wouldn't trade it for anything else. Tired, dirty, gassy from constipation, pocked here and there with diet-deficiency sores, he remembered battleship *West Virginia*, his first duty, followed by destroyer *Bagley*. It was possible to be exclusive, even snobbish on either one, but on a vessel the size of an S-boat it just didn't work. He sat down to the diesel-flavored tea Tayco brought him. As the steward's mate eased out the doorway of the tight little space and Guy lifted his cup for a gulp, he caught a glimpse of a bare ass in the forward battery room where the crew slept, some weary sailor climbing into his moldy bunk. It was hard to stand on ceremony in close quarters like these, where a long distance away was arm's length.

Schab discovered he could drink warm beer if he really tried, since the alternative was to let Rocky swill what was left by himself. Monday-morning quarterbacking began. It was every submarine sailor's right to criticize, and Gierhart expressed the opinion that Captain Coe had to be the greatest navigator but should never have stayed at periscope depth so long, letting everybody take a look, while the tanker was sinking. In Gierhart's opinion, if *39* had gotten out of there faster, she wouldn't have been bombed or depth-charged. There were those who agreed and those who didn't.

Fremantle, the seaport town for Perth, began to seem like a real place that the boat might get to in the not too distant future. Maybe four days with luck, five at most. It seemed to matter less that the mattresses had become so foul they followed the decaying food over the side, leaving only canvas bunk bottoms to sleep on. It didn't even matter much that the coarse cloth rubbed blisters under arms and on backs of legs to a bloody mess and that the only stuff left to dry up the sores was cornmeal and baking soda. Almost all drinking water had been coming from the rainfall rig on deck, and there was never enough. Nobody wanted to remember how long it had been since the tatters that passed for clothing had been washed. They were even running low on the rubbing alcohol they dabbed here and there on the rankest portions of their filthy hides to keep down the stench. But what the hell, it was all there waiting for them in Fremantle. Oranges, lettuce, milk, ice cream, meat, potatoes, showers, new clothes. Just over the horizon. And then the new-found contentment that had lasted since Sunda Strait, all of three days, was shot to hell.

Bernard had dreamed about it so often that it was still a dream when it actually happened—at first. Then it rapidly became a nightmare. On the twenty-fourth day of patrol, 9 March, the port engine began to vibrate and pound so violently that the engineers had to stop it. Because of broken securing bolts, they found the flywheel wobbling like a drunken sailor. Emergency repair efforts were begun immediately. Tella, Bloom, and Spencer fell to, and Bernard worked with them around the clock, wondering what sleep was like, grateful to find an occasional cup of coffee magically appearing at his elbow when Rocky had loudly proclaimed there wasn't any more. Spencer found that all taper bolt nuts were tight, indicating that some of the taper bolts were broken. The engineers conferred and decided that at least a week would be required to remove and replace the broken bolts. This would mean the complete removal of the clutch, which would put the port motor out of commission during this time.

"But we got no spare bolts aboard," Dean pointed out. "We can't do it."

"It don't take a genius to figure that one out," Tella snapped, tying his wringing wet sweat towel around his wringing wet neck. The sudden change from hope to hopeless did not improve tempers.

As senior chief machinist's mate, Spencer summoned up his dignity. Trying to smooth troubled waters before they kicked up 20-foot waves, he said quietly, "Maybe we could make a temporary repair by using small studs placed between the crankshaft flange and flywheel. Then the remaining unbroken taper bolts would take the load. What do you think, sir?" Bernard, an ever-deepening frown carving a line between his brows, nodded assent.

The work went on for three days in heat close to cremation point. Although the boat was traveling on the surface now, the temperature of these crystal waters was excessively high, with brilliant, hide-frying sunshine day after day. It was the kind of tropic weather longed for by vacationers, but the *39* crew would have preferred overcast. It would have kept them both cooler and harder to detect by enemy aircraft. Thin men grew skeletal. Rationed water became more strictly rationed. Bernard didn't have to worry about forcing down mutton stew anymore; his ulcers made even plain rice an effort. Scuttlebutt was rife that the old boat might never make it to Australia, and nobody wanted to bet on how long it would take to be rescued, if ever.

On 12 March they thought they could get the engine operating, at least under a light load. With twelve ⅜-inch studs installed and the engine reassembled, it was time to test the repairs at two-thirds speed. Placing his scarred and greasy palms in prayer position, Tella muttered, "Come on, God, give us a break." Bernard added, "Amen." Breath-holding was the order of the day as the engine started up. At the end of one minute, the machinist's mates dared take their eyes off it and look at each other hopefully. At the end of two minutes, they were smiling. At the end of three minutes, a heavy bu-bang bu-bang bu-bang was suddenly heard, and upon stopping the engine, they found all the studs broken and the flywheel very loose. Nothing more could be done. It would have to be one engine, making no more than 7 knots. The remainder of the 1,500 miles from Sunda Strait to the port of Fremantle was bound to be a long hard pull.

As if they didn't have burdens enough, the starboard main engine clutch showed symptoms of breakdown, dragging when thrown in and out, slowing up the shift to motor or engine considerably. The engineers suspected some misalignment of assembly in the overhaul done at the navy yard in Soerabaja, but there was no way to investigate until the end of the patrol, if it ever ended. Bernard couldn't shuck off the nagging worry of what would happen if the starboard engine went, and he wasn't the only one. Even Hendrix, famous for cheerfulness, had little to say by way of pep talks. Bone thin COB Nave coughed half his sleeping time away, and the irrepressible Schab withdrew into a shell that nobody knew he had. The only living things aboard that thrived were the cockroaches. They had made Asiatic Fleet S-boats extra-hazardous duty even in peacetime; now they ran wild, slithering along pipes overhead and dropping down on the bare bellies of sleeping men. Les Dean didn't thrive, but he was happier than anyone else. He disliked *39* so heartily that he took a perverse satisfaction in knowing that the old pigboat had blown it.

The unwise became experts, advising the wrung-out engineers, "Why doncha do this, why doncha do that," until blasted by, "Scram, godammit, or I'll bash your brains in with this wrench." Schoenrock, who had never had a long fuse, lost his temper more often. When a complainer pushed his untouched chow aside, saying, "I could really go for shit-on-a-shingle now—I never appreciated that stuff before," Schoenrock, frequently profane himself, exploded. "You foul-mouthed slobs, can't you even call ground beef on toast by a decent name?" Nobody laughed. Zeke Matthews's heart went out to him as he watched the coolie and ricksha, tattooed on Rocky's thigh, speed up to a trot while the cook stomped around the galley in frustration.

But as each day passed the atmosphere lightened because the starboard main engine clutch continued to hold together. A few optimistic souls began cracking jokes and dusted off old chestnuts that made people groan, "Sure hope the Aussies got a set of new stories to tell. If I hear that one about the hunting dog sleeping under the rocking chair again. . . . " But nobody really minded. The weather freshened; the submerged pallor that persisted even under the sunscorch changed to a more normal hue; officers and crew began to look alive despite beggarly rags, open sores, jutting ribs and vertebrae, and skin too loose for the meat underneath. They still smelled, of course, but they were so used to it now that they scarcely noticed it. The boat had begun to develop a sick-sweet stench of putrefaction from mold, decay, and slime.

On the morning of the thirty-third day, 18 March 1942, at 0820, *39* sighted a steamer bearing 24 degrees, range eight miles on parallel course. At 0827 Coe ordered calls exchanged with an Australian bomber, and Radioman Rice directed the plane to the steamer. The bomber circled the vessel, found it friendly, and reported back. It was as though the redhead had been superstitious about taking for granted that the boat was in safe company at last. There wasn't a soul aboard who didn't agree with his wariness. By 1330 they had sighted a total of 18 Allied steamers, one cruiser, and four destroyers, either entering or leaving the port of Fremantle. At 1712 the submarine exchanged calls with the signal station on Rottnest Island and was directed to proceed into the harbor. Torpedo and engine room hatches were opened, and men were allowed to come topside. As the boat completed passage through the minefield, a cheer went up.

The time was 1830, and one of western Australia's spectacular autumn sunsets was in progress. The reflection from subtle reds and pinks masked the beat-up main deck structure and hull, crusted with moss from prolonged submergence. It brought a blush to haggard faces, making them look young again. In a few minutes cool breezes dissolved tensions that had built for months. Men smiled at each other but didn't say much. They didn't have to; their feelings were understood. The moment passed, and minds turned to practical needs: food and sleep, showers, new clothes—no self-respecting sailor could go on the town like this. And there, a gift from heaven, was the U.S. light cruiser *Phoenix*—snappy, clean, untouched, new, stocked with small stores from home, in harbor, and at hand for necessary purchases. "Um hum," Schab murmured. "Fremantle, here I come."

9. A Hard Act to Follow

By the time *S-39* had gotten her paperwork squared away and her weary men assigned to sleeping quarters, what was left of the night was used for showering, scrounging a late meal from the cooperative Aussies, and grabbing a few hours' sleep in cool, clean, comfortable beds. It was enough for starters.

At dawn's early light, Gugliotta donned his grimy rags, which he hated to feel next to his clean body, and was ready to hotfoot it over to *Phoenix* to get new skivvies, shorts, shirts—the works. But, like Swede Bloom and his chief's cap, Guy, who had made lieutenant junior grade in late November, had been unable to get his collar insignia. So he borrowed from Larry Bernard, fastening the bars onto his threadbare collar. It was unthinkable that a three-month veteran JG should board trig and trim *Phoenix* without proper indication of rank. Then he worked his feet into his only footgear, moldy leather sandals that had warped during the night from having dried out for the first time in months, and fastened rusty buckles on ankles scabbed over from blisters. Finally, he settled his cap straight on his forehead in approved regulation style, trying to ignore the green stains that pocked its cover. He knew he'd be among friends soon and that *Phoenix* would see to it that he had apparel fit for an officer and gentleman.

Coe had been told that all other S-boats had been sent to Brisbane and would operate out of that port in the future, as would *39* as soon as she received voyage repairs sufficient to make the journey from the western to the eastern coast of Australia. The flywheel was the biggest concern, but a week or so of work was expected to do the trick. There would be no rest for the weary—relief crews were unavailable—but S-boat sailors weren't accustomed to luxury. Just being in port was enough. In Brisbane the boat would receive more extensive repairs.

Guy thought about this as he made his way to the *Phoenix* and also thought about the scuttlebutt that had immediately run through the crew, tired as they were, and spilled over to the officers, to the effect that Coe would leave them almost at once, be awarded a Navy Cross, and get command of a fleet boat. Seasoned, successful skippers were at a premium, and now that everyone knew the terrible attrition of the Java Sea and Sunda Strait battles, it was inevitable that *39* would lose the highly qualified Coe.

The *Phoenix* loomed large, and Guy noticed a number of *39* boat sailors heading for the after gangway as he began climbing the forward gangway. It was nice to see a handsome, unscarred ship for a change. When Gugliotta reached the quarterdeck, he faced aft and saluted the colors smartly, and then, facing forward, saluted the officer of the deck: "Request permission to come aboard, sir."

There was a noticeable pause as the OOD looked the JG up and down.

Suddenly the submariner realized that he was standing on a spotless quarterdeck with clean, gray-painted barbette and shiny brass fittings which showed up every defect in his bespotted, besmudged, besweated, khaki shorts, shirts, and water-warped sandals. In the eyes of the frit of an OOD, who had still not given him permission to come aboard, Gugliotta was scarcely recognizable as a naval officer. But finally the salute was returned, with a condescending "Permission granted."

Don't do me any favors, you S.O.B., Gugliotta muttered under his breath. But aloud he said only, "Can you direct me to small stores?"

As he listened to instructions, it was Guy's turn to look condescendingly upon his informer. After all, the officer of the deck was an untried ensign, while he, Gugliotta, was sporting J.G.'s bars and was not only qualified in submarines but qualified to tell war stories as well.

Back on the dock, parcels under his arm, Gugliotta ran into Swede Bloom, who was wolfing a head of lettuce like an apple, having just gulped a quart of milk. Bloom related that with grim determination he had finally managed to buy a chief's cap but that he and other *39*ers had had similar experiences on board Phoenix. They'd been looked upon as subhumans. It hurt even more because they'd just heard the news that loving mother *Canopus* had been scuttled after a glorious servicing, above and beyond the call of duty, of her children and any other orphans she could assist in the embattled Philippines. But the submariners got back at *Phoenix* that night.

The city of Perth and its port of Fremantle, located at the mouth of the Swan River on the Indian Ocean, had an atmosphere in 1942 similar to the American West circa 1900. Remote both culturally and geographically from the more populated areas (regular air travel had not yet begun, and access required many show changes by railroad), it was open, friendly, and sometimes as rip-roaring as San Francisco in Barbary Coast days; there had even been a gold rush. The Aussies had felt abandoned after the British defeat at Singapore; most of their army was fighting oveseas; and the loss of warship *Perth* in Sunda Strait had made a large hole in their small navy. It was only sensible to extend a warm welcome to the American Fleet. Australians were among the most hospitable people in the world, anyway, and they found similarities of spirit and independence in their American cousins. Some frictions would inevitably develop as time went by, but the honeymoon was in full swing in 1942.

The sight of the old-fashioned saloons with their pert barmaids suited the female-hungry *39* sailors just fine. By evening, they had slept enough, scrubbed enough, gorged enough, and were sartorially decent enough to head for the nearest bar for some serious drinking. Whatever else they could find by way of recreation would come later. Schab and Matthews were joined by Christopher and Mattingly at a glossy mahogany bar that was in a state of perpetual polish from uncountable numbers of palms sliding along its surface to grasp a glass. Four more were added as the quartet reached out for whiskey and water. They would find it strange to down first gulps served Aussie style without ice, but youth and determination resulted in rapid adjustment. There were a number of Diggers—Australia's GI Joes—in the bar, waiting for transportation overseas, and, though their pay was minuscule compared to that of the Americans, they were first to stand drinks. In no time arms were thrown over shoulders, lifelong friendships had developed, and the Americans began learning "Waltzing Matilda." It was a happy scene.

Then the swinging doors disgorged a group of sailors from light cruiser *Phoenix*. They worked their way through the crowd and the smoke that had risen high enough to wreath the reclining nude over the bar in a blue haze that reached to her dimpled knees. They looked great, these sailors—well fed, spick 'n span, a credit to Uncle Sam—and nobody had any intention of bothering them. It was live and let live until some nosy guy (Schab said it was Christopher; Christopher said it was Schab) overheard one of them brag that "*Phoenix* came all the way here to the west coast of Australia unescorted."

It was an innocent enough remark, but unfortunately it was said in the presence of submariners who had come a long way riding an old tub that could scarcely crawl much of the time, in seas filled with enough enemy vessels to sink a fleet, which was pretty much what the Japanese had done. There was a brief silence, then a voice rang out, "Poor fellows, all alone were you in your eentsy-weentsy 10,000-ton new cruiser with all them big guns and turrets? Didja get seasick? How about the four planes you carry? Couldn't they protect you in all that great big ocean?" It didn't take much of this kind of palaver before an elbow dug its way into a rib, a foot was stamped on, and a fist smashed a jaw. The submariners found unexpected help from their Digger friends, many of whom had seen combat and were going back for more. Men who had hoped to spend the night in town with a pickup were picked up allright—by the shore patrol. Everybody agreed later on, though, that it was worth it.

Missing from the fracas was Chief of the Boat Earl Nave, who would have outswung, outshouted, and outcursed every man in the place, Aussie or U.S. The feverish spots on the cheeks of the gaunt chief, and the hacking cough that had given him no rest, had put him in sick bay upon arrival. It didn't take long for the doctors to diagnose tuberculosis and write orders to send him home fast for treatment in the States. A new COB was needed immediately. Paul Spencer, senior chief machinist's mate, was named.

One crew member who found out quickly how to wring the greatest amount of friendship out of the friendly residents of the Perth-Fremantle area was W.E. Schoenrock. When the crew had continued to bitch endlessly about the tea that nobody wanted to drink Rocky, in a snit, had tossed the bags into a five-gallon can which he stowed in a food locker. His first night on the town convinced him that almost any American in Australia was welcome, but an American with tea would be given no holds barred. Rationing was in effect, but nothing really mattered except tea. Rocky's coconspirator this time was Swede Bloom. The two of them divvied half the stash (saving the other half for Brisbane), and while other American sailors bought Johnny Walker Red Label scotch with American dollars, Rocky and Swede bought it with teabags. It helped romance along as well.

Within a few days the rumors about Coe became fact; it was confirmed that he would be leaving in 24 hours and given command of the fleet boat *Skipjack*. When Hendrix heard the news, he accepted Bernard's invitation to have a beer and then had another, a rare occurrence for the fitness-conscious ensign. But he explained it by confiding to Bernard, "I was lucky to get his boat for my first boat. I won't forget how he always said to make the best of what you've got and try to keep it in fighting shape. I learned good submarine from him."

Larry added solemnly, "We'll never have another like him."

Schab and Bixler would remember Coe, too. That same day, the two sailors were on deck watching the sailboats from the Fremantle Sailing Club. One of the craft, with a couple of girls on board, came nearer and nearer until the two young men could admire at very close range the wind-tossed hair, tight jerseys, and sparkling eyes that sought theirs.

"Hi," the girls called out. "Come on aboard, Yanks, and go for a syle with us."

"We can't," Bixler called back, wishing his heart out that they could. Suddenly Schab looked up at the bridge, and there was Captain Coe watching them. By this time the sailboat was almost alongside and, like the sirens of yore who seduced sailors into shipwreck, the girls cried out, "Come on, come on."

Embarrassed by the insistent invitation in front of the skipper, the two men glanced sheepishly at the bridge again and saw Coe jerk his thumb in the direction of the sailboat; "Go ahead," he said. They didn't waste a second scrambling aboard. It was a great farewell gesture on the part of the old man, and they never forgot it.

And then Coe was gone, and Lieutenant Francis E. Brown—Naval Academy 1933, from Reno, Nevada—became skipper of the *39*. His only S-boat experience had been a few months on board the *S-32* while she was being decommissioned in Philadelphia. He had served on board *Nautilus*, a 2,730-ton goliath, and had assisted in fitting out the USS *Seal* at the Electric Boat Company in New London, Connecticut, serving on board her for three years. He had also been division engineer officer for Submarine Division 15 before getting *S-39*. The old pigboat was a comedown, but she was, after all, a command—the thing dearest to any man's heart. Tall, slender, dark, and sporting a small moustache, Brown was a serious and intense type who had the same desire as any other skipper—to make a name for himself. With his engineering experience, he had no illusions as to the material condition of the boat he had inherited, but couldn't help showing that it was a shock to find out how truly bad it was.

Everybody was sorry to leave Fremantle and its cool weather. But there would be stops in Melbourne and Sydney before reaching Brisbane, where, it was hoped, *39* could be put into as close an approximation of fighting trim as possible. The crew were still a little punchy at the change from poverty to prosperity, and even reasonable souls not inclined to get in trouble, like Zeke Matthews, struggled with the sudden wealth of T-bone steaks, and abundance of women whose men had been away fighting the war for some time, and plentiful booze (which would be imbibed so freely by thirsty Americans that it would shortly become $20 a bottle for Johnny Walker, if you could find any).

On his last night in Perth, Zeke had enjoyed all of the above. War had taught him one thing—grab what you can while you can grab it. The *39* was scheduled to leave Fremantle on a Sunday morning at 0700, and at 0600 Matthews tried to shake himself awake, fell back for a snooze, then opened his eyes wide enough to glance at his watch. That was enough to propel him out of bed in a hurry. Slapping on his clothes as he raced down the quiet halls, he paused long enough to find out from a sleepy desk clerk that there were no buses running this early on Sunday. The frantic Matthews erupted onto the empty sidewalk, then galloped around the corner to Queen Street, one of the main arteries. By luck there was a cab available; he hailed it, climbed in beside the driver, and asked how much he'd charge to take him to Fremantle. He had about 20 minutes left before *39* shoved off. "Arf a pound," the cabbie said. Matthews asked, "Can you get me there by seven?" The driver replied, "If they catch me speedin' they'll tyke me bloomin' driver's license awy." Zeke glanced quickly at his wallet. "This is an emergency. I'll give you a pound and a half."

They were off. The morning sun sparkled on the Swan River like diamonds on blue satin, but Matthews didn't see it. There was a sweet-spicy aroma from the lemon-scented gum trees, but Matthews didn't smell it. He was staring either at his watch or at the road straight ahead. He wanted to yell, "Faster, faster," but these Aussies were plenty independent, and if he opened his yap and said the wrong thing, the driver might dump him then and there. The quiet kind who took his obligations seriously, Matthews dreaded missing the boat. Besides, there was a new skipper, and nobody'd had much time yet to find out about his policies. Zeke had the fare clutched in his hand long before they reached the dock. The moment they arrived he thrust it at the cabbie with a "thanks." The submarine was tied up alongside a freighter. As Matthews ran up the freighter's gangway, he shouted to the deck watch, "Is the *S-39* still around?" Upon receiving a nod, he shouted again, "Tell them to hold it till I get there." Sprinting across the deck, Matthews saw that there was only one mooring line left from freighter to *39*. It was better than a 50-foot drop at a 45-degree angle, a dizzying feat for a nonacrobat with a slight hangover, but Matthews didn't hesitate for a second. Duty called. Better lost than left. Grabbing hold with a will, he maneuvered hand over hand not daring to look down. He made it.

Unhappy Les Dean had hoped to be made happy in Fremantle by finding orders awaiting him to a fleet boat, any fleet boat. As *39* creaked her way through the marine traffic and headed out to sea, Dean's hopes receded with the shoreline. The east coast gave him no hope either, since he'd heard that there were only S-boats in Brisbane. Who wanted to exchange one pigboat for another? Maybe he'd get sick; people did. Look at the way Pennell and Parks had passed out in Java. Of course, they might be prisoners of the Japanese by now, and that was too high a price to pay for a transfer, but it was about the only thing he could think of that was.

In Oakland, Dorothy Reynolds had kept tabs on every bit of information she could find about the formation of the WAAC, the Women's Army Auxiliary Corps. It seemed that the corps was going through endless labor before actual birth took place. Finally it was announced that the first officer's candidates would go to Fort Des Moines, Iowa, for an eight-week training course starting 15 July 1942, after that, 12,000 enrollees would be accepted to meet the first year's quota. A June article in *Time* magazine showed pictures of some of the 13,000 women who had applied for the 440 officers' slots available in this first class. Dorothy's heart sank. Many are called but few are chosen, she reminded herself, but her determination was not lessened. And, although Dorothy didn't know it, General George C. Marshall ordered the plans expanded and training speeded up so that a large number of women would be available at the earliest possible date. The reason was simple: there was a manpower crisis in the services. Army ground forces were short 160,000 men, making WAAC expansion a necessity.

As Dorothy had anticipated, there were so many applicants for the pioneer enrollments that the corps could pick and choose. In addition, no other service had yet established a women's branch, so there were no competitors. Scoring high in aptitude testing, Dorothy breezed in but not without moments of tension. Since the number of applicants at first far exceeded training space, recruits were rigorously screened. They were required to show proof of their claims of work experience and willingly endure inquiries made at their schools, from the people they had given as character references, and even in police courts if that seemed advisable. Physical and mental requirements were astronomical compared to those for enlisted men. A make-or-break interview with a WAAC officer topped off the procedure. As she left, Dorothy heard one of the male recruiters whisper to a coworker, "Looks like another one of those female wackies has joined up." It was the first snide remark she'd heard about the corps, but it wouldn't be the last.

One of the happiest parts of all this took place when Dorothy came home from her interview, looked her conservative father straight in the eye, and announced that she was entering the WAAC. Her father stared right back at her for a long moment, then said, "I think that's great." Dorothy didn't realize that she'd been holding her breath until she let it go in a sigh of relief. Sympathetic to her daughter's desire to see and do, her mother simply said, "I'll miss you."

There was not much sleep in the household that night. Dorothy lay awake for hours, then got up and smoked a cigarette in the dark, worrying about the rigors of basic training that began at five in the morning and lasted until five in the afternoon. Among other subjects, she'd be studying military customs and courtesy, map reading, sanitation and first aid, defense against chemical and air attacks, company administration, and mess management. She wondered whether she should remove her cap in church or dining rooms where women usually didn't, or open doors for men who outranked her. She'd always loved military music and marching bands, so the thought of parades and drills and ceremonies didn't faze her. And anyway, no amount of hard work would be too much, because she'd been told for sure that Europe, Asia, Africa would all be available for WAAC overseas assignments.

She remembered the recruiting poster showing a male soldier with a gun and the head of a woman complete with cap and insignia. The legend read, "Release Men to Fight. Serve in the WAAC." It made her think of Ed Schab, and she wondered what was happening to him. Even though they'd just been kids way back then and kind of foolish, she'd never met anybody she liked better.

On the East Coast, Bobette Gugliotta was surprised one day in August 1942 to received a letter from her sister-in-law that did not concentrate as usual on the welfare of brothers Guy and Paul, the latter training as a paratrooper. Instead, Anne Gugliotta had an important announcement of her own to make. The librarian and Latin teacher had watched the formation of the WAAC with an interest equal to that of Dorothy Reynolds, but for a different reason. Anne was hoping the Navy would follow suit. After a bit of foot-dragging, it did.

On July 30, 1942, legislation was enacted that would enable women to become part of the Naval Reserve. The female branch was to be called the contrived mouthful, "Women Accepted for Voluntary Emergency Services," which would happily shorten into the appropriate word "WAVES." Anne was determined to join. She first applied for the enlisted corps but, at 35, was told she was "too old." Her hopes sank but quickly revived when, quick as a flash, the 4th Naval District, Philadelphia, enrolled her in officer's training. A few months later she would go to the Naval Reserve Midshipman School in North-hampton, Massachusetts, and after six weeks training proudly don an ensign's uniform. Women were beginning to come into their own in the armed forces.

By mid-April the *S-39* had made her way around Australia and was tied up at New Farm Wharf in Brisbane to begin repairs with tender *Griffin,* who had herself just arrived after a history-making voyage of some 12,000 miles. USS *Griffin* had completed conversion from a C-3 cargo ship to a submarine tender in the Brooklyn Navy Yard in August 1941. Commissioned under the command of Captain Stanley D. Jupp, she deployed to Newfoundland to support the U.S. Navy's undeclared war against German U-boats. There she provided facilities and services for U.S. submarines in the area and for the giant-sized, non-maneuverable French submarine *Surcouf.*

After Pearl Harbor, *Griffin* operated out of New London, Connecticut, for a few months until it was decided that she would proceed to Brisbane, where she was sorely needed for S-boat repair. In Panama she would pick up Captain Ralph W. Christie, who was to command submarines based in Brisbane, and Division 53—composed of *S-42, 43, 44, 46,* and *47*—which would join the tender on the long trip to Australia. *Griffin* carried a nucleus crew of 100 Navy regulars and approximately 800 reserves from the Detroit Armory. Among her regular crew members on this safari were gunner's mate K.M. Hurtt, machinist's mate Richard Ellis, and electrician's mate Paul Bryan.

Hurtt, Ellis, and Bryan, along with other experienced seamen aboard, were aware that S-boats had never been designed for anything more strenuous than coastal patrol. Would Captain Christie's strange armada be able to complete the 45-day journey that had scheduled only one stopover, in Bora-Bora, for refuel-ing? The painfully slow pigboats would make the expedition resemble the old race between the hare and the tortoise. *Griffin* and chicks averaged 8.7 knots during the lengthy journey. Miraculously, considering wartime dangers, the distance involved, and the frequent breakdowns that were par for any S-boat, Subdiv 53 made it all the way with only minor problems.

Hurtt, who had previously served four years in the Asiatic Fleet on flagship *Augusta,* had always nursed a secret desire for submarine duty and had requested it several times unsuccessfully. From the eminence of *Griffin*'s decks, he watched the little black specks when they surfaced. Their obvious fragility only reinforced his interest. He wanted sub duty and was determined to get it. Richard Ellis had grown up by the sea in Miami, Florida, and liked it well enough to join the Navy. After service school in Norfolk, Virginia, he was sent to Panama, where he served aboard an old four-piper destroyer, the USS *Tattnall*, until ordered to the submarine tender *Griffin*. That was the beginning of his interest in submersibles. Unlike Napoleon, who turned down a submarine built by Robert Fulton in 1800, Ellis made up his mind he would not turn down any opportunity to volunteer for sub duty. Paul Bryan, from Tunis, Missouri, had traded in an $18-a-week grocery store job (of which $16 went for room and board leaving 8 bucks a month for fun, games and clothes) to join the Navy, where he'd be paid $21 a month from which nothing would be taken. His first duty in 1936 was aboard USS *Wright,* a seaplane tender. While tied up in Coco Solo, Panama, not far from the sub base, Paul could see the squat underseas vessels and decided he wanted to go to sub school. But the school was full up, so he settled for the submarine tender *Griffin*. The near-miss had only whetted his appetite to wear dolphins and he was ready to take advantage of the first opportunity that presented itself. All three men would end up on *S-39*.

It was a whole new ball game for the *39* boat. Many seasoned crew members were leaving, or soon would be, to go to other boats where experienced men were needed among the newcomers. Frank Brown, himself new in the position of top authority aboard a submarine, was eager to succeed. Officers Dernard, Gugliotta, and Hendrix were eager to help him and tried not to make comparisons, mentally or verbally, between the new skipper and the old. Brown sometimes made it difficult for them because he implied that *39* was a loose arrangement badly in need of sharpening. He was hot for use of the deck gun and started making arrangements to get a fifth officer aboard, a gunnery expert who had served with him previously.

Brown had been a top man at the Naval Academy and was expert in engineering. In some ways his expertise, plus his fleet-boat experience, made it harder for him to accept the fact that S-boat machinery could leak and creak and still operate, even occasionally sinking something along the way. He liked things to be right and regulation, a difficult feat to achieve with a class of over-age boats that would be retired from patrol duty the moment there were enough fleet boats to take their places. Kind and optimistic Hendrix was impressed with Brown's knowledge of just what spare parts were needed and his ability to locate problems with machinery; nevertheless, he still worried that the new "old man" would be disappointed with the performance of vessel and personnel, since he was mentally geared to a by-the-book perfection not found aboard S-boats. Brown had something else to contend with. If fleet-boat sailors had their snobbery, S-boat sailors could give them cards and spades in the art. Pigboat people felt they had proved their worth. They had to be tough.

Fortunately for the officers, the inevitable readjustments were eased by the goodwill of the Australians and the pleasant living conditions. Brisbane's climate was far more tropical than that of Perth but didn't approach the heat of the Philippines or Java. American officers were welcome at any private club in the city, including the exclusive Tattersall's, where they could drink, eat, and fraternize with leading citizens. Dinner and dance invitations were plentiful for officers and crew, and excellent quarters were furnished at the Esplanade Hotel, an old but elegant Victorian establishment with superior food. Gugliotta, whose favorite meal was breakfast, took to "styke and aigs" or "brynes and aigs," lusty dishes that were routine starts for the day for trencherman Aussies, who were automatically served two potato dishes with each entree.

Guy found the city reminiscent of the U.S. in his childhood. Not all houses boasted indoor toilets or even bathtubs, and there were often open-air troughs for use as urinals behind pubs and saloons. Horse-drawn vehicles were not uncommon, although Brisbane had her share of trucks, buses, streetcars, and automobiles. But since all petrol was imported, strict rationing had begun in 1940, restricting private cars to 16 miles per week. The Americans were interested in an unusual device used to extend mileage. Mounted on the rear ends of commerical vehicles and some automobiles were generating plants that resembled miniature furnaces. Coal or charcoal was burned in a small cylinder approximately a foot in diameter and two feet high, giving off producer gas, which was then burned in lieu of petrol.

The Brisbane of 1942, with its narrow streets and row houses, was not a pretty town, nor did it boast unusual features, with the exception of a few homes built on stilts and some with iron filigree balcony railings However, it could have been subtitled "the Flowering City" because of the beautiful blossoming trees that softened its outlines and lavishly decorated its thoroughfares. Coral and tulip, frangipani, flame-of-the-Forest, and bauhinia were only a few of the many varieties, one or more of which were almost always in bloom. Rare wildlife—koalas, kangaroos, wombats, and emus—could also be seen nearby. At the shops in town, American servicemen bought star rubies, opals, and other stones at prices impossible in the U.S. When out sightseeing, they were proudly shown the Italian Renaissance–style City Hall, with its high clock tower, built in 1931.

Gugliotta and Hendrix, at Tattersall's one evening, made the acquaintance of Stewart Tait, who owned a department store in town. He immediately invited the young men to dinner at his home, where they met his wife and daughters. His brother, David Tait, who called himself the black sheep of the family, entertained the two submariners at Tattersall's with his stories of bushrangers (Australian bandits) and bunyips (lengendary creatures), part of the Aboriginal culture. David's ability to consume oysters—four dozen on the half shell, without batting an eye, washed down by vast quantities of ale—was awesome even by Aussie standards, and left the Americans properly humble.

Bernard lost his ulcers and gained weight, helped along by his friendship with a gentleman by the name of Pud Thurlow, who was manager of Brisbane's largest brewery, the Bulimba. With true down-under hospitality, Thurlow invited Larry not only to visit the brewery but to bring all his friends. Next was an invitation to dinner, where Bernard met more people and received more invitations. And everybody went to the races and took the Americans along. Australians were crazy over horses. Gugliotta had never been much of a fan but wisely forgot that he wasn't because of his kind host's enthusiasm. And with all the color and excitement, Guy actually found himself enjoying the Queensland Turf Club Run at Albion Park. He even managed to look knowledgeable when Stewart Tait advised him which entry to bet on because "his sire was Phar Lap, a gibber of a horse, more than 17 hands high, winner of Melbourne Cup in 1930."

The materiel condition of the boat was still the big concern. The repair work accomplished in Fremantle had held up well as far as the port main engine flywheel went, but had not corrected the apparent misalignment in the starboard main engine clutch assembly. A *Griffin* repair gang was turned loose on it, assisted by *S-39*'s ship's force. They broke it down quickly and gave it a thorough overhaul, knowing that speed was of the utmost importance, since the enemy was on the move. In March the Japanese had landed 3,000 men at Lae in Eastern New Guinea. Australia, the only remaining Allied bastion in the Pacific, was being threatened by Japanese submarines. The month of April saw enemy ships, planes, and men taking off from the Marshalls and Dutch East Indies to occupy harbors in the northern Solomons without a shred of opposition. Their plan was to cut Allied supply lines and isolate Australia. In the offing was a seaborne invasion to secure Port Moresby, New Guinea, and a move to Guadalcanal.

Griffin repair and the ship's force fell to on a dry-docking, bottom-cleaning, painting, and overhaul of all sea valves, trim pump, and C & R (ship's air) compressors. Then attention turned to depth-gage calibration and the welding of port engine exhaust piping. The officers who had been aboard during *39*'s three patrols felt that she would be in better operating condition when the work was complete than she had been at the start of the war. Maybe that wasn't saying much, they wryly admitted among themselves, since at that time she had gone without overhaul for so long.

For the crew, Brisbane was not as good a liberty as Perth in some ways. There was a mulititude of servicemen in the area, including a number of Diggers from a nearby army base. These soldiers got liberty at noon, making it harder for the U.S. servicemen to get quality drinks in quantity, since they couldn't make it to the pubs until 1600. Then Diggers started coming back from their ordeal in

North Africa to find that many of their girls had gone over to the newcomers and had Yank sweethearts—or husbands. Typical was Swede Bloom's experience. At a party one evening he met a sergeant in the women's army whose ancestry combined Australian and East Indian. She introduced him to her sister, and he fell head over heels for this attractive Indralian, not even needing teabags to have her return the compliment.

It wasn't that Americans were so special, but they started with a great advantage, No matter how little U.S. enlisted men were paid, it was more than Aussies got. A beer a day could wipe out a Digger, but a U.S. type could squire a girl to the National Hotel, buy a four-inch-thick, two-foot-long porterhouse steak dinner, then take her for dancing and drinks at the Princess cabaret—not every night, of course, but once a month was oftener than his Australian counterpart could afford. Brawls were not unknown. Even so, many lasting friendships developed between Aussie and American servicemen.

Ed Schab and Bob Bixler headed for the Princess cabaret for a little hoofing as often as they could. One evening they met up with a couple of good-looking girls. Schab, who had just come back from the dead so to speak, was in high spirits. The Red Cross had recently contacted the *39* boat to find out whether Edmund Schab was aboard. He had been reported missing by his family because no mail had reached them since long before the start of the war. Very much alive as usual, Schab was not missing in action but ready for it, and while he instructed the attractive Australian Mary Besperam in a few intricate jitterbug maneuvers, he bent her willing ear. When they exchanged names, Ed, with his old urge to stir up excitement, gave Bixler a solid kick in the shins under the table as he told Mary that he was called Ripper Schab.

The startled girl, a worry line between her brows, asked quickly, "What do you mean, Ripper?" The famous Jack of the same name was no doubt uppermost in her mind. Thinking fast, Schab explained, "It's a kind of nickname." He didn't want to lose this sweet chick. "I was christened Rip Van Winkle Schab," he ventured, then braced himself for the reaction.

It was a relief to learn that though Aussies spoke an approximation of the American language, they obviously didn't read American authors in school, because Mary Besperam brightened at once: "I understand. You must have come from a Dutch family."

Bixler whipped out his handkerchief, coughing and sneezing, unable to keep as straight a face as his buddy. Schab nodded his head without actually saying yes. From then on—and he saw her often—she called him Ripper. He never did tell her the truth. Later, letters came to the States for him addressed to Rip Van Winkle Schab in which she called him her knight in shining armor. She was a mighty attractive girl, and if it hadn't been for Dorothy . . . .

Tayco and Fabricante had indulged in the state lottery called by the odd name "Golden Casket Art Union"; Fabricante was secretly hoping to duplicate his success in the Philippines. He would probably never get to spend the lottery money he had salted away in the bank in Manila now that the Japanese had taken over, but if it could happen once, it could happen again. Australia was not as ideal for the mess stewards as it was for the rest of the crew. At home in the islands, there was a sizable group of Filipinos of status who owned businesses and were active in politics and the professions. There had been no such group in Java, but at least darker skins were no novelty there, and *mestizos* were accepted. In an underpopulated country like Australia, badly in need of settlers, there was continuing opposition in the 1940s, as there always had been, to non-British immigrants—including even those of European origin, let alone blacks, Orientals, or Polynesians—although there were a few. Brothels did not admit men of color, nor did they employ any but white prostitutes. Saloons, dancehalls, pubs were closed to them as well. Tayco and Fabricante found no colony here of their own compatriots or similar groups to welcome them into their homes or provide diversion. All they had was each other.

The Aussies seemed to take their women a lot more casually than Americans did. In Tattersall's Club for a farewell drink before going on their fourth patrol, Gugliotta and Hendrix noticed an Australian lieutenant who, though neatly dressed, had that scraggly-scrawny look about the face reminiscent of themselves when they came into Perth. The lieutenant downed beer after beer with an intensity that brought back memories to Guy, although near-teetotaler Hendrix hadn't scoffed the brew so rapidly. When they struck up a conversation, the lieutenant divulged that he'd arrived from Africa quite a few hours earlier and that the first thing on his mind had been grog. Making a beeline for Tattersall's, he'd been drinking his fill ever since. Finally, a little stiff-legged and sated, he excused himself: "Guess I'd better call the old girl. M'wife doesn't know I'm home yet."

There was mail in Brisbane. Long separated from their spouses, young officers like Gugliotta and Bernard read their letters threadbare and stared hungrily at new snapshots of their wives. The unwed crew, with or without girls at home, devoured their mail as well, wanting to hear what was going on, needing sustenance from friends and family, storing up home stuff because it was nearing time to make another patrol. There was no mail for Tayco and Fabricante. The Philippines were firmly in Japanese hands; even Bataan had fallen.

On 10 May, *39* got underway from alongside USS *Griffin* standing out the channel. HMAS *Bingera* escorted the submarine out of port and then *39*, as a routine courtesy, acted as target for the surface ship so that she could practice antisubmarine tactics. In another routine procedure that followed work done on hull closures or anything else affecting watertightness, *39* made a deep dive, submerging to 215 feet. Among other minor leaks they found a weep through the engine-room hatch coaming. Captain Brown concluded that they should not go deeper than 150 feet for depth-charge evasion until next upkeep, when the hatch skirt could be renewed. Gugliotta, Bernard, and Hendrix felt that the weep had existed for a long time. Less usual was an overheated bearing.

On the third day, a lookout reported a submarine periscope a couple of thousand yards away. Brown, on the bridge, decided to reverse course and go around the position. He gave as his reason that although enemy submarines had already been reported in the area, he did not consider the contact positive enough. Since *39* had tried-and-true lookouts who would hardly mistake a periscope at such close range, everyone was baffled by the decision.

Brown instituted a new procedure. Submerged to 85 feet, he ordered a periscope observation every 45 minutes. Previously, *39* had run at periscope depth in patrol area and had a look every 20 to 30 minutes unless the skies were crawling with enemy aircraft.

More minor casualties were reported: a broken rocker arm bracket, an overheated steady bearing, a leaky exhaust pipe. The last had been repaired by welding way back in October 1941 while a new one was being cast. The bombing of Cavite Navy Yard had destroyed *39*'s new pipe along with everything else, and she'd been making do ever since with what she had. The list of problems, old and new, grew as the fourth patrol continued; a flooded binnacle tube, a ground in the main motor power cable, the failure of the port engine air compressor. Some flaws had been taken for granted as endurable, if not desirable, but new ones were detected by the analytical eyes of a skipper accustomed to better mechanisms. On two points all agreed: the boat was over the hill, and improvements were needed.

Officers and crew had almost forgotten the dog-days heat of their metal kennel during their few short weeks of civilized living. Men like Dean and Gierhart kept thinking of air-conditioned fleet boats with the longing of a lover forced to accept a manatee when he'd been used to living with a mermaid. Constant overcast produced rain squalls and reduced visibility. When surfaced, *39* tried to carry a float (diverting engine power to charging the battery) to keep the battery at close to full charge, but the temperature of the motors gradually increased to 200 degrees, requiring frequent discontinuance of the float to keep motors and humans from dissolving.

All the old stenches returned, headed by bilge aroma, a mix of decayed fungus, sweat gone sour, and something indefinable but sick-sweet. Finger-length stud cockroaches, stunned but never decimated by fumigation, revived to sire new hordes. Prickly heat gone underground in Australia popped out red and itchy on butts, armpits, and backs of knees. Possibly the happiest soul on board was Schonenrock. To begin with, his almost inexhaustible supply of teabags had made him the undisputed sheik of Brisbane. And if clothes made the man, food makes the cook: Rocky was back to having quality material to work with; his refrigerator was operating; and he was able to set a good table. Zeke Matthews could once again chow down four times a day, faithfully tucking away hot soup, hot breakfast, cold lunch, and large hot supper.

One of the electricians, while testing switches in an attempt to locate a battery ground, accidentally turned on all the running lights. It lasted only five seconds, but since *39* and all others like her ran darkened ship at night, to be suddenly illuminated like a Hollywood opening scared the hell out of everybody, especially those topside. Christopher, who seemed to have a way of being present during these cases of indecent exposure, was acting as lookout. Later he told an interested audience, "Almost peed my pants. Lucky I suffer from sub complaint [chronic constipation], or it could have been worse." The preventive remedy was to remove all fuses for topside lights. If they weren't there, they couldn't turn on.

And then the submarine developed a noisy trim pump. Since it was used upon submerging to move water among the variable ballast tanks, or overboard, to obtain the proper trim, the pump had to run quietly; otherwise, it could divulge the sub's whereabouts. A concerned Brown inquired among the engineers and found that the tender had reassembled the pump knowing the crank journal was out of round. Repairs had not been completed for lack of time. An attempt to keep down operational noise was made by reducing the bearing clearance each time the bearing was hammered out. The engineers cursed *Griffin* repair, claiming that one of *39*'s auxiliarymen could have fixed it properly. Mechanical problems had begun causing emotional problems, too.

The next few days were spent attempting to survey Misima Island off New Guinea. This was easier said than done. Visibility was poor; the seas were heavy, and there were strong currents and winds, with skies swathed in solid overcast. When the weather cleared enough that Misima could be sighted through the haze, *39* saw a periodic flashing white light near Umoni on the north coast. There was little doubt that the Japanese had started populating the island. Next came a reconnaissance of nearby Deboyne Island to ascertain whether it would be a likely amphibious landing spot for the enemy. The seas had moderated somewhat, enabling *39* to circle Deboyne and report no activity in the lagoon and no ships sighted. Brown noted that there were no possible landing beaches except in a limited stretch along the west coast. Neither the Japanese nor the Allies were likely to use this island.

Advance scouting came under the heading of "special missions" and was important to the future success of the war effort. Although originally intended for patrol in their own coastal waters, S-boats were far more suited to this kind of work than to sinkings, which required exceptional skill plus exceptional luck to perform successfully. But at this crucial stage in the conflict, with a shortage of men and material, every ship was pressed into service regardless of age or suitability.

Everything was interesting and exciting to newcomer Dick Ellis, ma-

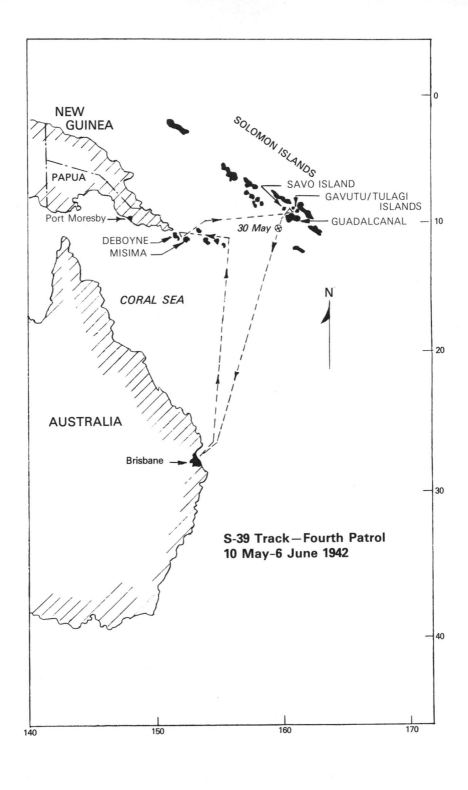

NEW GUINEA

PAPUA

Port Moresby →

SOLOMON ISLANDS

SAVO ISLAND

GAVUTU/TULAGI ISLANDS

GUADALCANAL

— 10

DEBOYNE

MISIMA

30 May ⊗

CORAL SEA

N

— 20

AUSTRALIA

Brisbane →

— 30

**S-39 Track—Fourth Patrol
10 May–6 June 1942**

— 40

0 —

140   150   160   170

chinist's mate, making his first patrol. Good-natured Kutscherowski showed him the ropes, and Ellis was soon standing motor-room and lookout watches. A couple of times he found his heart in his mouth and his stomach right behind it. Once, when *39* was at periscope depth in rough seas, she porpoised. When Dick felt the tremble as her two propellers reared up out of the water, screws spinning, those seconds seemed forever, and for a few more seconds Ellis wondered if he wanted submarines after all. "That ain't nothin'," Kutscherowski assured him. "I been down in really rough seas as deep as a hundred feet when we porpoised. It takes forever comin' up with the old boat shakin' all the way like a dog what just had a bath."

One night on lookout with Bernard, Ellis spotted a patrol craft. The exec reported it to Captain Brown, and *39* submerged. Eager for action, Ellis was disappointed that no contact was made. He wasn't the only one. Later on when they resurfaced, the seas had turned so rough that waves were slapping over the conning tower, making the bridge a skating rink. Man overboard would have been man drowned. Bernard and Ellis had body lines tied to handrails, but that didn't prevent them from being smashed against the after bridge structure with each big wave. Ellis lost his footing and took a smack in the back that would ache off and on for the rest of his life.

The port engine flooded, an old problem caused by leaking engine exhaust system valves. Repairs made in port between patrols never lasted long. On this occasion a crack in the piping was also found. Fogged periscopes were the next but not unusual difficulty; they were seldom sealed properly after being overhauled. But the fogging made it difficult to see out, hardly a condition to be desired for an arthritic pigboat prowling for prey and needing all the help she could get. A brand-new disaster was the flooding of the magnetic compass in the conning tower, which happened so rapidly that it was impossible to prevent sea pressure from breaking the glass compass face and crushing the float. *Griffin* got the blame for this, too, her name inevitably prefaced by "Sonuvabitch." The *39* was dredging up all the uglies she could find on this fourth patrol and wasn't finished yet.

A spark of badly needed interest was ignited when Schab, on radio watch, received a message from the squadron commander directing *S-39* to a rescue task. It was probably to pick up Australian coast watchers whose job was to report enemy activity; these were scattered throughout the Solomon Islands. But for some unexplained reason, the assignment was canceled and the submarine continued on her way.

Her primary objective was to bombard a Japanese airfield on Gavutu Island near Tulagi, capital of the Solomons. Allied aircraft were also scheduled to bomb the area. The weather was perfect, clear with calm seas, but the small densely forested island presented no point of aim for the designated target. Shortly after sunset it was impossible to make out the island at all, though a dim light flashed a few times in the interior. No aircraft, enemy or Allied, appeared. The submarine set course for Guadalcanal, where Allied aircraft were also scheduled to bomb. Again, no aircraft appeared.

While the boat was submerged, the exhaust system leak put sea water in the cylinders of the port engine, polluting the lube oil in the crankcase. This necessitated daily renewal, which used up so much oil that the boat was running short. Since 39 had to have enough to make it back to Brisbane, it looked as though she would be forced to leave the area, shortening the patrol. Nobody was sorry to go.

Then the port engine stopped. Frank Brown, Larry Bernard, and the engineers knew that this meant bad trouble. Each engine had its own attached air compressor, and the problem was located there. A full ground in the main motor power cable turned up, caused, like so many of their problems, by the eternally hot, humid atmosphere of the old boat. And on 1 June, the port main engine air compressor failed again from the carrying away of all second-stage piston rings and a scored and worn second-stage liner. The captain and exec decided to substitute the C & R compressor used for general air charging. It worked effectively, and they hoped it would hold until they reached Brisbane. It was the only bright spot. Given the list of mechanical defects, it was probably just as well that the patrol report read, "nothing sighted." The sea was starting to claim S-39 with seepage into vital organs.

On Saturday, 6 June, 39 moored to USS Griffin for more major surgery and patching up after a disappointing, tedious, and spiritless excursion. In his patrol report Brown recommended that if operations were to be continued in these unsurveyed waters, fathometers be installed; he requested that the officer complement be increased to five and a pharmacist's mate added; and, being a slender man who had sweated away the usual 15 pounds or so, he suggested that habitability would be greatly increased by the installation of an air conditioning unit. Only the request for an additional officer was granted. Bernard, Gugliotta, and Hendrix, discussing it among themselves, knew they had needed another since the start of the war because of extra duty required of them when they were not on watch. With five officers aboard, they could each have a normal one-in-four watch instead of one in three, giving them a chance to get enough sleep so that they could function without the nagging weariness that had been their lot for so long.

10. Sailor, Rest Your Oar

By midsummer of 1942, approximately half the crew of *S-39* that had left Manila the previous December had gone elsewhere. Old hands—among them Schab, Bixler, and Stowaway Johnson—were being drained off, many disseminated among fleet boats with new personnel to train. Some of the replacements were experienced sailors but new to submarines, like Gunner's Mate Hurtt, who finally persuaded *Griffin* to let loose of him and *39* to take hold. He found her as crummy, beat-up, and uncomfortable as an S-boat could be, but he didn't care. Hurtt was right where he wanted to be at last.

Paul Bryan was also determined to finagle a submarine assignment. As part of a *Griffin* repair crew, he found himself working on the carcass of *39* with Peterson; they struck up a friendship and made a couple of liberties together in Brisbane, winding up one night as the only sailors in a bar full of Aussie Diggers. The evening concluded with a jaw-punching, glass-breaking free-for-all, and suddenly Bryan (who would shortly earn himself the nickname "Blackout" for his ability to booze himself into oblivion) found himself in the crew of *S-39*. Bryan settled into submarines eagerly. He'd always wanted to be where the action was instead of repairing it after it happened.

A disgusted Les Dean, watching the happy faces of new arrivals and the happy faces of those departing, could only grind his teeth in frustration. He wanted off *39* so bad that it had become a pain in the groin.

Gugliotta, Hendrix, and Bernard were pleased to hear that Red Coe, in command of *Skipjack,* had returned from a successful patrol; sinking three cargo vessels would net him another Navy Cross. They had a beer at Tattersall's to celebrate the good news and let nostalgia creep in for a few minutes, but they couldn't tarry long. There was not as much time to enjoy life in Brisbane as they would have liked. Captain Brown was determined to get the boat into fighting trim as quickly as he could pressure *Griffin* into doing it. His engineering background made him highly qualified to spot *39's* infinite faults but unaware that "fighting trim" could not have the same meaning as it did for fleet boats. Chief Engineer Bernard worked harder than everybody else, and everybody else worked like dogs. The five weeks of labor would be called "extensive overhaul" in Brown's report. Unfortunately *S-39* seemed to require this after every patrol instead of the more routine "upkeep" needed by boats in better condition.

A fifth officer reported aboard, Gunner Paul Hodgson, a warrant officer who had served on USS *Seal* with Frank Brown.

There were several human casualties. Dick Ellis's first patrol was also his last. The hospital in Brisbane claimed him; when well enough, he would be assigned once more to submarine repair work. Radioman Frank Gierhart developed such a severe pain in the gut that *Griffin* kept him in sick bay, thinking he had appendicitis.

Communications was shorthanded with only Rice and C.I. Tatum, a newcomer. Then along came J.T. Lebow, who was available and qualified. He reported aboard shortly before *S-39* was ready to go on her fifth patrol. Since leaving Java, J.T. had had a number of adventures. He had dipped in and out of badly bombed Darwin about the time she was abandoned as a naval base. Fremantle came next and when tender *Holland* came in, Lebow was aboard once more, helping set up communications. He was just settling into the Perth area, enjoying all the hospitality, when a friend talked him into a job delivering new decoding machines to Allied ships and stations in Australia and giving crash courses on their operation and minor repair. This special duty enabled Lebow to see the continent with a thoroughness rare even for those born down under. He went to Sydney, Melbourne, Canberra, Townsville, and Brisbane, then on to New Zealand, enjoying every minute of it and making friends he would have for the rest of his life.

When the safari was over, he was assigned to the sub tender *Griffin* just after she came in from the States. No shrinking violet, Lebow often made his own luck and was selected, once again, for special duty in Sydney. Arriving in the capital of New South Wales, he met up with a prostitute named Shirley he'd known in Honolulu. Shirley had come to Australia on a family matter: her aunt had opened one of the biggest beauty parlors in Sydney with a whorehouse as a sideline. One evening J.T. attended a party there. Behind the blackout curtains an elegant chandelier lighted the green baize tables, and Lebow, who loved to roll them bones, could hardly wait to get a pair of ivories into his fist. It was his night: when it was over, the crap game had netted him more than $3,000, which translated into about 10,000 Autralian pounds. Americans could send only $300 dollars home at a time by money order, so J.T. had a pocketful to do something with.

The cathouse in Sydney proved so successful that Shirley's entrepreneurial aunt, a creative businesswoman, decided to branch out where there were lots of Americans with lots of greenbacks. Brisbane was a natural, and who would she pick to get the show underway but her own flesh and blood—Shirley. J.T. had been told that all this was in the offing, and it suddenly occurred to the Texan that he could get rid of some of his money by investing in a sure thing. He gave Shirley 1,000 pounds and told her to pay him back a fair profit after the business got underway. Lebow, attached to *Griffin* in Brisbane, figured that collection couldn't be more convenient.

The enterprise was a big success. The price was $3.20, of which the girl kept $1.20. J.T. observed that, though there was plenty of free stuff around, sailors on leave often did not have enough leisure to pursue it. In the same amount of time, or less, that it took to make an amateur conquest, a guy could visit a pro, get drunk, shoot craps, end up in a fight—in other words, have a tremendous time on the town that would vent enough stored-up energy to make the 90 percent boredom of the next patrol more bearable. J.T. managed to get his share of the profits sent back to the States each month through contacts with a National Exchange Bank in San Francisco. Shirley paid up regularly and continued to do so long after the war had ended.

Then something happened that J.T. hadn't planned on. With all his moxie and know-how, he fell in love with an 18-year-old Australian girl, a seamstress by the name of Claire Hanson, and he wanted to marry her. But the old peacetime ruling was still in effect, that Asiatic sailors were not allowed to marry without special permission from their commanding officer. The self-confident, 22-year-old Lebow felt that he'd known plenty of women in plenty of different places and had the experience and judgment to make up his own mind; nevertheless, he had to consult his new skipper. He was turned down. This did not endear Lieutenant F.E. Brown to J.T. Lebow.

S-39 was due to get underway for post-repair trials on 13 July. She made it on the 14th—for the first time. The work done on her by *Griffin* had included overhaul of 11 units on main engines, port engine air compressor, main engine clutches, ship's air compressors, HP (high pressure) pump, trim pump, air manifolds, auxiliary motors, and engineering sea valves. The insulation resistance of the main power cables was increased, and the engine room hatch skirt reinforced. The binnacle and miscellaneous piping were repaired; removal of A-frames and antenna mast trunk, and renewal of port engine exhaust pipe were accomplished. If all this proved satisfactory, she would proceed on her fifth patrol.

Submerging in lower Moreton Bay disclosed some minor pressure hull leaks of the type pigboat sailors had lived with before, so they surfaced, exercising at Battle Surface, and commenced swinging ship for a check on the magnetic compass, which would have to be used if the gyro compass should go out of commission. Captain Brown, who was not easily pleased with the work done on *39* by the tender, decided that the trials were satisfactory and set course to stand out the channel. Although nobody craved going on war patrol, the irritations and hard labor of the extensive repair period, under a skipper who seemed not to savvy the meaning of the words "stay loose," made Hendrix say to Gugliotta, "Never thought I'd be glad to go to sea, did you?" Gugliotta answered laconically, "I'll tell you when we get back."

K.M. Hurtt and Paul (Blackout) Bryan, who had waited so long for sub duty and were about to make their first patrol, agreed with Hendrix. Bryan had found submariners a less temperamental lot than the "prima donna flyboys," but he was a little confused by his new skipper.

At last quarters, before departure, Brown assembled officers and crew to announce, "We're going to the Coral Sea to get information on Jap strength there." Pausing, he stroked the trim black moustache on his long upper lip. Normally thin, he looked extra slender, as though he had not regained all the weight loss on the previous patrol despite an extensive period in port. His officers knew he had been conscientious about getting the boat into good shape. He had frequently applied the same zeal to correcting small defects taken for granted in the past as he had to large ones. In the process he had worn himself down, as well as other people.

"We think the enemy is trying to cut off Australia by an island-hopping strategy." Brown paused again for emphasis. Newcomers Hurtt and Bryan, wide-eyed and eager to start their novitiate, waited expectantly for the skipper's next words, hoping to be inspired. They weren't disappointed. "We will be patrolling off the southeast coast of New Ireland. There's supposed to be a squadron of Jap destroyers there, and we'll shoot those damned cans right off their sterns."

Hendrix murmured to Bernard, "Looks like the captain is a real shoot-'em-up boy." Bernard, who was fighting a lousy cold he'd picked up in Brisbane, couldn't resist croaking, "Look out, fellas, the Yanks are coming." He was feeling that irrestible urge, straight out of the Old West and Deadwood, South Dakota, to lighten the atmosphere when it got too heavy.

Captain Brown's desire for action had probably been reinforced by hearing that both the fleet boats he had served on had recently enjoyed successful patrols during a period when verified submarine sinkings were not plentiful. On 28 May, USS *Seal* had sent a cargo ship to the bottom off Palawan. On 25 June, USS *Nautilus*, Brown's first assignment after sub school, had sunk a destroyer.

The skipper's ambitions for *39* were admirable, but the patchwork pigboat, living up to her reputation, didn't cooperate. An hour after she had reported her trials satisfactory, the port engine stopped because of an overheated fuel pump, and the bridge rudder angle indicator began stripping and jumping gears. The affirmative was canceled, and the submarine returned to moor once again alongside *Griffin* with the weary resignation of the ailing seeking more of the same medicine that hadn't cured in the first place.

On 15 July the repairs were again complete except for final reassembling of the C & R air compressors, but the ship's engineers could finish that job at sea. The idea was to get out on patrol, they did. By the next day the hard-working crew had reassembled the port air compressor, but when they attempted to charge air, the third stage would not charge. Then the starboad engine stopped because of another air compressor casualty. The work done by *Griffin* had been less than satisfactory. Each time the tender's name was mentioned, the hot humid air was splattered by words to match.

The grime-blackened, bone-weary engineers, headed by Bernard, worked through another 24-hour session and discovered a cracked air compressor block. Effective repairs would require a new block, second-stage piston, and second-stage liner. Consulting with Bloom, Bernard heard that the only repair possible by *39*'s crew would consist of putting renewed rings in the second-stage piston—which would give maybe 24 hours' operation at most. Bernard reported this to Brown, who had no choice but to return yet again to New Farm Wharf.

They spent another 12 days alongside *Griffin* before post-repair trials and training dives in lower Moreton Bay once again proved satisfactory. Finally, on 3 August, *39* stood down the channel for the third and, they hoped, last attempt to reach their patrol station. Hurtt and Bryan were afraid to believe it; so was the skipper. The exec was less concerned. Bernard had been coping with a constant lightheaded feeling, and now he developed knife-edge pains that shot through his chest when he coughed. The only remedies on board, aspirin and APC capsules, didn't seem to help. He was aware that a decoded COMSUBRON-5 message had given *39* the information that there was a Jap submarine about 90 miles distant, but in his present state, the news hardly seemed anything to worry about. Then there was a fuzzy period when all he remembered was that he was stretched out in his bunk, that somebody put a little glass tube under his tongue, and that a voice said, "He has a temperature of 101." He was sure he was hotter than that because he'd been burning up for so long.

Brown called Gugliotta into the wardrom, "Guy, while Larry's out, you'll be acting exec."

"Yes, sir. How do you think he's doing?"

"Spencer says he has catarrhal fever, which adds up to a very heavy cold, A lot of the crew seem to be developing the same ailment. Spencer says he's doled out so much aspirin and APC that at this rate the supply may not last out the patrol."

There had been general rejoicing within the boat because she was finally running well and on her way at last to do her job. News of Bernard's illness dampened spirits, and somebody was heard to mutter in the after battery,

"Maybe we weren't meant to go out on this patrol." J.T. Lebow, still resenting Brown's refusal to give him permission to marry his Australian sweetheart, thought the whole fiasco no more than the skipper deserved. Les Dean, nursing a cold of his own, figured between sneezes that serving aboard *39* was enough to make anybody sick. The clear weather, changed along with morale, becoming overcast with intermittent showers. The seas began to build up. Then heavy rains and heavy seas developed, the gray-green swells looking like flawed bottle glass.

A few days later, still en route to the patrol area, Bernard became so ill that Brown ordered Radioman Rice to send a message to CSS-5 reporting his condition and requesting instructions. The squadron commander ordered *39* to take the executive officer to Townsville, about 600 miles away. Traveling on the surface, it took the pigboat almost three days to reach Grafton Passage, where she transferred Bernard to HMAS *Bendigo*. The Australian corvette would take Larry to an Army field hospital for further treatment of pneumonia.

With the exception of a minor problem in the port engine, quickly corrected, *S-39* had never been in better mechanical shape, at least in the recollection of Hendrix and Gugliotta. Monk said, "Maybe the captain's nitpicking over every little defect has paid off."

"He knows machinery," Gugliotta agreed. "Even if *Griffin* doesn't love him, he finally got them to do the work he wanted, the way he wanted it done."

"I hope Larry's okay. We're back to only four officers again. Good thing we have Hodgson." A worried look had replaced Monk's smile, but then his usual optimism took over. "Let's say it'll be smooth sailing from now on. Anyway, I've got Schab's gun."

Gugliotta gave him a quizzical look, "What do you mean by that?"

"Before Schab left, he very solemnly handed me a gun he'd found when we boarded a bombed-out ship in Corregidor just to take a look around. He'd kept it all slicked up but didn't say why he was leaving it with me."

"Maybe it was like a good luck piece that had carried him through safely," Guy speculated. "Maybe he figured that you, staying aboard *39,* needed it more than he did anymore."

The two officers looked at each other and laughed, then Monk said, "Maybe he was right."

Shortly before leaving on patrol, Allyn Christopher had received word from home that a kid he'd gone to school with was working at Army headquarters in Brisbane. It was cause for rejoicing, and Christopher had never been known to pass one up yet. Besides, any soul from your hometown automatically became a buddy way out here even if you'd hardly known him back in the States. Allyn was eager to show his friend the places that cost the least money where you could have the best times.

Climbing the stairs of Lennon's Hotel to the floors occupied by the Army, he remembered that he'd been invited to a dance at the Addie Cantwell Studios on Adelaide Street. A very nice setup—maybe his friend would like to go, too. He never found out. Christopher met with resistance at the door to Army headquarters. No enlisted allowed. It left the same sour taste in his mouth that he remembered from Manila. Now, asleep in his bunk, he was dreaming that MacArthur, garbed in a tight sailor suit with flared bellbottoms, was waltzing with an army mule. When the general spun around, everybody laughed because a tail was sprouting out his rear. Amid loud applause, Christopher took a bow and announced to the crowd that he'd always known the general was a horse's ass.

Suddenly Christopher sat up straight in his bunk, wide awake and scared. He couldn't figure out why. It hadn't been a spooky dream; on the contrary, he'd enjoyed it. The boat was pitching like an old lady riding a rocking horse, but that wasn't unusual. Lately this ancient crate had a way of getting folks down until they were mush steaks. As a messcook, Allyn had seen tough hunks of cow whacked with the side of a cleaver until they were buttery as filets but drained of flavor or substance. The *S-39*'s constant state of repair that never repaired could beat you to a pulp easy. Look at what had happened to Mr. Bernard. And almost everybody else was getting a lousy cold, too, himself included. Coughing to prove his point, Allyn started turning over in his bunk, but the sea did most of the work for him. As his forehead slammed against the bulkhead, he told himself it wasn't like the good old days. Hell no, it wasn't. The Japs were out there now.

That same day, *S-39* received a message assigning her to a new patrol area along the west coast of Bougainville Island. Everybody considered this the signal for action to begin. Faces sparkled with interest, though the eyes of those who'd been through it before grew wary for a moment with combat caution before they joined in the general refrain: "Hooray, at last we'll be getting a crack at the bastards." The scuttlebutt ran swiftly through the boat that there would be plenty of Japanese tincans, troop transports, the whole shebang, and that they, the *39*, when they reached patrol area, would be right in the midst of it. The Japs were making preparations throughout the Solomon Islands for a big push. The *39*'s job was to locate landings and prevent same.

"Cri'sake, if the old man really knows what's important, which I doubt," Lebow said in his cocky way, "what we ought to aim at is a big fat merchant ship. Can't you see barrels of gasoline, oil, coal, cobalt, tanks, antiaircraft guns, and those vats of rice—all going under."

"Ha, I'll say," Kutscherowski added excitedly, "and chopsticks too. Hey, that would be hard on them if they din't have no chopsticks to eat their rice with."

"Especially if they didn't have no rice," Lebow said in disgust, then added caustically, "J'ever hear of fingers?"

The *39* proceeded on the surface for several days. The wind and seas, which had subsided to moderate, changed back to heavy, making officers and men a little edgy. There were numerous low-hanging clouds, and visibility was poor. Bryan said, "If we can't see them, they can't see us," but nobody was comforted. The enemy's sophisticated equipment gave them an instant advantage, no matter what the weather. Besides, there was the Jap sub they'd sighted a few days back. Where was she now?

"On 14 August at 0000, when the ship's dead reckoning position was well clear of Adele Island at the easternmost tip of the Louisiade Archipelago, the course was changed to 005 degrees (T) in order to head directly for the patrol area. Gunner's Mate Keeven Hurtt had been alternating as messenger, helmsman, and lookout. Making the rounds from control room to conning tower to bridge, he was constantly fighting the rough seas. As a particularly big swell slapped him against the hatch skirt, he was unpleasantly reminded of running headlong into a typhoon on the cruiser *Augusta*. He'd been trying to secure a gangway stowed on the quarterdeck, when a huge wave broke over the port side as the ship rolled at a steep angle to starboard. Engulfed, Hurtt began sliding across the deck, sure he'd had it. Then his left leg accidentally threaded behind a fuel tank vent line which came through the deck and angled up the aft side of the starboard catapult silo. He was held fast until the ship righted itself and other deckhands retrieved him. One close shave like that was enough. And anyway, he was developing an aversion to immersion in tropical waters after seeing a rainbow-hued sea snake, longer than his arm, casually swimming beside the sub after they'd left Mr. Bernard in Townsville.

Hurtt was getting weary now. Fighting the motion of the boat all the time was the equivalent of climbing a couple of mountains. One more chore to go, and then blessed sleep. He had to check the temperature and security of the ammunition locker. As he made his way to the recessed watertight box, built into the forward ballast tank at deck level in the aft port corner of the torpedo room, he had no idea, of how soon he'd be back here and under what circumstances. Yawning as he glanced at the individual cans that each held a round of 4-inch, 50-calibre fixed ammunition, he was glad they were already stowed. The stowage procedure had to be exact or you'd be left with a couple of extras and no place to put them. That had happened a few days before. Hurtt had worn out all his cuss words and finally exploded, "It's like trying to fit ten pounds of horseshit into a five-pound bag." He hadn't known Mr. Hendrix was behind him until he heard a chuckle. Thank God it hadn't been the captain. Hurtt still forgot now and then how small a submarine was. But he didn't forget that *S-39* fired torpedoes at the enemy and engaged in gunfire, and that they were only a hairsbreadth away from the patrol area where she'd likely be doing both in a very short time.

Gugliotta had the watch. He had always prided himself on being inventive but not fanciful. To him, inventive meant the ability to take quick action in an emergency, while fanciful could mean letting imagination run wild enough to create an emergency. Tonight was the kind of night when imagination could get out of hand. It was clear but totally black; no horizon line showed between sea and sky. The moon might have taken itself off to another solar system trailing the stars in its wake. Yet the phosphorescence of the tropical sea flowing around the hull of the submarine as it moved at its best speed caused an eerie atmosphere. It was as though a witch's hand had deliberately drawn a silvery outline around the boat to betray its presence to an enemy known to be almost supernaturally expert at seeing in the dark.

The strong following wind carried voices out of hearing almost immediately, making it difficult for the bridge watch personnel to communicate one with the other, and effectively forcing each to commune with himself as he kept his eyes glued to binoculars, searching his section of the horizon. The captain's night orders had stressed that the bridge watch keep a particularly alert lookout for enemy ships, since *39* was approaching islands that the Japanese had to control if they were to isolate Australia. The watch was trying, only they couldn't see anything. It was like peering into a well, or black velvet. The blackness of the tomb was another analogy, perhaps the most unpleasant one of all. Swede Bloom, who'd just come up for a breath of fresh air, caught the mood immediately and thought, I wonder what it feels like to be torpedoed. He hoped he'd never find out.

Gugliotta's inner time clock told him that his watch was almost over; there was that release of tension around the belly area, as if a whole bunch of nerves had suddenly untangled. Turning the watch over to Gunner Hodgson at 0145 was even more relaxing. In a few moments Guy was in the wardroom writing up the log and drinking a cup of coffee, which he intended to follow up with a bowl of Schoenrock's good soup before getting to bed.

The captain, expecting a current to set toward the northwest because of the heavy seas and wind, had remained in the control room with occasional visits to the bridge until turning in around midnight. After threshing around in his bunk for half an hour, he finally dropped off, reminding himself not to drink so many cups of coffee.

J.T. Lebow, on radio watch, had just finished adjusting his earphones and was feeding paper into the typewriter to copy the "fox" schedule: a radio broadcast in code sent out from submarine headquarters at night, when submarines were on the surface. The "fox" gave orders to individual boats, but the entire schedule was sent to all so that radio silence did not have to be broken by receipt. As Lebow typed away, he was also running through one part of his mind the dodges he might use when they got back to Brisbane to get off *S-39* and reassigned to some other boat. He wouldn't even hold out for a fleet boat. Another S-boat would do—any S-boat.

Paul Bryan, seated at the controllers, was about to adjust the rate of charge.

He was beginning to hope that he'd soon have a chance to see some of the action the captain had promised. The old hands that were still on board *S-39* told again and again how it had been on the early patrols. Bryan wanted to be able to compete.

Navigator Hendrix, who hadn't had his usual quota of setting-up exercises lately, was wakeful. He dropped into the wardroom for a word with Gugliotta, but Guy, who had just finished the log, was beginning to think sleep and found himself yawning. With Larry gone, they were on the short end of shut-eye again. It was going to take more than Monk to keep him awake.

On the bridge, Gunner Paul Hodgson was looking through his binoculars when Smith, one of the lookouts, reported that he thought he saw breakers dead ahead. Hodgson spun around, training his glasses on the same spot, and saw what appeared to him to be a low-hanging cloud on the horizon.

Swede Bloom had been checking around the motor room with the man on watch, Jack Neighbors, to find out how the air compressors had worked during the last charge. A soft-spoken man, he had to shout to make himself heard above the noise of the engines. As Swede made his way back through the after battery room, a typical early morning conversation was in progress between two coffee drinkers. "That jerk wasn't only a brown-noser", one said, "he was a suck-ass . . . " "Good God, what was that?" There was a loud scrrunch like a giant retching, followed by a jarring shock that made the boat shudder from stem to stern, throwing men and equipment to the deck. Swede didn't have to ask what it was; he grabbed hold of the heavy wooden guardrail mounted in front of the main switchboard and held on tight. He'd been through it all before on the *S-36*. It sure as hell wasn't the torpedoing he'd been thinking about earlier. The time was approximately 0220, 14 August, 1942.

Most submariners are light sleepers, and the captain was no exception. His first realization when his restless sleep was abruptly terminated was that the engines had stopped. Swinging himself upright, he heard the words "Rig for collision" being passed. In a matter of seconds he clambered up the hatch and onto the bridge, noting that the ship was taking a port list and beginning to pound. It was a very dark night, and for a moment the white crests of breakers ahead caught his eye before he picked out Officer of the Deck Hodgson.

"What's wrong?" Brown shouted hoarsely, trying to make himself heard above the grind of metal and the crash of waves.

"We're aground, sir."

"Didn't you see the breakers?"

"At first I thought they were low clouds on the horizon, captain, then I wasn't sure and ordered Back Emergency, just as the ship struck the reef."

The *39* had hit the coral heads under the worst possible conditions. There were strong following seas and winds, and it was near high tide. About one minute after Brown reached the bridge, the starboard screw started backing, and approximately three minutes later the port screw did the same. The starboard screw was ineffective because as each swell subsided it was out of the water. Brown ordered, "All stop," then passed the word that the ship was aground. In the motor room Jack Neighbors muttered to himself, "Holy Jesus, I forgot to disengage the air compressor clutches when we started backing down, and the compressors have been running backwards for about five minutes."

On the bridge, struggling to keep his footing and be heard against the roaring sea and wind, Brown shouted, "Secure from collision, set the special sea detail, do not open any hatches, keep watertight doors on the latch and manned." This would put the best men at each watch station, have telephones manned at all stations, including the bridge, and a man standing by at each watertight door to shut it immediately, if so ordered, because of flooding or similar threat.

Swede Bloom, who had immediately gone back to the engine room when he felt the familiar crunch, reported to the bridge, "We had trouble disengaging the port engine clutch, sir, when we shifted to backing on the motors. I think there's misalignment on the port side. We also had trouble engaging the port tail clutch."

Brown ordered, "Blow number three main ballast tank, forward and after trim tanks, and the forward fuel group dry." Chief of the Boat Spencer carried out the order, which would lighten the boat and perhaps enable her to pull free. But *39* continued to pound heavily on the rocks almost directly under the bridge on the starboard side and the deck gun on the port side. Instead of working clear, it became more and more difficult to keep her from swinging broadside to the sea and swell.

At 0315 Brown ordered, "All stop" and "Flood number three MBT and after trim tank." To Gugliotta, who was on the bridge with him, he added, "Maybe that will hold the stern into the sea and prevent riding any further on the reef until daylight." One of the boat's periodic lunges cut off further conversation as the dripping men stood fast under another deluge of water. When Brown could be heard again, he said, "Guy, I'm going to write a message that I want you to send to CSS-5 telling them we're aground off Rossell Island." Gugliotta encrypted this and had Lebow transmit it as a priority message to the squadron commander in Brisbane.

By this time *39* had swung to a heading of 330 degrees (T). Fearing she might capsize, Brown made preparations for landing the crew. He issued orders for all hands to wear life jackets, and Monk Hendrix and Keeven Hurtt began taking jackets and Momsen Lungs out of the stowages to pass forward from the motor room. Hurtt had hoped for action on his first patrol, but not this kind. Being encased in a submarine with layers of water above and below you was different from meeting the enemy face to face, stranded on a reef, wearing a life jacket which was hardly bullet proof—and there were those snakes and sharks besides. Some of his thoughts must have showed on his face, because when he looked up, he saw Hendrix grinning at him and heard him say, "Cheer up, Hurtt, everything's going to be okay." Hurtt grinned back but didn't say anything. He couldn't. It was like being on a roller coaster way back here in the stern. If he'd opened his mouth, he might have vomited.

As a further precautionary measure, the captain ordered Hodgson to supervise getting the wherry ready and the two portable rubber boats inflated. Hurtt, Christopher, and Signalman 2/C May lurched their way up the hatch to the heaving deck to lend a hand, where Hodgson awaited them. The men pried the superstructure hatches open, ungriped the wherry and manuevered it out of storage.

It was 0400. The dark was broken only by shadowy gray life jackets encircling the chests of those at work, and foam flecks that broke off with the push and pull of each breaker, spattering white blossoms on the heaving bosom of the sea. No star twinkled; no moon shone. The constant struggle against the slipperiness of the deck and the motion of the boat made it seem as though the men were doing some strange tribal dance accompanied by drum-thump of pounding surf and squeal of metal.

Hurtt and Christopher were about to inflate the rubber boats when somebody yelled, "My God, watch out," and glancing up, Keeven Hurtt saw a wall of water bearing down on him. The cruel sea had spewed up a monstrous wave that crashed upon the helpless men, washing May and Hodgson overboard, snapping the lifelines secured about their waists. When the water drained off and those on deck were able to detect objects in the black and turbulent sea, they saw Hodgson crawling back aboard, but May was floundering and flailing as he cried out for help. Brown shouted from the bridge, "Throw him a line."

The stunned man was pulled aboard gushing blood from a slash down the back of his left leg from buttock to knee. Swept over the port side, he had apparently hooked one of the metal pipe projections that had held rail stanchions. His right leg was damaged as well, but it could not be determined in the dark whether it was broken. Most important was to get the groaning May below and stanch the blood.

The wherry had also been lost in the accident, and the whole incident increased tension throughout the boat. Brown ordered Spencer, in the control room, to "flood number one main ballast tank" in an effort to alleviate the pounding. Navigator Hendrix was told, "Fix our position as soon as you can," and to Gugliotta the captain said, "Get all your secret publications and records ready and burn them." Guy went below to carry out the order, saving only the effective cipher strips and key lists that were in use. As dawn broke, he stuffed the other papers in a metal can and set fire to them on the after part of the bridge. When he reported back to Brown, the skipper said, "Pass the word to all hands to stand easy on station. We'll make another attempt to get off later in the morning." The dawn matched the greasy-gray of the faces aboard *S-39*. It didn't lift spirits, even though the list of the ship had eased to about 5 degrees port. The only advantage to sunrise was that it enabled the men to see that they were a couple of hundred yards from the reef and that there was a lagoon beyond.

The captain's thin face was haggard. He hadn't left the bridge for hours. He was eagerly awaiting the coffee that little Fabricante brought as far as the heaving deck, then gratefully turned over to the sure footed Hendrix, who was on his way up to the bridge. Although Schoenrock, anticipating the slosh, had filled the cup only half full, there still weren't more than a few gulps left by the time Monk handed it over to Brown, saying, "There's more where that came from, sir. Rocky also sent you this." Monk's smile was as big as ever as he reached inside his life jacket and brought out a squashed, napkin-wrapped sandwich. Then he reported, "By bearings on Rossell and Adele Islands, we're 3.2 miles west of Adele but . . . "

At that moment Matthews, acting as lookout, interrupted excitedly, "Captain, Captain, there's a ship dead ahead 6,000 yards." A look through the binoculars brought the order "Man the deck gun" and word spread like wildfire throughout the beat-up submarine that an encounter, when least desired, was about to take place. Navigator Hendrix had taken his bearings before visibility was clear enough to see a relatively small object. But when down below plotting, he saw the wreck charted and, to everyone's relief, now explained that the vessel, though real, was another unfortunate victim of treacherous waters. It had been there since 1923.

At 0640 Lebow had just turned over the radio watch to Rice and was heading for the galley to wolf down one of the triple-deckers Schoenrock was turning out when he heard Rice say, "Hey, Lebow, looks like the answer to the message we sent to CSS-5 is coming in. Call Mr. Gugliotta." Gugliotta got to work decrypting. Headquarters asked for details: damage to ship, state of tide at time of grounding, and the like. It also urged an attempt to save the torpedoes when jettisoning weights. Brown ordered all ammunition, all provisions except enough to last two days, and miscellaneous weights (such as torpedo loading equipment) to be thrown over the side. In addition, No. 9 fuel oil tank, the only large tank that remained full, was to be blown dry, as well as all variable and main ballast tanks to lighten the boat as much as possible. The skipper was going to make another try at backing out during high tide. But the *S-39* dispatch to CSS-5, detailing the information previously requested, also prognosticated that there was no hope of getting off without help.

In the control room, Peterson swiped his dirty hand across his dirty forehead, then called for Bryan to relieve him. He had been on the main motor controllers and wanted to make an overall inspection of the batteries, main motors, and electric plant in general. Although he found nothing abnormal, he was worried that it wouldn't continue that way for long.

At approximately 1030, Brown ordered, "All back full." They continued backing and twisting for almost 40 minutes. The submarine moved about 50 feet but again listed to port 30 to 35 degrees. As the angle increased, Fabricante and Tayco went on their knees sending out their own messages for help and, though nobody else had their unselfconscious approach, many a man welcomed the assistance.

Peterson's fears began to materialize—the forward and after batteries were approaching the low voltage limit. Brown ordered the main ballast tanks and after trim tanks flooded to try to hold position. Gugliotta, making his way to the bridge, struggled with the unpredictable motion but finally got there. Looking over the side, he reported, "Air bubbles are escaping from the main ballast tanks, sir, probably holed from the violent pounding the hull has taken." The grooves on Brown's face, from nose to mouth, deepened. Gugliotta was beginning to feel sorry for the skipper. These were hard lines for a first command.

In the radio room, Lebow was back on watch. He and Tatum and Rice had been trying for some time to get the information through that had been requested by CSS-5, data that would determine when and if *39* could expect help. But they were having trouble making contact and had been sending blind to NERK: that is, any or all navy ships or stations. Suddenly a voice said, "Hello there, this is Radioman Daniel F.B. Dweyer, RANR, on Thursday Island. What can I do for you?" The Aussie voice with its flat, nasal twang was the nicest music J.T. had heard for a long time. He explained the dilemma and was given a "Goodo, shall do," reassuring words that bore fruit some hours later.

After testing out the engines, Brown ordered a battery and air charge on both engines. Then at 1455, *39* received a message. By this time, officers and men were worn down almost to the stubble on their chins, including the radiomen who had been rotating more rapidly because of the increasing danger of falling asleep and missing some vital communication. Tatum and Lebow were sprawled on the deck dozing, having succumbed to the constant motion that was giving dry heaves to many a gut.

"Hey, guys," Rice said excitedly, "hey, you guys, its's CSS-5 Serial 35." The two men were alert immediately as Rice added, "Get off your duffs and on your feet. Get Mr. Gugliotta to break it down."

Tatum picked himself up off the floor, held on for a second to steady against the pitch, then took off. In a few minutes Gugliotta arrived and decrypted with all speed the welcome news that HMAS *Katoomba* would arrive 15 August. In the meantime, every effort was to be made to free the ship and, if these were unsuccessful, all personnel were to be removed and the vessel destroyed.

The seas throughout the afternoon were heavy from south-southeast, and 20- foot breakers innundated the submarine. At each swell, *39* pounded heavily, with tearing and grating noises. Like an old human with a fatal illness, the boat was slowly being drained of personality and becoming a carcass. Though remission was still possible if help arrived in time the reserve and normal lubricating oil tanks had begun to leak. It was noted that the forward battery showed no rise in gravity charging in parallel. At 2200 no progress had been made on the forward battery, and the attempt to charge it was abandoned. An overcharge was started on the after battery, but vital signs were failing.

On Saturday, 15 August 1942, at 0930, a last attempt was made to break free. All 12 torpedoes were fired onto the reef after removing detonators, exploder mechanisms, and gyros. The men blew all possible ballast, then tried backing on both motors. But the stern was so high that the screws repeatedly came out of the water; with practically no movement away from the beach, the ship swung rapidly to starboard, almost broadside to the swell, despite all twisting effort. She took a rapid list of 45 degrees to port and continued until she reached approximately 60 degrees. Bryan and Peterson, in the control room, were trying almost as hard as the ship was to keep her from rolling over, sweat streaming down their bodies. "Jesus," Bryan grunted, "this is really shoveling shit against the tide." With each swell, tons of water broke over the conning tower, and the jolt had become so severe that Brown, with Hendrix and Gugliotta beside him, ordered, "Flood number three, MBT, number nine, fuel tank, and after trim." Then straightening himself against the pitch, voice hoarse with fatigue, he added, "Maybe that will make the stern swing into the sea."

It didn't. Men who hadn't braced themselves were slipping, sliding, and grabbing for something to hang onto. Prayers came thick and fast from Tayco and Fabricante, and others were openly joining in. Every man on board knew that each succeeding pitch could force the ship to roll clear over. Brown said to Gugliotta, "Pass the word that I'm not ready to abandon ship yet but any man who so desires has my permission to try to swim to the reef." No man left. The sea had abated somewhat, and Brown decided to get the injured May, plus any nonswimmers to safety before wind and surf picked up again. He discussed the most feasible method of doing so with his officers. Hendrix, calling on his years of experience on Chesapeake Bay, said, "Sir, I can swim to the reef, then haul the two mooring lines over as a riding line for the crew." His offer was accepted. Tying a marker buoy line to his belt, Monk took the plunge. The treacherous undertow and the swirling crosscurrents of the heavy surf were plainly visible to Brown and Gugliotta on the bridge. It was easy to see that only good swimmers could qualify for the job, but even Hendrix, after reaching the reef, was having difficulty pulling in the six-inch mooring lines.

"He needs help," Brown said to Gugliotta. "Pass the word for another strong swimmer." The volunteer was through the hatch and ready to go in a matter of minutes. It was Schoenrock. Diving in, he was instantly swallowed by an angry, frothing sea that made the human body seem almost too frail to fight its way. But suddenly Rocky was clambering onto the reef, assisted by Hendrix, and they started hauling in the mooring line. They managed to secure it to one of the torpedoes resting on the reef but signaled that they needed more help to make it permanent. Brown asked for more good swimmers, who would be able now to use the mooring line to get across, one at a time, in a hand-over-hand operation. Soon there were enough men on the reef to make the line permanently secure.

But one more volunteer was needed to take a small line over with which to pull the rubber raft back and forth. Paul Bryan was happy to take on the job. It would get him out of the motor room, where there was no way to avoid close quarters with Peterson. Although he had come aboard *39* as the result of a friendship with the chief electrician's mate, they had had a falling out almost as soon as the patrol started, and it had galled Bryan ever since to have to work with him.

As Bryan sped up the hatch, he flashed the positives through his head: I'm not afraid of water, I'm a pretty good swimmer, and I'll be shut of the motor room. But the moment he reached topside and saw breakers crashing over the bridge, he wondered if he hadn't made a mistake. Having spent most of his time below since the ship went aground, he had been largely unaware of how conditions had worsened. Water was one thing, but walls of it falling on you every few seconds. . . . He didn't have time to finish the thought. A slimy-wet rope was thrust into his hands, not the small one he'd expected but a one-inch line. Nobody had to tell him that some 40 yards of this would be a hard drag, especially when it was caught and sucked back by waves. Also, the captain had ordered crew members to wear shoes and dungarees when making their way to the reef; coral cuts were well known for causing infections hard to clear up in the tropics. The soaked shoes and pants would be another drag. But there was no time to think about that now.

Tying the line around his waist, he plunged in. The waves were coming big and fast. Paul fought to swim high enough up one so he could body surf in. It wasn't working. Each time he semiscaled a wall of water, a combination backwash-undertow whacked him down again. All he was getting was a bellyfull of salt water. He didn't know how long he could hold out. The rope acted like the dead weight of a drowning man clutching his rescuer and forcing him down, and the rough fiber sandpapered his flesh each time it pulled against his waist. He glanced back at the submarine through green-gray foam that made it waver as though already a ghost ship. He saw someone thrust an arm out and point a finger at the other side as much as to say, "Bryan, get the hell over there."

For some reason, the peremptory motion affected him like an order barked in his ear. With a mighty effort he grabbed hold of the line that was already secured on the beach and managed to hang on to it long enough to battle through the vortex of water. Willing hands helped him onto the reef and somebody cried out, "Hey Bryan, like the Aussies say, good show, cobber, we was rootin' for ya."

In a short while May, protected by a strong swimmer on either side, was safely transported to the reef. Bryan felt good that he'd cut loose and done something that showed positive results. It had worked off resentment, too.

The next order of the day was to gather the nonswimmers and use the second, and last, rubber boat to convey them to safety in the same way. The first boat was kept on the reef to make May as comfortable as possible while waiting for the Australian corvette and also, if needed, as a conveyance for the injured man to HMAS *Katoomba* after she arrived. The hauling-in line, devised from a heaving line and bunk lashings for tending it from the submarine, was then attached to the second boat. Actions such as these, which under ordinary conditions would have been considered simple line-of-duty matters, were accomplished under circumstances that made them feats. Some officers and men had been without sleep for 24 hours under exhausting physical conditions. Continually drenched in salt water or slaving below in the heat, constantly trying to balance against the unceasing pound and pitch of the ailing ship, feet slipped more often and fingers fumbled, while red-rimmed eyes blurred and each man drained his reserves of strength, often to help others.

Among the nonswimmers who answered the call was Fabricante. Finding it hard to believe that a Filipino, born and raised by the sea, wasn't accustomed to the water, the mess steward was asked, "Are you sure you can't swim?" Shrugging his shoulders, the little man answered sadly, "Maybe, sair, a little bit. But in that boat I be going to ride." He did. Nobody grudged him the lift; he didn't have the height or weight to pit against the cauldron of the sea. Soon all eight non-swimmers were across. The group on the reef was growing.

The captain retained officers Gugliotta and Hodgson aboard and a dozen or so senior crew members. By 1200 all others had made it to the reef. Now everybody could start worrying again about the arrival of *Katoomba*. She was long overdue. If there was any hope at all of pulling *39* off the reef, even with assistance, it would have to be soon. Rivet heads were developing leaks throughout the ship, and the pressure hull worked with each swell. The seas were again building up from the southeast, making her pound more heavily.

At 1310, HMAS *Katoomba* was sighted. A cheer went up from the reef, and Captain Brown said, "At last we have a chance of getting her off." Now a series of messages was sent back and forth by searchlight.

1325 from *S-39:* "Have you cable to help tow?"

1330 from *Katoomba:* "I have cable and tow wire."

1335 from *S-39*: "Can you pass tow wire to us?"

1337 from *Katoomba:* "I will try and anchor off you and will float wire down on Carley Float" [small raft].

1338 from *S-39*: "Have rock reef astern that we have to go over."

Suddenly, miniature detonations like firecrackers on Chinese New Year rent the air, causing heads to swivel and frayed nerves to jump. Jettisoned ammunition had come drifting back with the tide, and the pounding of the submarine set it off as though in celebration. The elation on Brown's face brought about by the arrival of *Katoomba* was wiped off instantaneously as he awaited the next message from the corvette.

It was seven minutes in coming, the longest interval yet. But it seemed more like seventy, because nobody on the bridge had anything to say. It was just as well, since the screeching wind, accompanied by the groans of the injured ship and the slosh of water pouring over her wounds, made conversation impossible.

At last the message light flashed again, and faces brightened.

1345 from *Katoomba:* "Have you a towing hook aft?"

1349 from *S-39*: "Will have to use cleat."

1354 from *Katoomba:* "If I get you off can you steam?"

1358 from *S-39*: "I think so but need escort."

This was beginning to sound more like it. But as though to give the lie to Brown's words, an explosion, strong enough to supersede the constant pounding shook *39* with earthquake force, causing consternation everywhere. In the engine room, deck plates jumped, and Swede Bloom reported, "That last one seems to have holed the main engine sump. We're pumping but are unable to gain on the leak." Les Dean allowed himself a surge of hope. Could this be the end of the old bitch? A 4-inch shell had exploded under the engine room, and salt water was gaining so rapidly that Dean was pleased to report to the captain, "Sir, we won't be able to run the engines even to charge the after battery or to charge air."

The tall, gaunt captain had been clutching the handrail on the inside of the bridge for the last hour against the pitch of the ship. So had acting exec Gugliotta. After the terrible explosion subsided, Guy noticed that Brown's white-knuckled grasp on the rail had loosened as though he were about to relinquish his hold. It was prophetic, because a few seconds later the skipper ordered a new message sent to the corvette.

1418 from *S-39:* "Now have hole in compartment and unable to steam. Ready to evacuate."

1421 from *Katoomba:* "Does this mean submarine will have to be destroyed?"

1425 from *S-39:* "Yes, the boat will have to be destroyed. Am starting preparations now."

Brown turned to Gugliotta: "Go ahead with the procedure we discussed earlier, Guy."

At the moment, the *Katoomba's* location was to windward of the submarine. Because of heavy seas, strong winds, and sandy bottom, she signaled back that the anchor would not hold, and the chances of maneuvering her whaleboats near enough to the reef to bring the men out alive were nil. Brown asked if a Carley Float would help. The answer was "no." *Katoomba* next

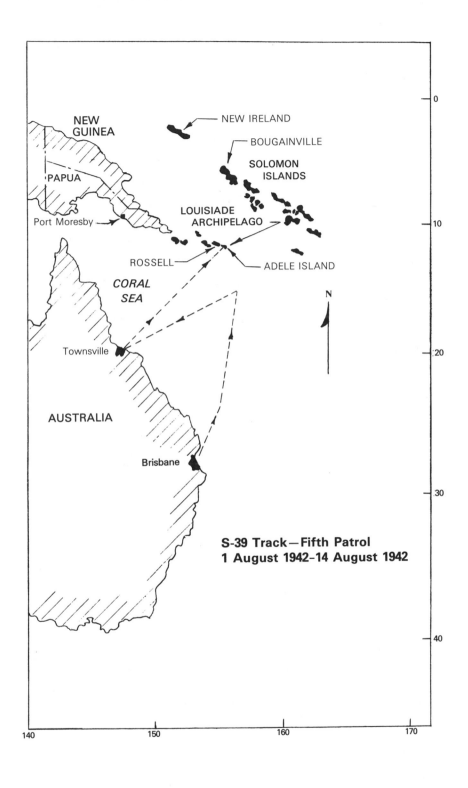

NEW IRELAND

NEW
GUINEA

BOUGAINVILLE

SOLOMON
ISLANDS

PAPUA

Port Moresby

LOUISIADE
ARCHIPELAGO

ROSSELL

ADELE ISLAND

*CORAL
SEA*

N

Townsville

.20

AUSTRALIA

Brisbane

.30

**S-39 Track—Fifth Patrol
1 August 1942–14 August 1942**

.40

0

10

140   150   160   170

inquired if it was possible for the men to cross to the other side of the lagoon, the lee side, where there was a narrow space that the rescue whalers could enter between Adele and an adjacent small island. The answer was a relieved "yes." *Katoomba* began changing locations.

Below decks, Gugliotta carried out the captain's orders. He had retained several empty ammunition cans and now loaded them with the crew's service records, ship's log, quartermaster notebooks, and other important documents and records. He also tucked in his wife's baby shoe, a good luck talisman given him by his mother-in-law and carried on patrol ever since. The waterproof cans would be secured at intervals to heaving lines and hauled onto the reef.

Destruction proceeded. Rice wielded a sledgehammer on radio and sound gear. Hodgson and Hurtt destroyed the deck gun, bashing in the threads of the breech, plug, recoil mechanism, and so on. Then they disassembled the machine gun and threw all its parts, along with pistols and rifles, over the side. Peterson, discarding more conventional methods, jumped on the master gyro with both feet, smashing it in with a will; it had always caused him trouble. And since he had an audience that needed a laugh, he urinated on it for good measure. In the engine room Swede Bloom directed the necessary destruction, which Dean carried out with zest and Matthews felt bad about. Starboad air compressor and main engine were backed down with the jacking gear engaged and the cylinders filled with water. The port engine could not be rolled by the motor, either ahead or astern, indicating that the desired destruction had already occurred.

Arnold bashed in periscope lenses, while Gugliotta, assisted by Neighbors and Christopher, strewed rags, paper, clothing, and bedding throughout all compartments and drenched the mess with fuel oil. Control room litter was sloshed with alcohol. Officers and men ripped, tore, and macerated with a vengeance, doing their best to make sure that nothing on the *39* could be dissected and analyzed in a post mortem that might aid the enemy. It was as macabre as an All Hallows' Eve celebration at graveside.

The *Katoomba* had signaled that she would try to make two rescue trips with the whalers before she had to put out to sea for the night for fear of Japanese submarines. Captain Brown sent Hendrix and some of the men to wade the three-quarters of a mile from the reef across the lagoon to meet the whalers. The injured May was propelled in the rubber boat. The next step was to get the remaining crew members on the reef before total darkness set in. The wind had not abated, the overcast was unrelieved. It would not be a bright and starry night.

On board *39*, last-minute preparations for departure were being made by the remaining crew. Swede Bloom's biggest worry was his chief's cap. After the struggle he'd had to find one, he couldn't afford to lose it. Besides, replacement wouldn't be easy. Supplies of that sort were not keeping up with the number of Americans pouring into Australia. Reaching for the Momsen Lung he'd be using now that they'd run out of life jackets, he figured the only thing he could do was to clamp the cap on his head as tight as he could force it without cutting his ears off, and hope that by some miracle it would stay on until he made it to the other side. His watch was no problem; following the lead of Kutscherowski and others, he secured it in a condom. First aid gear was placed in empty ammo cans, fresh water in milk cans. Most delicately handled, most carefully packed of all, were the half-dozen bottles of booze—some brandy, some whiskey. If ever a bunch of fellows needed a shot of good medicine, it would be the gang who spent the night on the reef.

Gugliotta passed the bottles to Bloom, one by one, with utmost care, working hard not to drop the precious stuff on the heaving deck. Cut-up pieces of blanket cushioned each bottle before it was nested in a milk can with its mates. Individuals had already taken smokes over to the reef, but more packs, along with matches, were stashed anywhere and everywhere they would fit. Almost everybody had the habit, and it would help to make a long night shorter. Anyway, a pull on a bottle and a drag on a butt went hand in hand.

Swede inflated the Momsen Lung, then buckled the strap that went around the neck and the one around the waist. Now it was up the hatch and over to the reef. Like everyone else at first view of the Niagara Falls they had to plow through, Swede felt a moment of trepidation, but there was no turning back. Yanking hard on his cap, he reached out and grabbed hold of the line; as he began his first hand-over-hand movement, the waist strap on the Momsen Lung broke, and a 20-foot wall of water collapsed on him. The lung floated up to his neck and snaked around his throat, tightening rapidly. He couldn't breathe, he couldn't swallow. He lost his grip on the line, and the next wave tumbled him over and over with the ease of an elephant tossing a peanut. The message flashed through his mind, I'm going under.

The men on the reef weren't making a sound; neither were the few left on board the submarine. Swede had disappeared. It was an eerie scene. Twilight made the overcast day darken faster, smudging the waves, the dying vessel, the drained men into a colorless painting where one entity overlapped the other. And then there was a shout, "I see him."

A miracle had happened. As they hauled him onto the reef—jostling each other in their eagerness to pull him to safety, peeling off the waterlogged lung, turning him this way and that to make sure he hadn't been slashed by coral— Bloom, after a long spew of briny, croaked, "Anybody see my cap float in?"

Nobody had. But that didn't discourage the stubborn Swede. As soon as attention switched to others fighting their way across, he walked down the reef, already under water in spots from the incoming tide. Lo and behold! battered, scratched, scraped, but intact—there was the cap, bobbing against the coral. Bloom clamped it on his head, figuring it would be as good as new once it dried out. And if it wasn't, he didn't care. He'd wear it anyway. Another miracle had happened.

Back in 1938, Keeven Hurtt's mother had sent him a newspaper clipping which stated that Belfry, Montana, his birthplace, was the biggest Navy town in the U.S. on a per capita basis: of its population of 250, nine were in the Navy. Keeven didn't know what the other eight guys were doing right now, but he was discovering the marvels of a tropical coral reef. There'd been nothng like it back in Montana, where he'd been accustomed to Big Sky wonders. Now he was glimpsing Big Sea wonders, too. Paul Bryan had suggested that the men on the reef should mound loose coral to use as a head rest during the night. It sounded far from comfortable, but Hurtt decided to gather some for later and give it a try. As he stooped down, his first surprise was the many different shapes and colors of coral. Duty aboard flagship *Augusta* had never brought him eyeball to eyeball with an atoll before. Being shipwrecked was a hard way to find beauty, but Keeven, who loved the great outdoors, was willing to accept it on any terms. Despite the fading light, as each wave washed in, tropical fish flashed red, purple, gold, midnight blue, grass green—every color Keeven had ever seen. He forgot weariness and laughed aloud as he watched a hermit crab in a tide pool hold out a sea anemone in his claws like a little old man offering a flower.

But he couldn't stay too long. First of all, with night coming on there was the herd instinct. Everyone ought to get together and stay together, even though the tides were not expected to rise much. Keeven had wandered down the reef, and now he started wandering back. Canned goods, their labels soaked off, kept washing in, some splitting open on the sharp coral. From the load dumped overboard to lighten ship, there was plenty of food to stave off hunger, even though the menu might be canned white potatoes, canned sweet potatoes, and canned macaroni. It was, for sure, catch as catch can.

When Keeven rejoined the men, they had already grouped themselves into a circle around the rubber life raft as a substitute for the traditional campfire. Joking seemed to be increasing in proportion to increasing darkness, although with lack of sleep it was not up to par. Kutscherowski called out, "Hey, push that there raft over, and let's stack it with different kindsa canned stuff. Then we could have a watchacallit, a bordamorg, I mean a morda . . . "

"You mean a smorgasboard," Christopher cut in.

"Howdja know that word?" Ski asked admiringly.

"I'm a Scandahoovian, you big jerk."

"Yeah, that's right. I forgot," the good-natured pug replied. "Anyhow, it would give us sump'n to do until somebody gets here with the whiskey."

"That's gotta be any minute now. There's only a couple of them left besides the captain," Jack Neighbors said.

As Gugliotta started for the hatch, he took a last look around. The *S-39*, partially interred in her natural element and partially cremated internally, would be undistinguishable from any other grounded sub. Her hull number had been painted over at the start of hostilities, and all other distinctive marks defaced or removed within the last 24 hours. But his automatic head-swivel had caught something. Over the door to his stateroom was a three-inch bakelite plaque that read, *"S-39."* He knew it was stupid to go back for that. The deck was a slippery mess, and the list of the ship so severe now that even a few steps were an enormous effort. And he probably wouldn't be able to pry it loose with only a penknife as a lever. He went back. Maybe it was because he was acting as exec for the first time. Maybe it was because he was just a damned souvenir hunter. Maybe it was because she was his first submarine. Somehow it seemed indecent to leave it. It came off easily.

And then there was no one left aboard *39* but Captain Brown. Silence fell on the group as they turned to watch the figure on the heaving bridge fire a Very's pistol down the hatch. They knew that this pyrotechnic flare would immediately start a blazing fire in the control room that would spread rapidly through the other alcohol- and oil-soaked compartments. The intense heat generated, although it could not burn much more than a couple of hours because of insufficient oxygen, would be enough to start fires in the electrical wiring and distort most of the machinery and equipment that had not been mechanically destroyed already. From the atoll, Bryan watched the destruction and figured that if a Jap wandered by, he wouldn't get much information from the old *S-39*. But he wondered whether it was the enemy's policy to take prisoners or just to shoot 'em down. He wasn't the only man thinking about that, despite the presence of the Aussie corvette.

When the captain joined them, it was a very quiet crowd on the atoll. Nobody knew what to say. "Gee, cap'n, sorry we lost her" didn't seem appropriate. And "What will happen after we get back to Brisbane?" wasn't much better, since everybody knew there'd be an investigation. Fortunately, Brown gave Gugliotta the high sign to break out the whiskey, and the awkward moment passed in a lip-smacking, soul-healing gulp of 100-proof that eliminated the need for speech and blunted fears that the enemy might surface.

By the time a couple of bottles had been downed, the reef was in total darkness, the men in high spirits, and a songfest in progress: "Sweet Adeline," "Down by the Old Mill Stream," "That Old Gang of Mine," "Lost in the Cradle of the Deep" had all been sung so often that J.T. Lebow called out, "How about Casey Jones for a change? Anybody know that one?"

Everybody knew it. They sang it, and sang it, and sang it, and passed another bottle around, leaving one for morning, when they figured to need a pick-me-up. Even Les Dean joined in, his relief was so great at not being a *39* boat sailor anymore. Around midnight, euphoria wore off and reality began to set in. The wind had been increasing, and the tide had risen steadily. Rice muttered to Bloom, "The water's past crotch level already and don't look like it's about to go down yet."

It wasn't. When it reached waist level, nobody could keep a match dry enough to start a cigarette, so they lit one butt from another, trying to keep a smoke alive. The mounds of coral they'd gathered for pillows had long ago been scattered by the restless sea, but the water was too deep to sit down in anyway. It got cold, especially when the liquor wore off. Most of the men were shirtless, and their dungarees had been soaked for so long that the cooler night temperatures turned cloth into a chilling poultice against the skin. Men fell asleep standing up, then slumped down into the water where they were picked up by their comrades and shaken awake to groan and keep on standing—until the next time. It was warmer in the water than out, but that made drowning a very real possibility, like a person collapsing in the snow and freezing to death under the illusion that he was cozy and safe.

Bryan rescued somebody, then somebody rescued him. He tried thinking of things he was going to do when he got back to Brisbane, but all he could think of was sleeping for a week when he got aboard the Aussie corvette. Around 0230 he thought the tide had finally stopped rising; an hour later he was sure of it. When the first gray light of dawn seeped into the sky, the water was only ankle deep.

Adversity is a great leveler. They all looked the same, with ashen, stubbly, salt-rimed skin. Like babies' diapers, the wet pants and shoes looked no different from one another. Half-closed eyes showed no color, and the drawn, hungry look around their mouths was uniform. But Swede Bloom was still wearing his cap, and when the captain said, "Look, there's a whaleboat coming in from the *Katoomba* on the other side—let's walk across the lagoon to meet her," renewed hope restored individuality. Then somebody called out, "Pass the bottle. We need strength for the walk."

During the night, when the water had been at its highest, Gugliotta had helped Fabricante stay afloat. Now, as the lieutenant prepared to lead a party across the lagoon, he felt a sharp tug at his pants. Looking down he saw the mess steward with a tentative half-smile on his face; Fabricante pointed to the lagoon, then raised his arms. Guy understood the pantomine. The water was too deep. It would be up to the mess steward's chin at times. "Hop on," Gugliotta said, bending down. The little man clambered onto the lieutenant's back, and grabbed hold. Like some prehistoric, two-headed marine animal, the oddly assorted pair started wading toward food, rest, safety, and the *Katoomba,* accompanied by the slosh-slosh and rising voices of yakking, joshing men, animated by the excitement of rescue.

Behind them, smoke still rose from the smoldering guts of the *S-39.* In the torpedo room and the forward battery, the doors to the men's lockers swung harder and harder, faster and faster as the pound increased and the boat broke up. No lock had ever secured any of the doors. Whatever a man had of value was kept there, was safe there, was never touched by anyone else.

Phase one of World II in the Pacific was almost over, and the S-boat sailor, with integrity and determination, with humor and stamina, had played his part. Retreat was not defeat.

Afterword

HMAS *Katoomba*, after setting course at 1130, 16 August 1942, with all *S-39* officers and crew on board, arrived off Townsville on 19 August, then berthed and commenced fueling. The exhausted submariners had slept most of the way, but upon arrival, according to the *Katoomba*'s War Diary, "*S-39*'s crew victualled on board all day. At 1935 *S-39*'s crew left ship for railway station. . . . In conclusion may I add my admiration for the exemplary conduct and behaviour of *S-39*'s personnel and particularly for the captain, Lieutenant F.E. Brown, USN, and the 26 other officers and men who remained standing over knee-deep on the reef throughout a dirty squally night." The entry is signed by *Katoomba*'s commanding officer, Alan P. Cousin, Commander RANR.

Each of the 52 submarines lost during World War II has been assigned (by name) to one of these United States. *S-39* is assigned to Maryland, where special attention is given her memory by members of the Submarine Veterans of World War II at chapter meetings throughout the state on the yearly anniversary of her loss.

The *S-39* is credited with sinking the two vessels described in the text, on her first and third patrols, in *United States Submarine Losses, World War II* (Washington, D.C.), originally prepared by the Commander Submarine Force, U.S. Pacific Fleet, 1946. JANAC (Joint Army Navy Assessment Committee) credits only the third-patrol sinking.

One of the purposes of the nationwide SubVet organization is to "perpetuate the memory of those shipmates who gave their lives in submarine warfare." Among these is pioneer Captain James Wiggin (Red) Coe. After leaving *S-39*, Coe commanded the *Skipjack* on three successful war patrols and was credited with sinking four Japanese *marus* (merchantmen). Subsequently, he put *Cisco* in commission. *Cisco* failed to return from her first patrol out of Perth, Australia, and was presumed lost in September 1943. There are many references to Coe throughout submarine literature. His name appears among "Top Skippers of World War II by Number of Confirmed Ships Sunk"; see Clay Blair, Jr., *Silent Victory* (Philadelphia, 1975). A rest camp at Subic Bay, P.I., was named for him in 1945, as well as a street at the submarine base in Pearl Harbor.

There were war casualties also among the officers and men rescued from the *S-39*, who were spread throughout the submarine force and participated in war patrols until the end of the conflict. Lieutenant Frank Brown, who went on to command *S-44*, was lost with that submarine in October 1943, when she was sunk by destroyer gunfire off the Kurile Islands; C.I. Peterson, then an ensign, was lost with Coe on USS *Cisco*; Schoenrock and Arnold were serving on board the USS *Tullibee* when she was presumed lost in May 1944.

Others appearing in *Pigboat 39* who are known to have passed on, some during the writing of this book, are William Hiland, Earl Nave, Pop Bridges, George Lautrup, Dorothy Reynolds Schab, Charles (Monk) Hendrix, John Mattingly, and Roy Klinker.

The fate of the British military that *S-39* was sent to rescue is described by Denis Russell-Roberts in *Spotlight on Singapore: Rape of an Island Fortress* (London, 1966), pp. 165-67. In a personal letter to Larry Bernard, Lt. Col. Russell-Roberts states, "I am in touch with two living survivors of that British party on the island of Chebia. . . . they, with five others, left the island on the 14th May 1942, leaving behind a further ten or twelve men who were too sick to accompany them. This bid to escape in a self-made native sailing boat failed, and the escapees were subsequently interned in Singapore. Those remaining on the island were finally picked up by the Japs and also made prisoners of war. . . . Many others had died on the island."

As for the *39* boat herself, the latest information we have is from Robert K. Piper, Royal Australian Air Force historical officer, who writes: "Rossell Island is a very remote area of PNG [Papua Territory, New Guinea]. However, when I . . . was around Milne Bay about 1970, there were rumours that the *S-39* had washed off the reef and ended up on the beach partially submerged in sand." It is my hope that this book will brush back the sand from the stories of those who served aboard her.

Bibliography

Personal Communications

Antipolo, Lottie. Letter to Rachel Coe, 10 March 1946.

Bernard, Lawrence G. Interview with author, Santa Roša, California, 21 Nov. 1981. Transcript with author.

Bernard, Mrs. Lawrence G. (Caroline). Interview with author, Santa Rosa, California, 21 Nov. 1981. Transcript with author. Letter to Mr. and Mrs. Carl Mayn Smith, Urbana, Ill. 25 July, 1940.

Bixler, Robert H. Letter to author 1 July, 1982.

Bloom, Lyman C. Interview with author, Los Altos Hills, California, 5 Jan., 1982. Transcript with author. Letters to author, 16 March, 28 July, 1982.

Browning, Joseph S. Letters to author, 28 May, 6 June, 1983.

Bryan, Paul L. Letters to author, 2 Jan., Feb. 7, 29 March, 19 Dec. 1982. Tape to author, 29 March 1982.

Chapple, Wreford G. Telephone conversation with author, 9 Aug. 1982. Interview with author, San Diego, California, 7 Sept. 1982. Transcript wih author.

Christopher, Allyn L. Interview with author, Sacramento, California, 17 Sept. 1981. Transcript with author. Letters to author, 8 Jan., 14 Feb., 25 April, 1982.

Coe, Mrs. James W. (Rachel). Interviews with author, Santa Barbara, California, 12, 13 Jan. 1982. Transcripts with author. Letters to author, 1982-83.

Dean, Leslie. Letters to author, 31 March, 31 July, 3 Nov., 1982.

Ellis, Richard E. Letter to author, 20 April, 1982.

Gierhart, Frank W. Interview with author, Sacramento, California, 18 Sept. 1981. Transcript with author. Letters to author, 5 Feb., 21 Feb., 21 Nov., 14 Dec., 1982; 31 Jan., 7 April, 1983.

Gugliotta, Antoinette F. Letter to author, 10 March, 1983.

Gugliotta, Guy F. Letters to author from 7 Jan. 1941 to 29 Nov. 1941.

Hoy, Bruce D. (Curator, Aviation, Maritime and War Branch, National Museum and Art Gallery, Papua, New Guinea.) Letter to author, Sept. 1983.

Hurtt, Keeven M. Letters to author, 8 Jan., 7 March, 18 Dec. 1982.

Johnson, Leonard W. Letters to author, 13 Jan., 5 Feb., 12 Feb., 1982.

Klinker, Roy C. Interview with author, Piedmont, California, 14 Aug. 1982. Transcript with author.

Lautrup, George W., Jr. Letters to author, 21 April, 5 May, 1982.

Lautrup, Mrs. George W. Letters to author, 11, 25 July 1982.

Lebow, J.T. Letters to author, 14 Feb., 8 March, 1983.

Lebow, Mrs. J.T. (Minnie Jeanne). Letters to author, 16, 22 March 1983.

Mackenzie, John M. (Naval Historical Officer, Australia Department of Defence). Letter to author, 26 Oct., 1983.

Matthews, Edward F. Letters to author, 29 Dec., 1981; 5 Feb. 1982. Tape to author, 5 Feb. 1982. Transcript with author.

Mayn Smith, Mrs. Carl. Letter to Caroline Bernard, 25 April 1981.

McKnight, George. Letter to author, 3 Feb. 1982.

Neighbors, Jack C. Letter to author, 26 Dec. 1981.

Parks, Thomas R. Interview with author, Los Altos Hills, California 14 Mar. 1982. Letters to author, 30 Dec., 1981; 14 Jan., 1 Feb. 1982.

Parks, Mrs. Thomas R. (Corenne). Interview with author, Los Altos Hills, California, 14 March 1982. Transcript with author. Letter to author, 27 Feb. 1982.

Pennell, James F. Telephone conversations with author, 28 Sept. 1982; 23 April, 6 Sept. 1983. Letter to author, 28 Nov. 1982.

Piper, Robert K. (RAAF Historical Officer). Letter to author, 21 Sept. 1983.

Russell-Roberts, Denis. Letters to Larry Bernard, 15, 16 Nov. 1966.

Schab, Edmund G. Interview with author, Los Altos Hills, California, 9 Jan. 1982. Transcript with author.

Schab, Mrs. Edmund G. (Dorothy). Interview with author, Los Altos Hills, California, 9 Jan. 1982. Transcript with author.

Triebel, Charles O. Interview with author, San Diego, California, 9 Sept. 1982. Transcript with author.

Triebel, Mrs. Charles O. (Jo). Interview with author, San Diego, California, 9 Sept. 1982. Transcript with author.

Documentary Material

Air Facilities in the Western Pacific (chart), June 1941. War Plans Section, M.B. Quantico, Va.

Doritty, R.E. "Diary while on Board USS *Sailfish* (SS-192). 8 December–31 December 1941. Manila."

Hendrix, C.N.G. "War Patrols of USS *S-39* and USS *Sturgeon* (SS-187)." Recorded Interviews, 10 Aug. 1944. Pearl Harbor Office of Naval Records and Library.

National Archives, Navy and Old Army Branch. Washington, D.C.

"Action Report: Stranding and Loss of the USS S-39 (SS-144), Report of." Commanding Officer to Secretary of the Navy, 22 Aug. 1942.

"First Endorsement to Action Report." Commander Submarine Division 201, 23 Aug. 1942.

"Second Endorsement to Action Report." Commander Submarine Squadron Five, 28 Aug. 1942.

Booklet of General Plans. USS S-39 (SS-144).

"Brief Summary of USS S-39 War Patrol Report #1." 21 Dec. 1941.

"Second War Patrol, Report of, USS S-39." 22 Jan. 1942.

"USS S-39 (SS-144), Report of 3rd War Patrol." 18 March 1942.

"4th War Patrol Report, USS S-39." 10 June 1942.

"USS S-39 (SS-144), Report of Fifth War Patrol." 24 Aug. 1942.

"Narrative of Events, Asiatic Fleet Leading up to War and from 8 December 1941 to 15 February 1942." Admiral Thomas C. Hart, 11 June 1942.

"Supplementary of Narrative." Admiral Thomas C. Hart, 8 Oct. 1946.

Sackett, E.L. "History of USS Canopus." Office of Public Information, Office of the Chief of Naval Operations, Washington, D.C. 1947.

Books

Alsberg, Henry G. *The American Guide*. New York: Hastings House, 1949.

Barnard, Marjorie. *A History of Australia*. New York: Frederick A. Praeger, 1963.

Blair, Clay, Jr. *Silent Victory: The U.S. Submarine War against Japan*. Philadelphia: Lippincott, 1975.

Casey, Robert J. *Battle Below: The War of the Submarines*. Indianapolis: Bobbs-Merrill, 1945.

Cope, Harley F. *Serpent of the Seas: The Submarine*. New York: Funk and Wagnalls, 1942.

Dictionary of American Naval Fighting Ships. Vol. 6. Washington, D.C.: Naval History Division, Office of the Chief of Naval Operations, 1976.

Fisher, Robert C., and Leslie Brown, eds. *Fodor's Australia, New Zealand, and the South Pacific, 1978*. New York: David McKay, 1978.

Great Cities of the Word. Maplewood, N.J.: Hammond, 1958.

Gunther, John. *Inside Australia*. Edited by William H. Forbis. Evanston, Ill.: Harper and Row, 1972.

Hackerl, C.J. *Subron Five's Equatorial Cruise*. Manila: Sugar News Press, 1938.

"Hobby, Oveta Culp." *Current Biography* (1942), 386-88.

Holmes, W.J. *Undersea Victory: The Influence of Submarines on the War in the Pacific*. Garden City, N.Y.: Doubleday, 1966.

Hoyt, Edwin P. *The Lonely Ships: The Life and Death of the U.S. Asiatic Fleet*. New York: David McKay, 1976.

Huxley, Elspeth. *Their Shining El Dorado: A Journey through Australia*. New York: William Morrow, 1967.

Ind., Allison. *Bataan, the Judgement Seat: The Saga of the Philippine Command of the United States Army Air Force, May 1941 to May 1942*. New York: Macmillan, 1944.

Kimble, David L. *Chronology of U.S. Navy Submarine Operations in the Pacific, 1939-1942*. Bennington, Vt.: International Graphics Corp. 1982.

Lewin, Ronald. *The American Magic: Codes, Ciphers and the Defeat of Japan*. New York: Farrar, Strauss and Giroux, 1982.

Lockwood, Charles A. *Sink 'Em All*. New York: E.P. Dutton, 1951.

Mellnik, Steve. *Philippine Diary/1939-1945*. New York: Van Nostrand Reinhold, 1969.

Morison, Samuel Eliot. *History of the United States Naval Operations in World War II*.

Vol. 3, *The Rising Sun in the Pacific, 1931–April 1942*. Vol. 5 *The Struggle for Guadalcanal, August 1942–February 1943*. Boston: Little Brown, 1948, 1969.

Parr, Charles McKew. *Over and Above Our Pacific*. Binghamton, N.Y.: Maundeville House, 1941.

Pike, Douglas. *Australia: The Quiet Continent*. London: Cambridge Univ. Press, 1962.

Polmar, Norman, and Thomas B. Allen. *Rickover: Controversy and Genius.*: New York: Simon and Schuster, 1982.

Roscoe, Theodore. *United States Submarine Operations in World War II*. Annapolis, Md.: United States Naval Institute, 1949.

Russell-Roberts, Denis. *Spotlight on Singapore: Rape of an Island Fortress*. London: First Tandem Book Limited Edition, 1966.

Silverstone, Paul H. *U.S. Warships of World War II*. Garden City, N.Y.: Doubleday, 1965.

Stafford, Edward Perry. *The Far and the Deep*. New York: Putnam, 1967.

Talbot, Frederick A. *Submarines: Their Mechanism and Operation*. Philadelphia: Lippincott, 1915.

Treadwell, Mattie E. *The Womans Army Corps*. Washington, D.C.: Special Studies, Office of the Chief, Military History, 1954.

The Submarine in the United States Navy. 3rd ed. Washington, D.C.: Naval History Division, Office of the Chief of Naval Operations, 1949.

United States Submarine Losses, World War II. Washington, D.C.: Naval History Division, Office of the Chief of Naval Operations, 1963,

Vreeland, Nena: Geoffrey B. Hurwitz; Peter Just; Philip W Moeller; and R.S. Shinn. *Area Handbook for the Philippines*. 2d ed. Washington, D.C.: Foreign Area Studies of the American University, 1976.

Younger, R.M. *Australia and the Australians: A New Concise History*. Adelaide: Rigby, 1970.

Periodicals

Abercrombie, Thomas J. "Perth—Fair Winds and Full Sails." *National Geographic* 161 (May 1982): 638-66.

Bredin, Dee. "Java Assignment." *National Geographic* 81 (Jan. 1942): 89-119.

Ferrin, Lynn. "Mabuhay! The Philippines." *Motorland*, Jan.-Feb. 1983, 20-22,38.

ISWAS (Submarine Squadron Five, Manila), 3 April 1938.

Simpich, Frederick. "Return to Manila." *National Geographic* 78 (Oct. 1940): 409-51.

"Facts about the Philippines." *National Geographic* 81 (Feb. 1942): 185-202.

Time. 11 Aug. 1941, 52-53; 12 Jan. 1942, 57-58; 25 May 1942, 72; 8 June 1942, 71-72; 22 March 1943, 50 (News reports re the establishment of the WAAC).

Walker, Howell. "The Making of an Anzac." *National Geographic* 81 (April 1942): 404-56.

Index

air compressors: poor efficiency corrected, 86; failure of, 186
Albay Gulf, 89, 91, 94, 100
amah: children's nurse, 17, 21, 22; knitting, 22
Americans in Australia, 180
ammunition, jettisoned, 203, 204
Andrews, Jim, 56
annual military inspection: preparations for, 62, 64; *S-39* makes good score, 68
Antipolo, Lottie: Jean Coe's amah, 40, 41
Army-Navy Club, 17, 27, 28, 48, 52, 56
Army-Navy game, 87
Arnold, _____: destroys periscope mechanisms, 206; lost with *Tullibee,* 213
Asiatic Fleet, 6, 7, 11; and misconception of its strength, 85
attack: on Cajogan Island, 90; on Japanese cargo ship, 91-95; on submerged submarine, 127; on Japanese tanker, 148-53; by Japanese submarine, 160
Australians, 171, 181

Baguio, 19
balut, 87
battery. *See* main battery
battle stations submerged: for practice, 34; for attack on cargo ship, 91-95; for attack on tanker, 149-56
battle surface action: procedure for, 25-26; conducted on SS *Montanez,* 89
Bellamy, John, 69-70, 103-04
Bendigo, H.M.A.S., 192
Bernard, Caroline (Mrs. Lawrence G.), 1, 3, 5; and nipa hut living, 16, 17, 18; and dying

ricksha boy, 32-33; hires a professional worrier, 34; with monks in Tsingtao, 37, 38; with incapacitated Larry, 39; and voyage to Manila, 47-48; and stranding adventure, 48-49; illness of upon return to U.S., 70-71; and Pearl Harbor Day, 102; receives telephone call from Larry, 133
Bernard, Lawrence G., 128, 157, 161; background and reports for duty, 1-3, 16; maneuvers *S-39* first time, 3, 5; shows Gugliotta cleanup routine, 66-67; and anticipated start of war, 82, 88, 89; as diving officer, 92- 94, 99, 148-49, 154; forages for food, 120-21; and main engine repair, 124-25, 131, 165-67; in Java, 132; calls Caroline, 132-33; sights possible target, 148; and captain Coe's departure, 172, 177; at Brisbane, 179, 181, 182; and word of Coe's continued success, 187, 190; illness of, 191, 192
Bernard, Lawrence and Caroline: pay call on Coes, 17-19; in Shanghai, 33- 34; and birth of son Lance, 49; reminisce on experiences in Philippines, 51
betting, 61-62
Bingera, H.M.A.S.: escort for *S-39,* 181
Bini-Boy, 66
Bittern, U.S.S., 105
Bixler, Robert H., 67, 95, 119, 180; upon approaching Shanghai, 35; and fond memories of captain Coe, 172, 173; transferred off *S-39,* 187
Blood Alley (Shanghai), 36, 101
Bloom, Lyman C., 161, 165, 169, 172, 180;

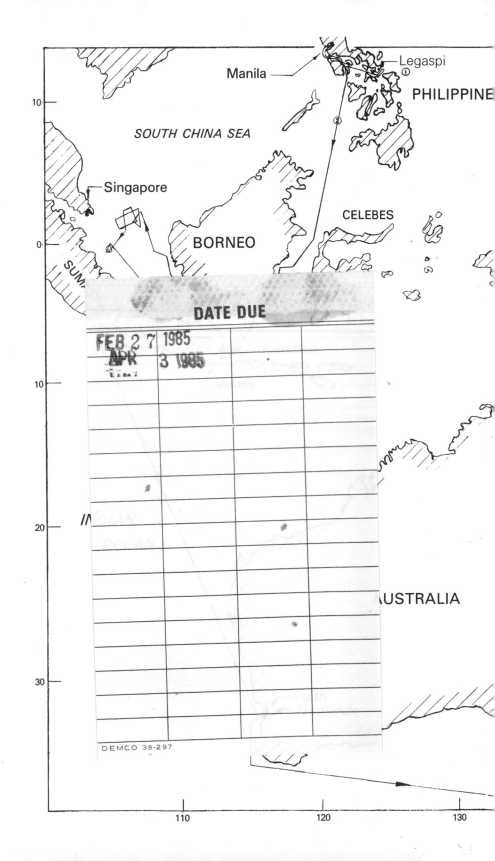